UNIVERSITY COLLEGE
WINCH

PROSOCIAL BEHAVIOU

D1495077

Dedicated to Elke

Prosocial Behaviour

Hans-Werner Bierhoff
Ruhr-University Bochum

PSYCHOLOGY PRESS
ALERE FLAMMAM
Taylor & Francis Group

First published 2002 by Psychology Press
27 Church Road, Hove, East Sussex, BN3 2FA

www.psypress.co.uk

Simultaneously published in the USA and Canada
by Taylor & Francis Inc,
29 West 35th Street, New York, NY 10001

Psychology Press is part of the Taylor & Francis Group

© 2002 Psychology Press

British Library Cataloguing in Publication Data
A catalogue record for this book is available from the British Library

Library of Congress Cataloging-in-Publication Data

ISBN 0-86377-773-2 (hbk)
ISBN 0-86377-774-0 (pbk)
ISSN 1368-4574 (Social Psychology: A Modular Course)

Cover design by Joyce Chester
Cover photograph: *I Know How You Must Feel, Brad . . .* © The Estate of Roy
    Lichtenstein/DACS 2001
Typeset in Palatino by Mayhew Typesetting, Rhayader, Powys
Printed and bound in the UK by TJ International Ltd, Padstow, Cornwall

Contents

Series preface

Social Psychology: A Modular Course, edited by Miles Hewstone, aims to provide undergraduates with stimulating, readable, affordable, and brief texts by leading experts committed to presenting a fair and accurate view of the work in each field, sharing their enthusiasm with students, and presenting their work in an approachable way. Together with three other modular series, these texts will cover all the major topics studied at undergraduate level in psychology. The companion series are: *Clinical Psychology*, edited by Chris R. Brewin; *Developmental Psychology*, edited by Peter Bryant; and *Cognitive Psychology*, edited by Gerry Altmann and Susan E. Gathercole. The series will appeal to those who want to go deeper into the subject than the traditional textbook will allow, and base their examination answers, research projects, assignments, or practical decisions on a clearer and more rounded appreciation of the research evidence.

Also available in this series:

The Social Psychology of Aggression
By Barbara Krahé

Attribution: An Introduction to Theories, Research, and Applications
By Freidrich Försterling

Attitudes and Attitude Change
By Gerd Bohner and Michaela Wänke

Preface

Most of the work for this book was done within one year. During that time I remember thinking several times that the project would never be completed successfully. I am still surprised that this prophecy proved false and that I am now writing the preface. In retrospect, my main challenge was to get through two bodies of research, one related to developmental issues and one to social-psychological approaches. After having followed both research traditions I have found that an impressive amount of knowledge on prosocial behaviour has been accumulated during the last 40 years, which is no longer fragmentary but contributes to a deeper insight into the psychology of altruism, empathy, and prosocial behaviour.

I am very grateful for the support I received from several people. Detle Fetchenhauer from the University of Groningen read most of the chapters and made insightful and very helpful comments on earlier drafts of the manuscript. In addition, I would like to thank Gustavo Carlo from the University of Nebraska, Lincoln, Tom Farsides from the University of Sussex, and an anonymous reviewer for their constructive feedback on the manuscript, leading to a substantially improved result. Moreover, Miles Hewstone made many very valuable suggestions. Gabriele Croitoru took care of the manuscript from the beginning until it was finished and was responsible for all of the correspondence involved. Gabriele Kourouma-Wilke checked the References and encouraged me to continue. Eleonore Hertweck was responsible for the English translation of the manuscript and in translating the chapters she made many helpful suggestions on how to improve the wording. My thanks to all of you. Finally, I want to thank all the staff from Psychology Press who were involved in the project including Rachel Brazil, Lucy Farr, Susan Rudkin, and Tanya Sagoo.

to support the assertions and arguments, instead of striving for completeness of referencing.

Obviously, this book on prosocial behaviour has been influenced by some of my personal biases. For example, the emphasis on processes of prosocial behaviour (empathy, guilt, and responsibility) is not typical of other treatments of this subject. Further, the fact that theories of prosocial behaviour are described after having discussed these processes, instead of before, may need some explanation. Because the theories make assumptions about the processes of prosocial behaviour, it should be easier for the reader to understand them if the processes are described first. Therefore, I have decided to treat these two topics separately, because from a didactic point of view it is more effective to introduce them in different chapters and to start with the processes on which theories are built, although it is clear that processes and theories are closely intertwined.

Prosocial behaviour and social life I

Issues of definition 1

What does it mean to act altruistically, and what is the difference between prosocial behaviour and altruistic behaviour? The terms "helping behaviour", "prosocial behaviour", and "altruism" are frequently used interchangeably. However, they may be distinguished for analytic purposes. Such distinctions refer to the motives "behind" the overt behaviour:

- "Helping" is the broadest term, including all forms of interpersonal support.
- The meaning of "prosocial behaviour" is narrower, in that the action is intended to improve the situation of the help-recipient, the actor is not motivated by the fulfilment of professional obligations, and the recipient is a person and not an organisation.
- The term "altruism" refers to prosocial behaviour that has an additional constraint, namely that the helper's motivation is characterised by perspective taking and empathy.

These three terms are closely interrelated. Their overlap is illustrated in Figure 1.1.

An example of "helping" is the customer service behaviour of a salesperson (e.g., informing a customer of the important features of a CD player; see Smith, Organ, & Near, 1983). In this case, helping is part of the role obligations of the salesperson. The meaning of "prosocial behaviour" is narrower, excluding all paid activities in the service sector. An example is the father who explains how to use the new PC to his daughter because he is aggravated by her constant questioning about what to do next. In this example, the daughter needs her father's help—he

FIG. 1.1.
Relationships between the concepts of helping, prosocial behaviour, and altruism. Bierhoff, H.W. (2001a). Prosocial behaviour. In M. Hewstone & W. Stroebe (Eds.), *Introduction to social psychology* (3rd edition). Oxford: Blackwell. Copyright © (2001) Blackwell Publishing. Adapted with permission.

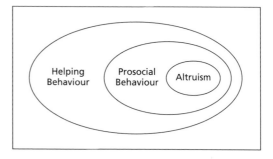

acts more out of anticipated personal distress than out of empathic concern. The ultimate goal of this egoistically motivated behaviour is to benefit oneself.

Finally, altruism is characterised by an emphasis on the needs of the other, concern about his or her well-being, and finding a solution for his or her problem. The definition of altruism in Webster's *New Encyclopedic Dictionary* (1993) is "unselfish interest in or care for the welfare of others". A good example is the biblical parable of the Good Samaritan, who could easily have left the situation but instead was concerned about the well-being of the victim of a robbery (Luke 10:29–10:37). The Samaritan had feelings of empathy and was only satisfied when he had made sure that something was done to reverse the harm inflicted on the victim. In this story the helper's ultimate goal is to benefit the other person. The parable is an example of altruistically motivated behaviour.

The distinction between prosocial behaviour and altruistic behaviour is in many cases difficult to confirm empirically. One reason is that feeling states such as personal distress and empathic concern cannot be observed directly. In the earlier example of pro-social behaviour, the behaviour of the father could also serve as an example of altruism. Only information about what the father thinks and feels allows conclusions about his motives. Furthermore, pro-social behaviour may be based on a mixture of egoistically motivated and altruistically motivated sources (Batson, Duncan, Ackerman, Buckley, & Birch, 1981). In many real-life examples, personal distress and empathic concern occur simultaneously.

Co-operation, solidarity, and support are other related terms, which are frequently used. "Co-operation" is used when the inter-dependence between people is emphasised (e.g., among members of a team). The term "solidarity" is used when a broader societal per-spective is taken. Solidarity action occurs in a larger social network. "Support" denotes any form of helping and may be taken as equi-valent with the term "help". However, in the context of "social support" it has a special meaning, in that it refers to the social network of a person (a network of communication and mutual obligation including friends, kin, acquaintances, and work associates; Burleson, Albrecht, Goldsmith, & Sarason, 1994).

In this book, the term "prosocial behaviour", which includes egoistically and altruistically motivated helping behaviour, is pre-dominantly used. When the issue is to emphasise that a particular behaviour is altruistically motivated, the term "altruistic behaviour" is used.

Forms of prosocial behaviour 2

Whereas the distinction between helping, prosocial, and altruistic behaviour refers to subtle differences beyond the overt behaviour of actors, quite obvious differences exist between different *forms* of prosocial behaviour, such as saving somebody from drowning, donating money to charity, or giving directions to a stranger in town. Certainly it would be very useful if these diverse forms of behaviour could be classified in a taxonomic system.

A descriptive analysis of prosocial behaviour shows that it may be organised along several dimensions (Smithson, Amato, & Pearce, 1983). The starting point is that the degree of perceived similarity between different helping episodes may be used to identify clusters of episodes that are considered similar. These different forms of helping were collected by Smithson et al. on the basis of examples that were found in empirical studies of prosocial behaviour. Students assessed the similarity between 62 helping episodes. In each comparison the similarity between two episodes was assessed on a 5-point scale. The study was conducted at the University of North Queensland, Australia. Every fifth episode is listed here (Smithson et al., 1983, pp. 28–29; numbers in brackets refer to the cluster that is represented by the episode, and which is described next):

- 5. Stopping to pick up a hitch-hiker standing along the roadside. (3)
- 10. Mailing a package for a stranger, who has approached you on the street explaining that s/he has to catch a train. (3)
- 15. While walking through a building you see a technician, who is working on some electrical equipment, receive a strong electric shock; you help the unconscious person by giving direct help or by calling for aid. (1)
- 20. Saving milk cartons, rinsing them, and turning them in to a group of university students collecting them for an art project. (2)
- 25. Donating money to a charity box. (4)

- 30. During a game involving the betting of money, you give another player (unfamiliar to you) who is almost broke enough money so that he or she can continue playing (one dollar). (4)
- 35. Volunteering to counsel high-school students after your lecturer has asked for volunteers. (2)
- 40. Giving change for a quarter to a stranger who approaches you on the street. (3)
- 45. You overhear one person giving another person directions; because you know the directions are incorrect, you step over and correct him. (3)
- 50. You are approached by a deaf person who hands you a note asking you to make a phone call for him/her; you make the call. (3)
- 55. You work extra hard for your supervisor at work, knowing that s/he is eligible for an award if productivity is up. (−)
- 60. A woman approaches you on the street and asks you to give her a hand getting her male friend to a first-aid station; you agree. (1)

At first glance it is clear that the episodes described are very heterogeneous. On the basis of similarity ratings, clusters of similar episodes were identified:

(1) Episodes 15 and 60 are examples of episodes consisting of a serious problem. This cluster was labelled "emergency intervention" and included 10 of the 62 episodes.
(2) Episodes 20 and 35 are contained in the second cluster, which was labelled "formal organisational helping" (14 episodes).
(3) Episodes, 5, 10, 40, 45, and 50 are part of the third "informal, casual, everyday help to strangers" cluster, which contains 18 episodes.
(4) Episodes 25 and 30 represent examples summarised under the cluster "donating and sharing", which contains 12 items.

Whereas nearly all of the episodes listed were included in one of the clusters, episode 55, which refers to an organisational context, was not. It corresponds with studies on dependency as a cue for prosocial behaviour that were conducted by Berkowitz and his co-workers (e.g., Berkowitz & Daniels, 1963). We will return to them in Chapter 20, when considering organisational citizenship behaviour.

In a second step of the analysis, the dimensions underlying the similarity ratings were identified by multidimensional scaling, which led to three dimensions that were immediately interpretable in terms of content (Smithson et al., 1983):

- The first dimension refers to *planned, formal help* vs *spontaneous, informal help*.
- The second dimension contrasts *serious situations* vs *not serious situations*.
- The third dimension is characterised by *doing, direct help* vs *giving, indirect help*.

The planned–spontaneous dimension refers to the social setting; the serious–not serious dimension refers to the need of the recipient; and the doing–giving dimension refers to the type of help (Levine, Martinez, Brase, & Sorenson, 1994).

Because the helping episodes were derived from empirical research on helping, the possibility exists that researchers used a biased sample of prosocial actions. For example, it might be easier to study certain forms of helping than others. Therefore, the list of studied forms of prosocial behaviour was compared with descriptions of helping used by ordinary people as represented in the dictionary. Although many of the considered verbs referred to the episodes used in the study, some helping terms (e.g., inspiring, encouraging, collaborating with) were not applicable to the examples of helping studied in psychological experiments—16 examples of helping were found that had not been investigated. These examples were described as episodes as before, including the following (Smithson et al., 1983, p. 40):

- Taking care of a friend who has come down with the 'flu by bringing him/her food, extra blankets, vitamin C, and getting the person's prescription filled.
- You tell your neighbour who doesn't have a radio that a storm is approaching the area.
- After a fellow student's ideas have been ridiculed in class discussion, you stand up and argue that the student is actually correct.
- While you are working together with others on a task you find interesting, your enthusiasm sparks their interest in it as well.

Most of these episodes are characterised best as personal help occurring between friends (Smithson et al., 1983). The newly derived forms of helping have the following characteristics:

- They are personal (vs anonymous).
- They are internally motivated (vs externally motivated).
- They occur between friends (vs between strangers or acquaintances).
- They are cognitively unfamiliar in the sense that there is no simple rule about what to do (vs cognitively familiar).

It comes as no surprise that such helping episodes are not regularly represented in social-psychological studies. Because research on helping behaviour is generally of an experimental nature, problems arise in subjecting the issue of personal help between friends to an experimental design. Other forms of data collection—like interviews and field studies—may be more efficient in dealing with these forms of helping.

In the next step of the analysis, the newly derived helping episodes were included in the similarity analysis. Multidimensional scaling indicated that the previously neglected forms of helping were represented by a fourth dimension, which is best described by *personal* vs *anonymous*. In summary, four dimensions seem to represent people's cognitive schemata in the domain of helping episodes: planned–spontaneous, serious–nonserious, giving–doing, and personal–anonymous. These dimensions were replicated in several samples. Although the four dimensions are not completely independent of each other, the correlations among them are quite low.

The special case of planned helping

The large majority of studies on prosocial behaviour focus on spontaneous helping. Planned helping, however, has been a neglected area (see Chapter 21). In this section, formal planned helping is contrasted with informal planned helping.

Amato (1985) conducted a questionnaire study on the personality and demographic determinants of planned helping. Respondents indicated their involvement in 33 activities of planned helping within the last 6 months. Examples are (Amato, 1985, p. 239):

- Bought a present for a friend or relative for no formal reason (i.e., it was not their birthday, anniversary, or Christmas).
- Purchased or picked up an item in town for a friend or family member who was not able to pick it up him/herself.

- Visited a person you knew was having a personal problem with the intention to talk it over or cheer up the person.
- Lent more than a couple of dollars to a friend or relative.
- Gave old clothes or household articles to a charitable organisation.
- Donated money to an organisation or agency which gives assistance to needy people.
- Donated money to a noncharitable, nonprofit community organisation (memorial fund, research organisation, school, hospital, etc.).
- Donated time to a noncharitable, nonprofit community organisation (memorial fund, research organisation, school, hospital, etc.).

The involvement in these activities was not dependent on specific circumstances because a retest 7 months later indicated high stability of responses. The data of the 33 items were reduced to two dimensions by multidimensional scaling, which represent formal, organisational activities on the one hand, and informal activities involving friends and family members on the other hand. The first four items in the list represent informal planned helping, whereas the other four items refer to formal planned helping.

On the basis of this distinction two subscales were formed which correlated quite low with one another ($r = .26$). Therefore, involvement in formal planned helping was relatively independent from involvement in informal planned helping. This distinction is further justified by the finding that the personality and demographic correlates of both subscales differed in part. Although social responsibility (Berkowitz & Daniels, 1964; see Chapter 11) correlated significantly with both subscales ($r = .23$ and $r = .24$), authoritarianism (Robinson & Shaver, 1973) was negatively correlated with formal planned helping ($r = -.32$) and correlated around zero with informal planned helping ($r = .07$). Authoritarianism reflects a negative attitude towards other people and approval of strict control. Individuals who tended to provide assistance to charitable organizations also tended to hold positive attitudes towards other people and to approve a more liberal view. In addition, they emphasised internal locus of control (Rotter, 1966). Formal planned helping seems to be at least in part the expression of abstract notions about human nature and about self-efficacy.

In contrast, informal planned helping was significantly correlated with positive mood state (Mehrabian & Russell, 1974). This positive mood effect may be the result of seeing the positive consequences of the help given. Informal planned helping seems to be based on involvement in kinship and friendship. Similar mood effects have been found in research on organisational spontaneity (see Chapter 20).

Only formal planned help increased with age and was more pronounced for married couples and for people who have children. In general, formal planned help was better accounted for by the personality and demographic variables than informal planned help. It seems in part to depend on the emergence of developmental tasks (Havighurst, 1953), in other words, those tasks that the individual has to solve during a certain life period.

People set priorities in their goals depending on developmental tasks. Marriage and having children may influence the likelihood that the individual will encounter instances of formal planned help. Age is an indicator of these developmental tasks (at least in the studied age range from 18 to 50 with most respondents in the younger age groups). Success with developmental tasks depends on opportunity structures (Wrosch & Heckhausen, 1999). The availability of these opportunity structures depends on age. They may influence the chances to fulfil certain role expectations which derive from kinship and the social network. People may adapt to this opportunity structure and adopt the strategy to set age-related goals in their involvement in planned help.

How helpful are human beings? 3

How often does prosocial behaviour occur in daily life? Is it a regular occurrence or does it happen only under highly specific conditions? The best evidence concerning these questions comes from observations of what people do if they are confronted with a situation in which their help may be needed. In order to standardise the observation situation, it is necessary to simulate an emergency without the passer-by noticing that a psychological experiment is being conducted. Such simulations can provide evidence about the extent of people's willingness to help.

In the following, results are typically reported as percentage of persons who act prosocially. This is a simplification in several respects: First, help increases over time, but in empirical studies a time limit is set, which frequently ranges between 120 and 180 seconds. Second, some bystanders tend to offer indirect help. For example, they ask for someone who might offer help. Indirect help is usually not taken into account in the figures that follow. Finally, the amount of helping is not considered as long as a yes–no criterion is used.

The frequency of helping probably depends on the form of helping behaviour. The concrete forms of help are quite different (see Chapter 2). Therefore, no general answer can be given to the question "How helpful are human beings?". Instead, the answer depends on factors like the vulnerability of the potential helper (Milgram, 1970) and the perceived costs of helping. In general, high vulnerability and high perceived costs tend to reduce the willingness to help.

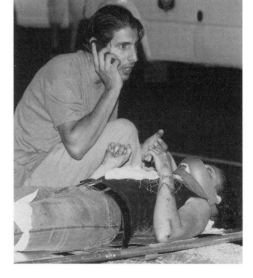

Credit: Popperfoto/ Reuters.

Helpfulness in nonserious situations

In a field study (Bierhoff, 1983), a person dropped his/her glove in front of a passer-by in the centre of a suburban town. The loss was arranged in such a way that the person dropped the glove about two metres in front of the to-be-observed target person. The experiment was designed so that it was very likely the loss would be noticed by the target person. The "loser" acted as if he/she did not notice losing the glove. In 72% of all simulations the target person drew the loser's attention to the lost glove and picked it up. As only a minority of people did not intervene, a high degree of helpfulness can be stated for this example.

In a second field experiment in the suburb (Bierhoff, 1983), a person let an object about the size of a fist fall out of a bag, so that it fell in front of the following passer-by. In this simulation the loser's attention was drawn to the lost object in 80% of the cases. These investigations were carried out in a busy part of town, so that several people were simultaneously present in the surrounding area. Occasionally, several people came running up at the same time to draw the loser's attention to his/her loss.

According to these results approximately 75% of the passers-by were helpful. This percentage is relatively high, showing that people certainly are not apathetic. However, one must consider the fact that the situations studied were favourable in terms of the two criteria mentioned earlier: low perceived cost and low vulnerability.

In contrast, an American study showed less helpfulness when a stranger asked if he/she could use the target person's phone because he/she had lost an address. This was especially true if men asked to use a phone in New York City (about 15% helpfulness), whereas helpfulness approached 100% if women voiced the same request in a rural area (Milgram, 1970). Obviously, the personal vulnerability of potential helpers played a role in connection with the low helpfulness in New York City. Therefore, willingness to offer low-cost helping decreases substantially if vulnerability is perceived as high.

More representative data on the likelihood of helping are available for four regions of the USA (Levine et al., 1994). In one study (dropped pen) the male experimenter dropped a pen behind him in front of a passer-by. The study was carried out in main downtown areas of 36 US cities. The proportion of passers-by who helped was .57 in the south, .43 in the north central, .53 in the northeast, and .45 in the west (see Figure 3.1). In another study (hurt leg) the experimenter,

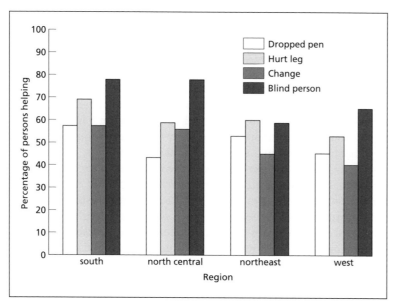

FIG. 3.1.
Percentage of helpful passers-by in four US regions (based on data from Levine et al., 1994, p. 76).

walking with a limp and wearing a leg brace, dropped a pile of magazines. In this experiment the level of helping was somewhat higher (see Figure 3.1). In a third study (change) the experimenter asked for change for a quarter. Level of helping was in the same range as in the first study. In a fourth study (blind person) a blind person was waiting at a traffic light to cross the street. In this experiment the level of helping was quite high. An inspection of the mean percentages of helping in Figure 3.1 shows substantial differences between regions on some of the helping measures. These differences are only significant in the change and blind-person studies. On both measures more help was given in the south and north central regions than in the northeast and the west.

In two further investigations (Bierhoff, 1983) the helpfulness of psychology students was investigated in connection with students' payment for participating in experiments. Students were usually paid 10 DM per hour for this kind of work. After psychology students had filled out a questionnaire, they were sent to an employee in order to receive a receipt for their participation. The employee informed the students—apparently on her own initiative—that she was trying to collect money for the care of latchkey children. The employee told students that money could be provided for these children if it was possible to save on the cost of subject participation. Because the experiments had to be carried out, the students were asked to participate in the experiment without getting paid, so that the savings could be donated to a good cause. (A similar procedure was employed by Miller, 1977.)

Students' willingness to participate in experiments without receiving any pay varied considerably. Whereas some students were not at all willing to participate without payment, others expressed their willingness to provide the money for 6 hours or even more. On average students offered a little less than 2 hours. A second experiment resulted in a similar amount of helpfulness, yet this time slightly higher. These experiments were designed in such a way that it was realistic for the students to believe they would have to keep their promise. Thus, it is likely that the students' responses to the request truly reflected their willingness to act accordingly. To work 2 hours for free in order to help others is a moderate offer—not overwhelming, yet it shows that the students were open to the appeal and that they frequently responded positively.

A 1996 replication involved 40 psychology students. The mean level of prosocial behaviour was an offer of 1.9 hours. Figure 3.2 shows the frequency distribution. Many respondents seemed to follow the strategy of offering something, but not too much. The percentage of students who did not help at all was 12.5% in this study. Therefore, the degree of helpfulness was very high if one considers the criterion of help vs no help.

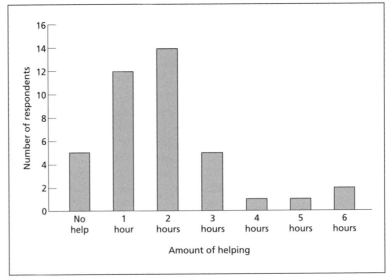

FIG. 3.2. Frequency distribution for number of volunteered hours. (Bierhoff, unpublished data)

Intervention in emergency situations

One might think that helpfulness is very high in emergency situations. That assumption is confirmed when potential helpers are direct witnesses of the accident itself. When, for example, passengers in a subway car in Philadelphia saw another passenger collapse (a student who simulated the incident), the willingness to help was overwhelming. Within 40 seconds, 95% of the victims received help (Piliavin & Piliavin, 1972). In a similar study in a New York City subway, a comparable amount of support was obtained. Observers who were eyewitnesses of an unquestionably serious accident almost always helped. More than one person intervened in 60% of the trials (Piliavin, Rodin, & Piliavin, 1969).

High intervention rates in emergencies are found as long as the cost of helping is relatively low. If blood was apparently coming out of the victim's mouth, the response rate was 65% within 1 minute after the incident. Blood increases the subjective cost of helping, which results in less and somewhat slower intervention of bystanders (Piliavin & Piliavin, 1972). In another variation, the collapse was simulated by an apparently drunken person (Piliavin et al., 1969). The rate of intervention dropped to about 20%. In the blood and the drunk conditions the subjective cost of helping is high, but why does the considerable difference in intervention rates occur? The pattern of response rates is explained by assuming that the costs of helping are counteracted by costs of not helping, which are probably high in the blood condition but low in the drunk condition (see Chapter 12).

In this kind of emergency intervention, males are more likely to intervene than females. For example, in the study in New York, 60% of the potential helpers were male; they offered help in 90% of the incidents in which help was offered (Piliavin et al., 1969). These figures are in agreement with a general trend of more help given by males than by females in emergency situations (see Chapter 4).

The response rates of passers-by are totally different if they do not observe the accident itself, but only see the victim lying injured on the ground after the accident. In 197 simulations of bike crashes on pavements and cycle paths in a German town, 27% of the bystanders offered help (Bierhoff, Klein, & Kramp, 1990). The position of the victim—next to the bike or under the bike—did not influence the results. There were only a few passers-by (about 1%) who seemed undecided about what to do at the scene of the accident and left without speaking to the victim. The typical response was either to address the victim directly or to pass or drive by the scene of the accident after a first short look. The observation protocols contained examples of both very helpful and very negative responses. For example, a bike rider who approached the scene of the accident on a racing bike shouted "Out of the way, out of the way" before making an evasive manoeuvre. In contrast, other passers-by offered to take the victim to hospital.

From this study the conclusion is that between one fourth and one third of the passers-by were willing to help, showing that willingness to intervene in such an emergency situation is relatively low. In this context another result is noteworthy, in that it points to the reason for not helping. We observed both single individuals and groups of two persons approaching the scene of the accident. The frequency of intervention was higher for single individuals than for groups of two people. Prosocial behaviour was obviously inhibited when several witnesses were present. One reason could be diffusion of responsibility, which occurs when several witnesses divide the total responsibility among themselves so that each witness feels less responsible for intervening (compared to the case where a single person witnesses the accident; see Chapter 15).

A comparison with intervention rates in a classical investigation seems to support the conclusions with respect to helpfulness towards a victim of an accident after the accident had apparently taken place (Darley & Batson, 1973). Theology students were sent from one university building to another within the course of an experiment. The students were supposed to tape a speech in the second building after they had been given the necessary information on which to base their speech. On the way they were confronted with a person who was lying in a doorway with his/her head bent downwards. While the theology students were approaching, the victim coughed twice and groaned. Forty percent of the theology students offered the victim direct help or took care indirectly by informing the experimenter. This percentage of helpers is comparable (although somewhat higher) to the level of helpfulness that we found in the bike accident simulation. Because it was not easy for the passers-by in our simulations to find a way to help indirectly, one type of helping behaviour was not available to them which was available to the theology students. Under these circumstances it seems realistic to assume that the degree of their direct helping behaviour would also lie in that range (about one third of the cases).

The likelihood of helping may be estimated on the basis of a summary of research into social inhibition of helping in emergency situations (Latané & Nida, 1981). In individual-alone conditions of simulated emergencies the overall helping rate was 50%. The same figure was found for groups of bystanders. In groups of bystanders the individual level of helpfulness was lower than the group level (see Chapter 15). The effective individual probability of helping was calculated as 22%. In correspondence with the hypothesis of social inhibition, the comparison with the 50% figure in the individual-alone conditions shows that people are less likely to intervene when they are group members.

The percentages of helping that were reported by Latané and Nida (1981) seem to be an overestimation of real-life helping. On the one hand, most of the data were obtained in psychology laboratories with psychology students as subjects. It is likely that this combination of artificial setting and the young age of subjects may increase willingness to intervene. In real life there is no experimenter to count on if you have a problem. Therefore, it is a justifiable assumption that intervention rates are overestimated in laboratory settings as far as their generalisation to real life is concerned.

The presented examples lead to a profile of helpfulness that illustrates what can be expected in different situations of prosocial behaviour (Figure 3.3). The profile is based on simplified estimates. The examples inform about the inferred general level of everyday helpfulness depending on the concrete circumstances under which helpfulness was studied. It is worth noting that the examples were taken from investigations in different countries. Although the results are compatible, the study of cultural differences in helping remains an important issue (see Chapter 5).

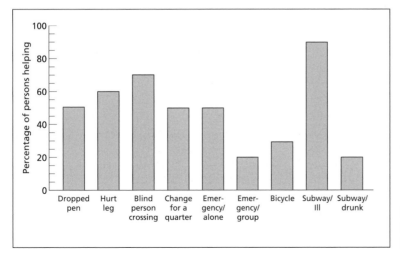

FIG. 3.3.
Hypothetical profile of helpfulness.

Culture, the individual, and level of helpfulness 4

The profile of helpfulness illustrated in Chapter 3 (Figure 3.3) suggests that the general level of prosocial behaviour only depends on the situation. However, this is an oversimplification because person variables (e.g., gender) and community variables (e.g. population size) are relevant. In addition, in the following sections time effects and social status are considered as moderator variables.

Gender differences

Even in toddlers, gender differences in empathy and prosocial behaviour are observed (Zahn-Waxler, Robinson, & Emde, 1992b) with girls being more empathic and boys more indifferent. These results are in correspondence with the stereotype of women as the prosocial gender (Eagly, 1987).

Credit: Art Directors and TRIP.

Empathy

The stereotype is in part confirmed by studies on empathy in children and adults. A reliable gender difference was found in questionnaire studies of empathy, most of which used the Questionnaire of Emotional Empathy (Mehrabian & Epstein, 1972). The difference favouring females is visible in a meta-analysis based on 16 studies (Eisenberg & Lennon, 1983). The meta-analytic gender difference in self-reported empathy is so strong that it would take more than 2500 studies finding no gender difference to turn the difference into an insignificant one (see also Lennon & Eisenberg, 1987, who considered 13 additional studies). Later studies using the Interpersonal Reactivity Index (Davis, 1994) also showed higher empathic concern of women compared to men (Davis & Franzoi, 1991; Erlanger, 1998).

Gender differences in empathy are partly dependent on the method of measurement. It has been found that physiological and nonverbal indicators of empathy do not show gender-specific effects favouring females over males (e.g., Fabes, Eisenberg, Karbon, Troyer, & Switzer, 1994b). This does not necessarily mean that verbal reports of empathy are coloured by stereotypic responding. It may also be possible that physiological measures as well as facial measures do not tap the same contents as verbal reports of empathy.

Guilt

A similar, even more convincing picture is found in research on guilt (Bybee, 1998). Strong and consistent gender differences were found in empirical studies of adolescents and adults, with females reporting more guilt feelings than males. This gender difference is interpreted against the background of decreasing guilt feelings with age in adolescents, especially in boys, and with respect to guilt over aggression.

A summary of empirical results indicates that between 2 and 10 years of age there is an increase in the number of incidents that elicit guilt feelings. During adolescence this development is reversed because guilt-proneness decreases between the 5th and 11th grade. Finally, in their twenties and thirties participants' guilt feelings are once again positively correlated with age (Bybee, 1998).

Socialisation practices for girls and boys deviate in important respects. For example, parents are more tolerant towards aggressive behaviour in boys than in girls, and they compare the behaviour of girls with higher moral standards than the behaviour of boys. As a consequence, in adolescence females report more about guilt over lying than males (Williams & Bybee, 1994). In contrast, males feel more guilty over aggression, reflecting their more frequent involvement in aggressive behaviour (e.g., fighting, causing property damage, injuring animals).

Another important gender difference emerges with respect to the persons who are identified as the reason for feeling guilty. Whereas females primarily refer to family members, males generally mention persons with whom they are only superficially acquainted (Williams & Bybee, 1994). Other gender differences have been found for responses to incidents that evoke guilt feelings: Women ruminate over such incidents more than men (Lyubomirsky & Nolen-Hoeksema, 1993).

Bybee (1998) gives nine possible explanations for the gender gap in guilt-proneness; the most important ones are as follows:

- Because males are more aggressive than females (Eagly, 1987) they block off guilt feelings and neutralise any remorse that occurs after transgressions.
- For males, aggression is more part of their gender role than for females (Spence, Helmreich, & Holahan, 1979). Therefore, there is a higher likelihood for males to consider aggressive acts normatively appropriate.
- For females, consideration, friendliness, and interest in others are normatively prescribed to a greater extent than for males. As a consequence, violations of interpersonal harmony elicit more concern in females than in males, leading to more intense guilt feelings in everyday encounters.
- Society in general and parents in particular are more tolerant towards male aggression than towards female aggression.

Prosocial behaviour

Girls tend to be more helpful than boys in a variety of tests (Eisenberg, Cialdini, McCreath, & Shell, 1987, for kindergartners, 2nd graders, and 5th graders; Eisenberg, Miller, Shell, McNally, & Shea, 1991 for 13–16-year olds; Grusec & Redler, 1980, for 7–8-year-olds; Rice & Grusec, 1975, for 3rd and 4th graders). However, other studies show either no gender differences in level of prosocial behaviour (Rushton, 1975) or complex statistical interactions with other variables (Rosenhan & White, 1967).

The inconsistency of results is at least in part resolved if the kind of prosocial behaviour is taken into account (see later). Mills and Grusec (1991), who found that girls were more helpful than boys, reported that girls attributed their prosocial behaviour to internal causes (vs external causes) less than boys. Girls may be more pressured by their social network to act prosocially and to internalise the ideal of altruism than boys.

Explanations of gender differences in prosocial behaviour may be based on an analysis of the content of gender roles. The social roles of men and women differ. For example, men are more likely to be firemen, policemen, or soldiers. Women are more likely to do the housework. Therefore, the distribution of men and women in different social roles is far from being equal. Eagly (1987) assumed that the unequal distribution of men and women in social roles is the basis of gender-role differences. The female gender role is characterised by interpersonal warmth, interest in social relationships, and interpersonal sensibility, whereas the male gender role is characterised by independence, self-control, and interest in success (Bakan, 1966; Spence et al., 1979). Because males are more involved in professional roles in general, and in risk taking in particular, the conclusion is justified that they acquire traits which are in correspondence with the roles that they predominantly occupy. In Bakan's (1966) terms, males are more oriented towards agency, whereas women are more oriented towards communion. A related distinction is that between instrumental vs expressive division of function (Parsons, 1964).

One assumption is that males are more likely to intervene if the helping must be performed in dangerous situations. If helping includes initiative and active intervention (e.g., in emergency crises) males intervene more than females. Those who have received awards from the Carnegie Hero Fund Commission for their outstanding courage and performance in saving the life of fellow beings are predominantly male. Only about 9% of these heroes are female.

From these and other considerations the prediction was derived that men are more helpful than women (Eagly, 1987, p. 52). On the basis of 99 empirical comparisons a meta-analysis confirmed this hypothesis (Eagly & Crowley, 1986). In 62% of the studies a gender difference was observed, with men being more helpful than females. The general gender difference in helping corresponds with the original finding in studies on simulated emergencies in underground trains, that the likelihood for men to intervene was higher than expected on the basis of the ratio of males and females present in the train (Piliavin et al., 1969). It also corresponds with the elevated likelihood of males intervening in real-life emergencies (Bierhoff, Klein, & Kramp, 1991).

Additional meta-analytic results throw light on the conditions in which there was a particularly strong gender difference in the direction of males (Eagly & Crowley, 1986). The difference was stronger when data were obtained outside the university, when the helping was observed by persons other than the victim, when other helpers were available, and when no direct appeal was made.

Furthermore, the likelihood of receiving help was higher for females than for males. Men were more likely to help women than

1000 inhabitants; 1000–4999 inhabitants; 5000–19,999 inhabitants; 20,000–300,000 inhabitants; and over 300,000 inhabitants. Six distinct helping measures were obtained:

- Complying with a request to name and write down one's favourite colour.
- Offering help to a person who fell on the sidewalk and cried out in pain apparently because he/she hurt his/her leg.
- Helping a person to pick up 20 envelopes he/she had dropped on the sidewalk.
- Donating to the Multiple Sclerosis Society.
- Correcting inaccurate directions.
- Nonresponse rate in the 1976 Australian census.

Referring to the dimensions of helping described in Chapter 2, the location of these six helping measures indicates that donating to the Multiple Sclerosis Society is high on giving (vs doing); completing the census form is high on formal help (vs informal); writing down one's favourite colour is at the nonserious pole of the serious–nonserious dimension; the hurt-leg episode is highly serious; and correcting inaccurate directions as well as picking up fallen envelopes are more spontaneous than planned. Therefore, the six helping measures represent different locations in the dimensional space that is described by planned–spontaneous, serious–nonserious, and doing–giving.

The level of helping was highest for writing down one's favourite colour. Next highest was correcting inaccurate directions, followed by Multiple Sclerosis donation and hurt leg, with a similar level of helping. The lowest rate of helping was obtained for dropped envelopes. These results indicate that the forms of helping included those that were very likely to occur and others that were quite unlikely to occur. Comparison of the helping measures across different population sizes led to unequivocal results: Willingness to help decreased from small to large communities. The largest decrease occurred in communities with a population between 20,000 and 300,000. The only exception to this general rule was the episode of dropped envelopes, which led to low rates of helping in all communities regardless of size (20% or less).

The results for census nonresponse rates in the Australian study did not follow the general pattern. Instead, nonresponse rate was highest in small communities and lowest in communities of intermediate size. Because Sidney and Brisbane showed a higher response rate than communities of intermediate size, the data pattern has a curvilinear shape. This result for census data is explained by the fact that the census was organised by the federal government, which is very remote from small communities in Australia. In addition, people in small towns may hold a negative attitude towards the federal government, which negatively influences their willingness to co-operate in a survey initiated by that government. Besides population size, nonresponse rates were also influenced by foreign heterogeneity of the population. Communities with a high proportion of foreign-born inhabitants had higher refusal rates. In addition, communities with high levels of tourism had higher refusal rates. These three predictors explained 30% of the variance in refusal rates.

Because other determinants of helpfulness besides population size were included in the analyses, it was possible to evaluate the relative importance of population size as a determinant of helping. Across all measures of helping, population size was the most influential variable, explaining, for example, 18% of the variance of the colour request episode. Foreign heterogeneity and tourism had only scattered effects. Finally factors such as social class and geographical isolation exerted no influence at all. The population size effect was still found when the influences of other community-level variables were controlled for in multiple regressions, documenting the robust-ness of its influence. These results confirm the information-overload hypothesis of Milgram (1970), as well as the diffusion of respon-sibility hypothesis, and lead to the conclusion that high levels of urbanisation are correlated with a low level of prosocial behaviour.

Although the study by Amato (1983) offers an elegant solution to several methodological shortcomings that were present in earlier studies, it is limited to one cultural setting—eastern Australia. Fortunately, a meta-analysis is available which overcomes these limitations (Steblay, 1987). A total of 65 comparisons between rural and urban areas were included in this analysis. The data included in the data base were collected all over the world, and 52 comparisons referred to the size of communities where the observed people lived, whereas the remaining 13 comparisons referred to size of the community where the respondent was born. As size of place of birth turned out to be irrelevant for helping behaviour, the comparisons reported in the following are limited to those that considered only the size of the current community.

If the classification of rural and urban areas as defined by the investigators is taken as the starting point, a stable rural–urban difference exists, because fewer people helped in urban areas compared with rural areas. However, this result is possibly misleading because a specific size of community (e.g., 60,000 inhabitants) may be labelled large by one investigator and small by another. Therefore, in this meta-analysis the classification variable was directly derived from the number of inhabitants. The communities were divided into seven levels of population size (numbers in parentheses refer to the number of studies that considered the level):

- smaller than 1000 (1),
- 1000–4999 (4),
- 5000–19,999 (23),
- 20,000–59,999 (14),
- 60,000–300,000 (7),
- 300,001–999,999 (14),
- larger than 1,000,000 (29).

Note that the classification system for population sizes used in the meta-analysis is more sensitive with respect to the larger population sizes than that reported by Amato (1983) and that it averages the results across different cultures. On the basis of this classification of population size, the negative correlation between size of community and helpfulness vanished (Steblay, 1987). Instead a curvilinear relationship emerged: Helping behaviour increased up to a population size of 60,000–300,000 inhabitants and dropped sharply in larger cities (over 300,000 inhabitants).

Further results of the meta-analysis indicate that the differences in helping behaviour depending on size of community were independent of the type of helping measure. To simplify matters, a dichotomy was derived by classifying all communities up to 50,000 inhabitants as rural and all communities of 100,000 inhabitants and larger as urban. Population sizes between 50,000 and 100,000 were omitted from these analyses. Following the three-dimensional taxonomy of helping (Smithson et al., 1983), each of the following helping measures was considered:

- Formal help (e.g., participation in a survey).
- Informal help (e.g., giving back overpaid change).
- Serious emergency (e.g., helping an injured person).
- Nonserious problem (e.g., changing money).
- Doing (e.g., making a call for a stranger).
- Giving (e.g., donating money).

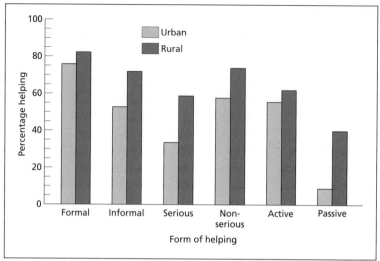

FIG. 4.1.
Rural–urban
comparison of
prosocial behaviour
(based on data from
Steblay, 1987, p. 351).

For each of these measures of help the analyses led to the same
conclusion: More help was offered in rural than in urban areas
(Figure 4.1). Therefore, the rural–urban contrast in helping was
independent of the specific measure of helping.

How can these results be integrated into the curvilinear trend of
data described earlier? The solution to this problem lies in the fact
that communities of 300,000 inhabitants and larger are over-
represented, and population sizes between 100,000 and 300,000
people are under-represented in the data base. As a consequence, by
averaging across all samples from communities of 100,000 people and
more, the very large communities where helping decreases out-
number the intermediate communities where helping rates are high.
So the comparisons in Figure 4.1 refer to the contrast between small
towns and large communities that typically have more than 300,000
inhabitants. If this contrast defines urban–rural differences, the conclusion is justified that people in large communities are more reluctant to help than people in small communities. But if the intermediate
range of population sizes (60,000–300,000) is represented in an
unbiased way, it becomes clear that the highest level of prosocial
behaviour in everyday situations is to be expected not in small communities but in the middle range of population sizes.

The results of the meta-analysis by Steblay (1987) offer only partial
support for the information-overload hypothesis (Milgram, 1970). A
better test of the hypothesis can be conducted if population density
(population per square mile) is used instead of population size

(Levine et al., 1994). Large, medium, and small cities from four regions of the United States were included in the study. Small cities had 350,000–650,000 inhabitants (e.g., Knoxville, Santa Barbara), medium cities 950,000–1,450,000 inhabitants (e.g., Indianapolis, Buffalo), and large cities more than 2,000,000 inhabitants (e.g., Houston, Los Angeles). Six measures of prosocial behaviour were considered. Five have already been mentioned (dropped pen, hurt leg, change for a quarter, blind person crossing, and lost letter). The sixth helping measure was donation to United Way which was derived from the statistical record.

An overall index of helping was formed by averaging across the six measures. The formation of an overall index of helping was based on the fact that the six measures of helping tended to correlate positively. The strongest correlations emerged between change for a quarter, blind person crossing, lost letter, and donations to United Way. Dropped pen and hurt leg (which only correlated $r = .06$ with each other) were not highly correlated with the other measures. Therefore, the alpha coefficient of internal consistency of .51 is quite low across the six measures. Omitting the hurt-leg measure would increase the alpha coefficient to .62.

The rather moderate level of correlations among the measures reflects the fact that they were intentionally selected to represent diverse measures of helping behaviour. Selection was based on the three-dimensional taxonomy of helping by Smithson et al. (1983). Donation to United Way represented giving, whereas the other five measures represented doing on the giving–doing dimension. Donation to United Way also represented planned helping, whereas hurt leg, blind person crossing, dropped pen, and giving change represented spontaneous helping (lost letter was in the middle of the planned–spontaneous helping dimension).

Results indicate that population density was a better predictor of helping than population size. The correlation was $r = -.55$. After partialling out population size, the correlation was still $r = -.44$. In contrast, population size had a correlation of $r = -.38$, which was reduced to $r = .04$ after partialling out population density. Population density turned out to be a strong concomitant of prosocial behaviour.

The cost of living was found to be a further negative concomitant of helping ($r = -.50$). However, the effect of population density was still significant even after partialling out cost of living ($r = -.41$). The negative correlation of cost of living with helping remained after partialling out population density ($r = -.33$). Therefore, population density and cost of living are two independent predictors of prosocial behaviour, although there is some overlap between both predictors.

In summary, these results offer strong support for the hypothesis that population density of a city is a concomitant of level of helping in that city. These findings support the information-overload hypothesis (Milgram, 1970) because higher density is expected to lead to more system overload. However, the evidence in favour of the hypothesis is limited because the study was based on a comparison between cities with more than 350,000 inhabitants (cf. Steblay, 1987). Alternatively, the results can also be explained on the basis of diffusion of responsibility (Latané & Darley, 1970) because higher density means a higher likelihood of diffusion of responsibility.

Although level of prosocial behaviour is relatively low in urban areas (compared with cities of 300,000, 400,000, or 500,000 inhabitants), rural areas are also characterised by a reluctance to act prosocially (Steblay, 1987). Therefore, the information-overload hypothesis is only viable if additional assumptions are made. For example, people in small towns may have a stronger ingroup orientation than people in larger communities. The combined effect of both assumptions (information overload plus ingroup favouritism) may explain the complete pattern of results.

Time effects

If people feel that they are vulnerable, it is a question of trust whether they are willing to help. In the United States trust has been decreasing over the years since the 1970s. This is true not only for generalised trust (Rotter, 1980) but also for political trust (Citrin & Muste, 1999). Although the decline in political trust halted in the early 1990s, towards the end of the 20th century mistrust was on the rise again.

Trust might be relevant to what people do in public. For example, nonresponse rates in surveys may be understood as an indication of mistrust. The increasing refusal rates in survey studies (House & Wolf, 1978) and in surveys dealing with opinions about political leaders (Tyler, 1986) point to a general trend which may be explained by the reduction in political trust. Such an trend towards mistrust may contribute to a reduced willingness to act prosocially in public. It is complemented by a decreasing level of interpersonal trust and an erosion of sense of community which—taken together—are inter-

Historically there was often a strong sense of community (as can be seen from this street party held in 1919 to celebrate the end of World War I a year earlier), but very close-knit communities are rarer within modern Western society. Credit: Popperfoto.

preted as a loss of "social capital" (Fukuyama, 1999). Finally, level of trait anxiety increased dramatically among adults and children between 1952 and 1993 (Twenge, 2000). All these trends in combination support the presumption that prosocial behaviour in public places has declined progressively in the second half of the 20th century.

It is difficult to predict what the future will hold. Will the trend towards interpersonal mistrust become stronger (because of increasing anxiety and decreasing social connectedness)? Or will the continuing process of urbanisation increase the magnitude of urban–rural differences, because the altruistic motivation of people living in big cities tends to be relatively weak?

Social status

Social status is one of the main organisational principles in society. Sociobiologists consider social hierarchies as universal characteristics of human societies (Hinde, 2001). How is social status related to prosocial behaviour? Whereas some results speak for the assumption that members of the upper middle class are more helpful than members of the working class (Feldman, 1968, for Boston, Athens, and Paris), there are also results that point in the other direction, e.g., the relatively high levels of helpfulness in Turkish slums of Istanbul and Ankara (Korte & Ayvalioglu, 1981).

Status does not seem to be a reliable predictor of helpfulness on a general level (Amato, 1983). But this does not necessarily mean that it is unimportant as a factor in helping. Presumably social status influences prosocial behaviour in interaction with other variables. For example, social class may be involved in similarity effects with middle-class people helping middle-class victims and lower-class people helping lower-class victims. Feldman's (1968) finding may result from the unintentional use of middle-class help-seekers, who were more accepted by middle-class than by lower-class people.

A related phenomenon is that leaflet distributors who had a conventional appearance were more successful than distributors who had a deviant appearance (long hair, old army jacket, etc., Darley & Cooper, 1972). The similarity hypothesis was confirmed in a further study in which conventional and deviant-looking students asked: "Excuse me, could I borrow a dime for a long distance phone call? It's kind of important" (Emswiller, Deaux, & Willits, 1971). Conventional-looking people helped conventional-looking petitioners more, whereas hippies helped hippies more.

Status is connected with cost of living which is negatively related to level of prosocial behaviour in a community (Levine et al., 1994). Although status as an isolated variable may have no general influence on prosocial behaviour, it may turn out to be relevant if there is a connection between status and living in a metropolitan area. Cost of living is highly correlated with per capita income across 36 US cities ($r = .82$), which also tends to correlate negatively with the overall helping index employed by Levine et al. (1994). Therefore, social status seems to be a negative predictor of helping in metropolitan areas.

Human nature vs cultural context 5

There has long been controversy about whether prosocial behaviour is the result of natural selection or of cultural institutions that were invented to increase individuals' solidarity and willingness to cooperate (Batson, 1983; Campbell, 1965, 1975). This controversy is even visible in the two papers by Campbell: Whereas in the earlier treatment altruism is understood as part of human nature, in the later treatment altruism is explained by the influence of cultural institutions that exert pressure on the egoistic human being.

In this chapter two explanations of prosocial behaviour are presented which focus on biological factors and cultural influences, respectively. By comparing these approaches, differences and similarities between biological and sociological explanations are highlighted. Because culture itself is the result of natural selection, it would be surprising if biological and cultural explanations did not fit together. This correspondence is rooted in the fact that evolution sets limits within which cultural variation occurs.

The biological perspective

Responsible behaviour and intention to help are concepts that are only applicable to human beings, not to nonhuman species. However, moral behaviour is the result of a process of evolution in animals which sets constraints on moral codes that control social behaviour in human beings (Hinde, 2001). What is recognised as responsible behaviour depends on internalised standards of behaviour. These standards are partially based on natural selection and partially on cultural settings. A key insight is that helping behaviour is likely to be based on natural selection, which is guided by reproductive success. Two biological mechanisms are relevant which are applicable among relatives and among friends, respectively. Prosocial behaviour is common among relatives. Altruism among relatives is best represented by parental care. Parents support their children and invest a huge amount of time and money in their well-being. Children support their parents when they are old with much energy and effort (although not necessarily with enthusiasm; Montada, Schmitt, & Dalbert, 1991).

Hamilton's theory of altruism between relatives (1964) explains how evolution may lead to the positive selection of prosocial behaviour. Reproductive success is not limited to one's own children but also includes children of relatives. Whereas own children count most, children of relatives count depending on their degree of relatedness. Relatives share genes with the individual. For example, the relatedness coefficient between parents and offspring is 1/2, and between siblings it is also 1/2 for diploid organisms. The probability that nephews or nieces share a gene with uncle or aunt is 1/4 (Ridley & Dawkins, 1981). Therefore, own genes are favoured by increasing the survival chances of genetic relatives. For example, two children of a brother or sister represent on average 1/2 of the genetic structure of their uncle or aunt in the next generation. As a consequence, the biological prediction is that prosocial behaviour is very likely among members of the family.

The ultimate reproductive success of an individual is represented by his or her inclusive fitness. Genetic fitness maximisation refers to personal reproduction (direct fitness) as well as to the reproduction success of relatives who share a certain proportion of genes with the individual (indirect fitness). Direct and indirect fitness in combination constitute inclusive fitness. In addition, the probability of altruism depends on the costs for the helper and the benefits for the help-recipient. Lower costs and higher benefits make altruism more probable. This is expressed in the following Hamilton inequality:

$$B * r > C$$

where B = Benefit, r = coefficient of relatedness, and C = Cost.

The inequality indicates that evolution favours altruism if its benefits multiplied by the coefficient of relatedness are higher than its costs. For example, help that provides four units of benefit to a sister and which costs one unit of benefit for the individual fulfils Hamilton's inequality. The lower the coefficient of relatedness, the larger must the gain in units of benefits be before it becomes advantageous for the individual who helps. Costs and benefits in this context are measured by the consequences of the prosocial behaviour. The coefficient of relatedness is a weighting factor which says how much the benefits of the help-recipient must outweigh the costs of the helper to ensure that the help is biologically meaningful.

But prosocial behaviour is not limited to relatives. Because human beings are social animals one may assume that natural selection has favoured co-operative tendencies on the individual level (Campbell, 1965). Human beings live in groups and achieve great advantages by co-operation. If the environment is dangerous and unpredictable, co-operation has great survival value. Studies on animals provide evidence that co-operation occurs depending on a scheme of reciprocity. Animals that are dependent on co-operation for survival share more of their food with those animals which have shared their food with them in the past (Hinde, 2001). The adherence to the principle of reciprocity is not limited to nonhuman species. It is universal among cultures all over the world (Komter, 1996).

The theory of reciprocal altruism by Trivers (1971) explains prosocial behaviour among friends and neighbours. The basic tenet of the theory is that prosocial behaviour is favoured by natural selection if it follows the principle of reciprocity and if the costs for the helper are lower than the benefits for the help-recipient. People in the social network who simulate co-operation, although they are only interested in profiting from the advantages (and not willing to sacrifice anything), constitute a real threat to the functioning of reciprocity in a social system. In fact, if the society is highly competitive, co-operation is meaningless, leading to the prediction that individuals are socialised to compete with each other (Hinde, 2001; see earlier). Reciprocal altruism is likely to occur if societies promote a co-operative climate that allows trusting relationships between initial strangers to develop over time (Voland, 1999).

The theory of reciprocal altruism does not predict the indiscriminate application of the principle of reciprocity. Instead, it predicts that reciprocity will flourish in a network of friends who take each other's perspective, vicariously experience each other's joys and disappointments (cf. Batson, Turk, Shaw, & Klein, 1995), and believe in each other's positive intentions to alleviate any distress that may occur in any member of the network (Hinde, 2001). For them, the principle of reciprocity constitutes a social contract to which they subscribe implicitly or explicitly.

The cultural context

The comparison of volunteerism in different nations has revealed that long-term involvement in prosocial behaviour varies widely between different countries (see Chapter 21). This result is an indication that large cultural differences exist with respect to prosocial behaviour. In the same vein, a comparison between Berlin, Bologna, and Warsaw revealed cultural differences in prosocial moral reasoning among 6th to 12th graders (Silbereisen, Lamsfuss, Boehnke, & Eisenberg, 1991). Cross-national variation in prosocial moral reasoning was also revealed in a comparison between Brazilian and American adolescents, with Brazilian adolescents scoring lower on internalised moral reasoning than American adolescents (Carlo, Koller, Eisenberg, Da Silva, & Frohlich, 1996).

One of the first studies on cultural differences in helping was conducted in Paris, Athens, and Boston, Massachusetts (Feldman, 1968). The study dealt with willingness to mail a stamped letter for a stranger who talked to the target person at a train station. The request by a native was fulfilled in Boston by 85% of the target persons, in Paris by 68%, and in Athens by only 12%. If a foreigner put forward the same request in Boston, the request was fulfilled in 75% of cases, in Paris in 88%, and in Athens in 48%. According to these results, Athenians differ significantly from the other city-dwellers in terms of their low helpfulness, especially towards natives. They seem to define their in-group very tightly and to react towards their Greek fellow countrymen in a rather unfriendly way (Triandis, Vassiliou, & Nassiakou, 1968).

These and other studies show that cultural variation in prosocial behaviour must be taken into account. In addition, cultural norms exert a significant influence on moral reasoning, which is mediated by different socialisation practices that affect the importance of self-gain, internalised moral standards, and empathic concern as motives for prosocial behaviour (Carlo, Fabes, Laible, & Kupanoff, 1999). For example, Brazilian adolescents scored lower on moral reasoning tests than American adolescents (Carlo et al., 1996; Hutz, De Conti, & Vargas, 1993). More research is needed on the interplay between cultural norms, prosocial motives, and prosocial behaviour.

Even highly industrialised countries—like Japan and Germany—differ from each other in respect to their values, social rules, and achievement motivation (Trommsdorff, Suzuki, & Sasaki, 1987). These cultural differences are represented on several dimensions (Hofstede, 1991). One important dimension of societal differences is the individualistic or the collectivistic orientation (Triandis, 1994). Whereas the Spanish, Greek, and Far Eastern cultures emphasise the connectedness of the individual with the group, the English, Germans, and Americans tend to prefer an individualistic culture in which the independence of the individuals is considered more important than their interdependence in a social network. Much research has been conducted in an attempt to identify similarities and differences between Far Eastern cultures and Western cultures (Shaver & Schutte, 2001). One difference is that in Western cultures the independence of the self is emphasised, whereas in Far Eastern cultures the self is considered as part of a social system (Earley, 1994; Johns & Xie, 1998).

In Far Eastern cultures a major part of everyday behaviour takes place in social systems such as family, school, and profession, and social roles are connected with obligations that determine everyday behaviour. This cultural collectivism is demonstrated by the different perspectives of Japanese and Americans on assignment of responsibility (Hamilton & Sanders, 1992). Whereas Americans understand responsibility as a personal issue of the transgressor, who is to blame for what he/she did wrong, Japanese consider the social context in which the transgression occurred, and avoid the well-known fundamental attribution error in which responsibility is primarily attributed to the actor who made the mistake.

One way to conceptualise the Western understanding of responsibility is to consider it as an example of the fundamental attribution error (Shaver & Schutte, 2001). This perspective is supported by the fact that the overattribution to dispositions of the actor is found only in Western culture but not in India or China (Miller, 1984; Morris & Peng, 1994). This leads to the insight that the fundamental attribution error is not as fundamental as originally assumed. Therefore, in psychological terms "correspondence bias" is preferable to "fundamental attribution error" (Gilbert, 1998).

However, the fact remains that Western culture tends to identify the wrong-doer with the transgression without taking the social context into account. As the comparison with Japan indicates, such a strong internal attribution bias in assignment of responsibility is not an expression of human nature but the result of cultural predilections which control individual thinking about transgressors. This cultural difference is also revealed in school (Shaver & Schutte, 2001): Whereas Japanese teachers delegate the responsibility for discipline and order to the students who themselves organise the social conditions of the classroom, the majority of American teachers take charge of the situation and ensure discipline in the classroom.

The same difference between Japan and United States is apparent in the legal system, which is more oriented towards achieving a compromise between opponents in Japan and more oriented towards identifying the guilty person in the United States (Shaver & Schutte, 2001). These differences are due at least in part to the application of the correspondence bias in Western culture. But they are also the result of institutional procedures in Japan that give high priority to interpersonal harmony and which value the social group over the individual.

In summary, principles of responsibility assignment are context-specific. Culture colours the type of communication about responsibility that is dominant among members of society. For example, it is likely that self-serving tendencies in the assignment of responsibility predominate in Western culture—self-deception and attempts to maintain face tend to dominate the discourse on responsibility. In contrast, in Far Eastern cultures communication about responsibility focuses on the individual as a member of a social group (Crittenden & Bae, 1994).

Another example that highlights cultural differences with respect to solidarity is that Chinese employees show not only a self-serving bias in attributions (which is also found in Western culture) but also a group-serving bias in their perception of their own work group, in that it is seen as better than the average work group (Johns & Xie, 1998). Such a bias was not found for Canadian employees. Chinese employees indicated not only that they themselves were better than the average member of their work group but also that the average member of their work group was better than the occupational standard. They showed solidarity with their work group, a tendency that was absent in Canada.

Is it possible to reconcile the biological approach with the cultural approach? On the one hand, principles like reciprocity and self-serving bias seem to be used in many societies, indicating pan-cultural human propensities. On the other hand, assignment of responsibility and solidarity are treated quite differently in different cultures, as the comparison between Western culture and Far-Eastern culture demonstrates. The latter result agrees with the finding that social responsibility is only moderately influenced by genetic factors (Neiderhiser, Reiss, & Hetherington, 1996).

Cultural variation and biological influence coexist with each other. On the one hand, cultural variations are limited by natural selection. On the other hand, biological propensities are put into perspective by socialisation. For example, religions in general seem to propagate prosocial behaviour of children towards their parents, but some have higher expectations than others. Therefore, the extent of obligations depends on the cultural system, although obligation to support parents is a universal phenomenon.

Measurement and generality of prosocial behaviour in children 6

Before turning to developmental trends, I will describe various techniques for the measurement of prosocial behaviour in children. Some procedures are illustrated using examples of prosocial behaviour in the school setting. Finally, I discuss the issue of generality of prosocial behaviour. Is it possible to predict prosocial behaviour on the basis of prosocial orientation, and how are different measures of prosocial behaviour related?

How is prosocial behaviour measured in children?

A researcher who is interested in preschoolers' prosocial behaviour might ask questions like: Do children help if a classmate asks for assistance? In which cases does a potential help-recipient reject a child's spontaneous offer to help? Before presenting the results of two studies that provide answers to these questions, I will offer some general comments on observational techniques. In observational studies of prosocial behaviour several methods are used which have common elements and differences. A general finding is that measures of prosocial behaviour in a given setting tend to correlate positively, although the correlations are only moderate in size.

Observation methods are used in field studies in kindergartens and preschool. An example is the description of the ecology of children's behaviour in preschool settings (Smith & Connolly, 1980). Non-interpretive motor patterns (e.g., simple smile, look around) as well as interpretive behaviour categories are taken into account. If the analysis of basic processes of social interdependence is pursued, specific units of analysis are appropriate. But researchers who are interested in the determinants of meaningful behaviour units like aggression or pro-social behaviour tend to use broader observational units. Each category is further explained by examples or subcategories. A classification

TABLE 6.1

Basic behaviour categories of prosocial and antisocial behaviour

Verbal co-operation	Physical co-operation	Verbal aggression	Physical aggression
Expressing positive verbal compliance	Expressing positive physical compliance	Expressing verbal noncompliance	Expressing physical noncompliance
Offering help	Giving help	Making demands	Taking an object by force
Making bids for mutual interaction	Engaging in mutual interaction	Threatening another	Using physical force against another
Making bids for reciprocal interaction	Engaging in reciprocal interaction	Expressing insults	Attacking another physically
Giving compliments	Giving nonverbal signs of approval	Verbally expressing dislike for another	Physically expressing dislike for another
Expressing friendship verbally	Expressing friendship nonverbally		

Source: Table from "Modification of cooperation and aggression through teacher attention to children's speech" by R.G. Slaby and G.C. Crowley, in *Journal of Experimental Child Psychology, Volume 23*, 442–458, copyright © 1977 by Academic Press, reproduced by permission of the publisher.

that focuses on prosocial behaviour and aggression is the taxonomic system of Slaby and Crowley (1977), which distinguishes between verbal and physical behaviour on the one hand and co-operation and aggression on the other hand. The 2 × 2 schema resulted in four behaviour categories, which were described by specific behaviour patterns (see Table 6.1).

Observational studies of children's social behaviour have been reported on regularly since the 1930s (Altmann, 1974). In many of these studies, time sampling was the applied procedure. This means that during a number of predetermined time intervals the occurrence or non-occurrence of specified behaviours is scored. In the meantime, a more elaborated taxonomy of sampling methods has been developed, which distinguishes between at least four different techniques (Altmann, 1974; Smith & Connolly, 1980):

- One–zero sampling is a new name for the old time sampling procedure. The resulting data show whether the specified behavioural category occurred or did not occur in the sampling interval.
- Focal-person sampling means that a complete record of one particular individual is obtained in each sample period. The

record includes all occurrences in which that individual is either the actor or the receiver. A variant is focal subgroup sampling, which is based on the continuous observation of each group member. With this method, it is possible to estimate the proportion of time spent on the behaviour. In addition, frequency scores may be obtained.

- Sampling all occurrences of certain behaviours means that all individuals who are present in the setting are observed and the occurrences of each behaviour category are recorded.
- Instantaneous sampling includes the repeated observation of an individual at preselected moments in time. Scan sampling is the application of instantaneous sampling to groups.

Each sampling strategy has its advantages and disadvantages in terms of amount of effort necessary to record the data and completeness of data recorded. One–zero sampling is the least efficient because the resulting data are hard to interpret and not useful as a replacement for frequency scores. The one–zero scores confound information on frequency and duration: as a consequence, their interpretation is difficult. The other techniques lead to unbiased estimates of time spent on the activity, frequency, or both (Altmann, 1974).

Methodological studies may contribute to our understanding of different observational techniques. In one such study (Yarrow & Waxler, 1979) about 4 hours of mother–child interactions at home were observed over 2 days. The observations, which followed the method of focal-person sampling, included various activities (e.g., free play, mealtime). Observational categories were specified in advance (e.g., attention seeking, obeys rules). In addition, frequency data on mothers' expression of warmth and demands were collected.

An alternative to the online recording of observational data is summary evaluation by raters after observing the mother–child interactions. Observers retrospectively rated the same categories on 5-point scales on the basis of the 4-hour observation period (Yarrow & Waxler, 1979). This rating technique is based on a process of abstraction that is characterised by an implicit categorisation of the observed behavioural sequences. Its objectivity can be heightened by giving examples of episodes that are relevant for the target activities, because one big problem is that observers tend to use their own idiosyncratic interpretation of the dimensions when making their ratings (Cairns & Green, 1979).

The more cognitive abstraction is required of the rater, the more the rater's cognitive processes influence the rating (Mischel, 1973).

This does not necessarily mean that summary ratings are invalid (Cairns & Green, 1979). The choice of method depends on the purpose of the study: If the focus is on broader behaviour categories that occur only infrequently, rating methods are very useful. In contrast, if the focus is on the ecology of behaviour, its elements, and their structural relationships, observational procedures are more useful. In addition, ratings refer to outcomes of development, whereas observational methods inform about the processes on which social patterns are built.

A third method is that a reference person for the child gives a rating of the child's prosocial behaviour. In the 4-hour observational study mentioned earlier (Yarrow & Waxler, 1979), mothers were asked to rate their children retrospectively on the same dimensions that were assessed by the observers (e.g., attention seeking). Therefore, they had to retrieve from their memory information that was relevant for the dimension rated.

It is likely that ratings are more influenced by implicit personality theories and expectations than the recording of online observations. To be sure, online recording of observation is also subject to biased information processing (e.g., halo effect, selective attention, and stereotyping), but the number of sources of bias seems to be larger in the case of summary ratings, because in addition to the same biases as online records of behaviour they have their own sources of error (Cairns & Green, 1979).

The three methods (online observation, summary ratings by observers, and summary ratings by mothers) were applied in a study on dependency on adults, compliance, and aggression by Yarrow and Waxler (1979). They considered research instruments as different samples of behaviour. Results indicate that the highest correspondence was observed between summary ratings of observers and mothers. For example, attention seeking correlated .37 between observers' rating and mothers' rating. Observed frequencies and ratings correlated lower.

In addition, prior to the observations an interview with the mothers was conducted which considered the same variables for which frequency scores and summary ratings were obtained during the observational periods. Although mothers' ratings and interview results correlated quite highly for attention seeking, low correlations were found for other dimensions (e.g., obeys rules).

Observational studies are specific in several respects (Yarrow & Waxler, 1979). The behaviour sampling is defined by time, by context, and by research instrument. For example, the sampling may be separated in time blocks of 15 minutes or 30 minutes. Results indicate that substantial stability of the relative position of children between successive samplings on dimensions such as seeking adult attention and aggression is only found when the length of observation is 1 hour and more. Yarrow and Waxler (1979) warn that even in 60-minute samples (and certainly much more so in 5-minute samples) "tremendous fluctuation in correspondence" (p. 48) may occur.

The frequency of specific behaviour categories and summary ratings thereof may also depend on the setting in which the observations are made. For example, observations of children's behaviour were made during indoor play and outdoor play (Yarrow & Waxler, 1979). Several categories were counted (correlations between both settings in parentheses): attention seeking (.39, $p < .01$); oppositional and aggressive (.50, $p < .01$); positive peer interaction (.24, not significant); co-operative and helping (.35, $p < .01$).

These correlations are positive although they are far from indicating high correspondence. Every setting is quite special, for example, rough-and-tumble play is more likely outdoors than indoors. Opportunities to express aggressive behaviour may be enhanced in outdoor settings, whereas co-operation and helping may occur more frequently in institutional settings like preschools. Therefore the selection of settings influences observational records. These results point to the relativity of empirical measurements in general and the measurement of prosocial behaviour in children in particular, although some consistency across measures is revealed (see also Hastings, Zahn-Waxler, Robinson, Usher, & Bridges, 2000).

A further method for the measurement of prosocial behaviour which seems especially applicable in schools is based on sociometric procedures. A comprehensive study of prosocial and antisocial behaviour of pupils in the 6th and 7th grades was performed by Wentzel (1993, 1994) who used sociometric methods. Prosocial characteristics were sharing, co-operating, and "helping other kids when they have a problem", whereas antisocial behaviour was related to "starts fights" and "breaks rules, does things you are not supposed to". Each student rated a unique set of 25 classmates for each behaviour that was assessed. Scores were obtained by computing the percentage of nominations received. In addition, pupils assessed their own prosocial goals in general and in school specifically. Academic achievement was measured by grade point averages and by the Stanford Test of Basic Skills as a standardised achievement test. Finally, teacher ratings of prosocial and aggressive behaviour were obtained.

Preliminary analyses indicated that pupil ratings and teacher ratings were correlated in the range of .26 and .37 for prosocial behaviour and .23 and .57 for antisocial behaviour, respectively. These results indicate that the understanding of prosocial and antisocial behaviour by students and teachers may be somewhat different, although some overlap in the assessments is obvious. Students who express a prosocial goal are perceived by other students as prosocial. In the same vein, their teachers also consider them to be prosocially oriented. Teachers rated "How often does this student show an interest in schoolwork?", "How often does this student work independently?", and "How often does this student show concern with evaluation?" (Wentzel, 1993, p. 359). These ratings were positively correlated between .57 and .66. They were also significantly correlated with grade point averages (ranging between .48 and .59) and with test scores on the Stanford Test of Basic Skills (between .32 and .50). Finally, teachers rated their preferences with respect to specific students: "How much would you like to have this student in your class again next year?" (Wentzel, 1993, p. 359).

Personal goals are defined as those things that an individual would like to achieve in a given situation (Wentzel, 1994, p. 173). Students' goal pursuit was measured by questions that began with the following phrase: "How often do you try to . . .?" (Wentzel, 1994, p. 175). Prosocial goals were to share and help peers with social problems and to share and help classmates with academic problems. In addition, goal pursuit related to social responsibility was measured by asking students how often they tried to keep promises and commitments made to peers. Peers and teachers also rated prosocial and responsible behaviour. Peer assessments of social acceptance were obtained using the question: "How much would you like to be in school activities with this person?" (Wentzel, 1994, p. 176). Finally, measures of social support were obtained relating to the support received by teachers and by peers. Items included "My teachers really care about me" and "My classmates care about my feelings" (Wentzel, 1994, p. 176). Results indicated that pursuit of prosocial goals was positively related to prosocial behaviour, to peer acceptance, and to social support.

As expected, academic behaviour and teachers' preferences for students were positively correlated. In addition, prosocial behaviour was a positive predictor of academic behaviour, whereas antisocial behaviour was a negative predictor. Antisocial behaviour was also a negative predictor of teachers' preferences for students. Finally, grade point average was influenced by academic behaviour, prosocial

Learning and development II

How does prosocial behaviour develop? 7

The development of prosocial behaviour is a continuous process that is not yet fully understood. This is due to a lack of longitudinal studies, which would allow a description of individual patterns of change in prosocial behaviour (see Magnusson, Bergman, Rudinger, & Törestad, 1994). Development encompasses inter-individual as well as intra-individual variation. Therefore, two approaches are viable for studying the development of prosocial behaviour:

- The first approach involves the search for the mechanism that influences development and which may be summarised in the form of general developmental laws. Here the focus is on intra-individual change accompanied by low inter-individual variation. Developmental psychology searches for such changes which occur during the entire life cycle. With respect to prosocial behaviour, primarily the development of children and adolescents has been studied so far.
- The second approach focuses on inter-individual differences in prosocial behaviour. The question is whether systematic relationships exist between personality variables and prosocial behaviour. An example is the issue of influences of the level of moral development on prosocial behaviour. In this approach special emphasis is laid on prosocial behaviour in natural settings. One important question is whether prosocial behaviour in everyday situations exhibits high generality across different situations or is situation-specific (see Chapter 6).

In the following, the question of general developmental change is emphasised (see also Eisenberg & Fabes, 1998; Zahn-Waxler & Smith, 1992). In addition, I address the issue of whether there are general principles underlying the developmental process.

Prosocial behaviour in the second year of life

Rheingold, Hay, and West (1976) documented prosocial behaviour of 2-year-olds. Later research based on mother's reports as well as on independent evidence collected by observers in simulated distress situations has basically confirmed the finding that 2-year-olds show prosocial behaviour (Zahn-Waxler, Radke-Yarrow, Wagner, & Chapman, 1992a), correcting the picture of the little monster that many parents cultivate.

The emergence of prosocial behaviour and empathic concern in the second year of life confirms the theory of empathy development proposed by Hoffman (1984, 2000) who considered the reflexive infant cry in 1-year-olds as the first manifestation of empathy. The fact that prosocial behaviour occurs quite early in life corresponds with the development of affective and cognitive competencies of the child in this developmental phase:

- Perspective-taking, which is a prerequisite of empathic concern, depends on cognitive capacities like symbolic representation and language acquisition—especially the use of emotional concepts—which develop during the second year of life.
- Likewise, self-recognition develops—a precondition for self–other differentiation in the second year of life (Zahn-Waxler et al., 1992a).
- Finally, emotional responses occur in response to the suffering of others. These resemble the emotional experiences of the victim and may be described as vicariously experienced sadness.

Children as young as 2 years may show concern when they see another child in distress. Credit: Photofusion/ Paul Doyle.

The development of prosocial behaviour is a slow process. In the first and second year of life base rates of prosocial responses are quite low. Mothers who were trained to record empathic and prosocial responses of their children reported that between the age of 13 and 15 months, natural distress incidents to which the toddlers could respond prosocially occurred about 9 times during the 3-month period; between 18 and 20 months the mean was about 7.5 incidents, and between 23 and 25 months the mean number of incidents was about 6. In addition, mothers reported that in 9% of natural distress situations that 13–15-month-old toddlers observed as bystanders, they responded prosocially (whereas in 15% of the incidents they showed self-distress). The percentage of reported prosocial responses increased substantially in the age range 18–20 months (21%) as well as 23–25 months (49%). These reports by mothers have been generally confirmed in distress simulations where observers rated children's prosocial responses (Zahn-Waxler et al., 1992a).

The development of prosocial behaviour has been systematically investigated as early as in 14-month-old children by Zahn-Waxler et al. (1992b) who studied a group of children at two time points 6 months apart. Because only twins took part in the study, it was possible to estimate the heritability of several components of pro-social behaviour. Children were observed at home and in the laboratory in the presence of their mothers. At each measurement time five tests of prosocial behaviour were conducted by the mother or the experimenter. For example, the mother pretended to have hurt her knee and vocally expressed some pain. The children were videotaped in these test situations. Responses that were coded included:

- Prosocial behaviour: The child tries to help the victim.
- Hypothesis testing: The child tries to comprehend what is going on (rated on a 4-point scale).
- Empathic concern: The child's facial, vocal, or gestural expressions indicate concern (rated on a 4-point scale).
- Self-distress: The child's facial, vocal, or gestural expressions indicate fear (rated on a 4-point scale).
- Indifference: Absence of involvement in the simulated distress.

Prosocial behaviour, hypothesis testing, empathic concern, and self-distress were positively intercorrelated, although the relationship for empathic concern and self-distress was rather weak ($r = .14$ and $r = 13$ for 14-month-old and 20-month-old children, respectively). In addition, the correlations between these four variables and indifference were negative. These results show that the simulated distress elicited individual differences in responses, which generalised across all measures obtained in the situation.

The positive correlation of empathic concern and self-distress is in agreement with the assumption that empathic concern originates from personal distress (Hoffman, 1984, 2000). Although personal distress and empathic concern share only very little common variance, they are obviously not mutually exclusive responses. In an overview of empirical research Eisenberg (2000) points out that in most studies the correlation of personal distress and empathic concern is around zero and sometimes negative. However, most of the studies were conducted in the laboratory in contrived situations, which presumably are less representative of real life than the situations investigated by Zahn-Waxler and her colleagues.

The test–retest correlations over the 6-month interval were low and only significant for hypothesis testing, empathic concern, and indifference. This low level of stability over time indicates that in the age range studied the individual position of each child compared to that of others on measures of prosocial behaviour and empathy varies considerably. A child who is rather indifferent at the first time point may respond quite prosocially at the second time point.

Children's empathic concern and hypothesis testing increased with age, whereas their indifference decreased with age. There was no change in prosocial behaviour and self-distress. The increase in empathic concern corresponds with the assumption that empathy increases with age (Hoffman, 1984). In addition, gender differences were found on all measures: On average girls scored higher on all indicators of prosocial behaviour, whereas boys scored higher on indifference. This pattern of results agrees with most research on gender differences in empathy, although the differences tend to be small and stronger in self-reports than in physiological measures and ratings of empathy on the basis of facial, vocal, and gestural cues, which tend to reveal no gender differences at all (Eisenberg & Lennon, 1983). Gender differences in empathy may be explained by either biological factors or gender-specific socialisation practices.

In addition, in a free-play situation and during a structured task the co-operative behaviour of the 20-month-old children was recorded. Children's level of reciprocity was assessed on the basis of their co-operative behaviour, which was higher during the structured activity than during free play. Substantial reciprocity was observed in both situations, indirectly supporting the assumption that reciprocity is part of human nature (Hinde, 2001; see Chapter 5).

Prosocial behaviour encompasses many behavioural categories including self-sacrifice, empathic concern, sharing, protection, rescue, and co-operation (Grusec, 1991; Smithson et al., 1983). Even in 2-year-olds a broad spectrum of prosocial categories exists ranging from verbal sympathy to combative altruism, hypothesis testing, instrumental help, indirect help, and sharing (Zahn-Waxler & Radke-Yarrow, 1982).

The early emergence of empathic concern and prosocial behaviour, not only among a subgroup of children but as a general trend

(Zahn-Waxler & Radke-Yarrow, 1982), has an important influence on the theoretical understanding of prosocial behaviour. First, the plausibility of biologically based theories such as sociobiology is increased. For example, empathy may have a high survival value because in a social species it is important to be able to comprehend friendly and hostile emotions of others (Zahn-Waxler et al., 1992b). Therefore, a biological preparedness for empathy is a viable hypothesis (Campbell, 1965; Hoffman, 1984). From the viewpoint of sociobiology, prosocial behaviour may contribute to the individual's inclusive fitness, which is based on the assumption that selfish behaviour that heightens the chances of reproducing one's own genes in the next generation occurs not only when the person attempts to secure an advantage for him/herself but also if the person attempts to secure an advantage for others who are related to him/her (Hamilton, 1964). People might strive to help others on the basis of cues (e.g., kinship, similarity, and familiarity) which signal that there is a high likelihood of genetic commonality (Archer, 2001; see Chapter 5).

Second, the social-cognitive competencies of children in the pre-school years are higher than originally assumed. Children are quite capable of forming social representations of reference persons around them, and applying them when others get into a situation where they may need help. Third, field studies have greatly advanced knowledge about the early onset of prosocial behaviour in 2-year-olds. In laboratory experiments it is not possible to fully simulate the child's natural environment. In addition, because the base rates of prosocial behaviour in 2-year-olds are very low and its occurrence is not predictable, data obtained by observers may be supplemented by reports of mothers who are carefully trained for the task of observing their children and reporting what has occurred in detail (Zahn-Waxler & Radke-Yarrow, 1982).

Genetic influences on empathy and prosocial behaviour

The comparison between monozygotic twins who share 100% of genetic information and dizygotic twins who share 50% of genetic information on the average allows an estimate of heritability coefficients. Results indicated that at 14 months of age, all responses to distress were significantly more similar for monozygotic twins than for dizygotic twins. At the age of 20 months the heritability coefficients tended to be lower. Additional analyses showed that at 14 months prosocial behaviour, empathic concern, hypothesis testing, and indifference revealed a genetic component. At 20 months, only empathic concern and indifference showed a significant genetic influence (Zahn-Waxler et al., 1992b).

These results point to a biological basis of empathy. Presumably there is a lower genetic influence in 20-month-old children because influences of socialisation increase with age. Because the evidence on heritability is not very strong, there is room for the influence of socialisation effects. The decreasing importance of genetic factors from 14 months to 20 months suggests that socialisation influences on prosocial behaviour continually increase during the early years of life.

Studies with monozygotic twins reveal a genetic component to prosocial behaviour. Credit: Photofusion/ Linda Sole.

Questionnaire studies with adults have led to the conclusion that a strong genetic basis of prosocial behaviour exists (Rushton, Fulker, Neale, Nias, & Eysenck, 1986). Heritability estimates were quite high: altruism 56%, empathy 68%, nurturance 70%, aggressiveness 72%, and assertiveness 64%. Because these conclusions are based on self-reports, they tend to overestimate the genetic component, as twins may develop highly similar cognitive schemas in answer to the expectations of the members of their social network. Such implicit theories of similarity may be stronger and more extreme for monozygotic twins than for dizygotic twins.

It is unlikely that genetic information directly determines prosocial behaviour. The interconnections are probably more complex and currently not fully understood. One hypothesis is that temperamental factors, which are inherited at least in part, play an important role. In addition, guilt is an emotion that is also related to prosocial behaviour (see Chapter 10) and which seems to be genetically determined. Children who are high on guilt may be more conditionable. In addition, children who experience more intense feelings may also experience more empathic concern when they observe the distress of others (Zahn-Waxler et al., 1992).

Temperament and prosocial behaviour

The importance of temperamental factors for prosocial behaviour in 24-month-old children was shown in a study in which temperament had been assessed when the children were 4 months old (Young,

Fox, & Zahn-Waxler, 1999). At the age of 24 months, the children were videotaped during two tests of prosocial behaviour which involved either the mother or a female experimenter. As in the earlier study, pain was simulated by facial, vocal, and gestural expressions. The coding categories included hypothesis testing, pro-social behaviour, concerned expressions, global rating of empathy, arousal level, and distress. Whereas concerned expressions is similar to the category of empathic concern, global rating of empathy is an overall assessment of prosocial behaviour and concern, and was highly correlated with prosocial behaviour and concerned expres-sion (up to $r = .81$). Whereas distress corresponds to the self-distress measure in the study by Zahn-Waxler et al. (1992b), arousal level is a new measure used in this study. It is low when the child ignores the victim and high when the child shows body tension and postural freezing.

Temperament was assessed at the age of 4 months on the basis of videotapes that showed how the infant responded to novel visual and auditory stimuli. Three ratings were derived from the videotapes: Motor arousal, positive affect, and negative affect. On the basis of these ratings three infant-temperament groups were formed: (1) high motor arousal, high negative affect, low positive affect; (2) high motor arousal, high positive affect, low negative affect; (3) low on all three ratings.

Results indicated that children in group (3) who exhibited under-arousal at 4 months also showed less arousal in the experimenter's pain simulation and less global empathy at the age of 24 months. The authors pointed out that underarousal is involved in antisocial behaviour and that empathy is negatively related to antisocial beha-viour (Miller & Eisenberg, 1988). Low reactivity in the temperament assessment at 4 months may be a predictor of later coldness, which leads to less empathy and more antisocial responses.

At the second time point when the toddlers were 24 months old social inhibition was measured in an episode with an unfamiliar female experimenter. Inhibition is related to shyness. High inhibition, defined as hesitation to approach an unfamiliar person, correlated with less prosocial behaviour and global empathy. In addition, the negative correlation of social inhibition with prosocial behaviour was higher in the experimenter distress situation ($r = -36$) than in the mother distress situation ($r = -02$). Social inhibition seems to be a negative correlate of prosocial intentions. Because of their beha-vioural inhibition, toddlers seem to hesitate to respond actively to the distress of the experimenter, whereas their response inhibition does not preclude that they turn to their mother when she is in distress (Young et al., 1999).

Age trends in prosocial orientation: 4–20 years

Data on base rates in the home environment are available for 4-year-olds and 7-year-olds (Grusec, 1991). Five types of spontaneous prosocial behaviour were recorded: help, showing concern and consideration, give/share, affection/praise, and reassure/protect. Mothers trained as observers reported that the mean number of prosocial responses per day was about .80 for both boys and girls, meaning that on average nearly one prosocial response occurred every day. The mean number of prosocial responses in 7-year-olds was somewhat lower, ranging between .38 (for girls) and .45 (for boys). In summary, these data indicate that base rates of prosocial behaviour increase from 2-year-olds to 4-year-olds. The reasons for the decrease in 7-year-olds may be that mothers no longer have as much contact with their child as when he or she was 4 years old.

The fact that young children develop an elaborate social understanding is underscored by studies on the comprehension of the emotional responses of other children (Fabes, Eisenberg, Nyman, & Michealieu, 1991; see also Fabes, Eisenberg, McCormick, & Wilson, 1988). Children in three age groups were interviewed: 39–48 months, 50–62 months, and 62–74 months. The interviews took place in a day-care facility after another child had experienced a visible emotion (happy, sad, angry, and distress) which was overtly expressed by words, laughter, crying, angry behaviours, and facial/tonal cues. The experimenter described the emotion in his own words and rated its intensity. Then a child who had observed the expression of the emotion was interviewed in reference to how the other child felt and why. A comparison with the experimenter's appraisal was used to estimate the accuracy of the children's appraisal.

Data analysis was based on distinguishing between social situations in which physical, verbal, nonverbal, control, and material causes elicited the emotional state. In general, accuracy of children's emotional appraisals increased with age from 69% to 72% and 83%. This high level of accuracy even among 3-year-olds attests to their high competence in identifying emotions. In addition, children were better at identifying the causes of negative emotions (85% correct) than the causes of positive emotions (64% correct). They explained positive emotional states more by external than by internal attributions, whereas the explanation of negative emotional states was not biased in such a strong way.

In summary, the causal explanations given by young children seem to be biased, especially for positive emotions, whereas the accuracy, defined as correspondence with adult appraisals, shows that the basic understanding of emotions in others develops quite early, building a basis for perspective taking and the development of empathic concern. In the following, three forms of helping are considered separately with respect to age trends: prosocial moral reasoning, sharing, and emergency intervention. Whereas prosocial moral reasoning focuses on the cognitive reconstruction of prosocial episodes, sharing and emergency intervention are examples of behavioural indications of prosocial tendencies.

Prosocial moral reasoning

The cognitive side of prosocial behaviour was investigated in a longitudinal study spanning 15 years from age 4–5 years to 19–20 years (Eisenberg, Carlo, Murphy, & van Court, 1995a; Eisenberg et al., 1991). The focus was on prosocial moral reasoning which is a variant of moral development (Kohlberg, 1984). Whereas standard moral reasoning focuses on the justification for conforming to or violating prohibitions, prosocial moral reasoning is based on the thoughts elicited by hypothetical moral dilemmas in which one has the alternative to help or not to help (Eisenberg, 1982, 1986). For example, the prosocial conflict may arise because helping means being late for an appointment. In general, five developmental levels of prosocial moral reasoning are distinguished:

(1) Hedonistic, self-centred orientation.
(2) Needs of others orientation.
(3) Approval orientation and stereotyped orientation.
(4) Empathic orientation.
(5) Internalised orientation.

These levels are understood as a sequence which starts with relatively primitive forms of reasoning and leads to elaborated, higher forms of moral reasoning. The level is estimated on the basis of a number of categories which are coded for the moral reasoning stories. These include:

- Hedonistic reasoning (e.g., orientation to benefit oneself; direct reciprocity).
- Pragmatic (orientation to practical concerns).
- Needs-oriented (e.g., "he is sad").
- Stereotypes of a good or bad person.
- Approval orientation (conformity with social reinforcement).
- Empathic orientation (concern for others, perspective taking, vicariously experienced emotions).
- Internalised affect because of loss of self-respect and not living up to one's values.
- Internalised value orientation (internalised responsibility, normative perspective).

Data on prosocial moral reasoning were collected at nine time points starting at age 4–5 and continuing into early adulthood (19–20-year-olds) with an equal number of boys and girls participating in the study. Hedonistic reasoning, which was very widespread among 4–5-year-olds, decreased with age. However, boys showed a slight increase in hedonistic reasoning during adolescence, and girls showed an increase at age 19–20 years. Needs-oriented reasoning increased up to age 7–8, stayed at that level until age 11–12, and decreased afterwards. Direct reciprocity increased until age 13–14 and decreased at the last time point when the adolescents were 15–16 years old. It increased again at age 19–20 years. A similar curve emerged for approval orientation, which also decreased at age 15–16 and increased slightly at age 19–20. Stereotyped moral reasoning increased up to age 13–14 and decreased slightly afterwards. Pragmatic reasoning showed a linear increase across age groups.

Most of the reasoning categories were used infrequently. Whereas at age 4–5 hedonistic reasoning was preferred, needs-oriented reasoning was dominant from age $5\frac{1}{2}$–$6\frac{1}{2}$ onwards. Many of the higher-level categories (e.g., concern for others, perspective taking, internalised affect, internalised norm) were not used at all by younger children. They first emerged at age 7–10 and increased from that age group onwards. An analysis based on the levels of prosocial moral reasoning was conducted for the last five time points, which cover ages 11–20. Results indicated that the level increased with age (see Figure 7.1). This result is compatible with other research that indicates a general increase in prosocial orientation with age (Fabes, Carlo, Kupanoff, & Laible, 1999).

Additional results indicated that girls scored higher on prosocial moral reasoning than boys. An intra-individual analysis showed that

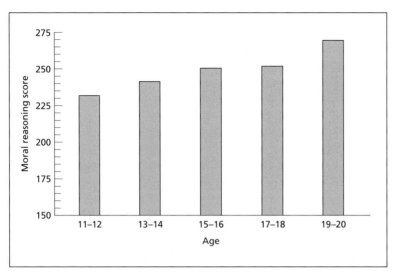

FIG. 7.1.
Level of prosocial moral reasoning as a function of age (based on data from Eisenberg et al., 1995a, p. 1188).

although most of the respondents conformed with the general pattern shown in Figure 7.1, some respondents showed a regression in their moral development. This longitudinal result is a warning against too optimistic a viewpoint based on the belief that prosocial moral reasoning generally increases during adolescence.

I will return to this longitudinal study in the context of the notion of the altruistic personality (Chapter 16). A critic may argue that prosocial moral reasoning says nothing about prosocial behaviour. At the last two time points a behavioural test of prosocial behaviour (filling out a questionnaire and returning it) was conducted. The levels of moral reasoning and prosocial behaviour were positively correlated ($r = .30$). In addition, hedonistic reasoning was negatively correlated with prosocial behaviour ($r = -.28$). These results, and others by Carlo et al. (1996) on Brazilian adolescents, show that higher levels of reasoning about prosocial moral conflicts are associated with more prosocial behaviour.

Whereas prosocial moral reasoning was originally measured on the basis of a content analysis of interview responses, a more objective paper-and-pencil measure has also been developed (Carlo, Eisenberg, & Knight, 1992). The PROM (Prosocial Reasoning Objective Measure) is based on several stories which focus on a prosocial moral dilemma of the protagonist. The task of the respondent is to select one of several items that accompany each story. The items represent different levels of prosocial moral reasoning. Respondents are asked to indicate the importance of several reasons why the protagonist should or should not help. For example, a Level 3 item is "It depends whether Mary's parents and friends will think she did the right or she did the wrong thing" (Carlo, Koller, & Eisenberg, 1998, p. 369). Results indicate that females prefer Level 4 and Level 5 items more than males, indicating that females express higher levels of moral reasoning (Eisenberg et al., 1995a). This result corresponds with those of the interview measure and adds to the gender differences in prosocial orientation which favour females over males (cf. Chapter 4).

In a sample of Brazilian adolescents, institutionalised adolescents (either delinquents or orphans) expressed lower levels of prosocial moral reasoning than non-institutionalised adolescents (Carlo et al., 1998). These results seem to indicate that there is a higher likelihood for institutionalised adolescents to have deficits in sociocognitive skills (cf. Crick & Dodge, 1994).

Sharing and related behaviours

In a cross-sectional study an increase of sharing was found in the age range 7–11 (Rushton, 1975). The results of another study with 1st to 4th graders also showed that generosity measured under neutral conditions increased with age (Midlarsky & Bryan, 1967) with 3rd and 4th graders donating more than 1st and 2nd graders. Sharing was correlated $r = .58$ with age in a study of 6- and 9-year-olds (Iannotti, 1978). A summary of pertinent research (Underwood & Moore, 1982a, p. 28) shows that most studies that included a broad age range showed a positive age trend of children's donations. Older children act more generously than younger children (see also Fabes et al., 1999; Moore & Underwood, 1981). This conclusion is also supported in a more recent study of 7-years-olds and 9-years-olds (Fabes, Eisenberg, Karbon, Bernzweig, Speer, & Carlo, 1994a): 2nd graders helped more than kindergartners.

Emergency intervention

Children's generosity may be contrasted with children's intervention in emergencies (Underwood & Moore, 1982a). Whereas emergency intervention requires courage and decision making under stress, donations are a more silent form of prosocial behaviour. In addition, in the taxonomic system of prosocial behaviour (Smithson et al., 1983) generosity and emergency intervention are both high on the spontaneous dimension, whereas they differ on the nonserious vs serious dimension and the giving vs doing dimension, with emergency intervention representing a serious situation in which *doing* is required.

Several studies indicate that the relationship between age and emergency intervention follows an inverted U-shape. Emergencies were simulated in a study in which more than 200 children participated, namely kindergarten children, and 1st, 2nd, 4th, and 6th graders (Staub, 1970). Children waited alone or in the company of another child in a room, where they drew pictures. They were informed that another child was present next door. After a while an emergency was simulated by pretending that the child next door had fallen from a chair. The children heard the chair tumbling over and the other child crying and moaning. The dependent variable was the number of children helping in each age group.

The lowest level of prosocial behaviour was observed in the youngest and oldest age groups (19% and 15%, respectively). In 1st, 2nd, and 4th graders the amount of helping was much higher. This result was obtained for children who were waiting alone. The same pattern of results was found for children who waited together with another child.

The increase of prosocial behaviour from preschool to 2nd grade can be explained by an increase in prosocial motivation which occurs in this age range. Such an increase may be expected because role-taking ability grows with age (Hoffman, 2000) and hedonistic reasoning sharply decreases in this age range (Eisenberg et al., 1991). In addition, needs-oriented reasoning and the necessary competence to attempt an intervention increase in this age range, facilitating actions to alleviate the suffering of the victim.

Whereas the increase in prosocial behaviour is to be expected, the decline in helping among older children comes as a surprise. This reversal in development may be understood on the basis of conflicting tendencies: Whereas prosocial behaviour is fostered by the development of role taking and concern for others, the major inhibiting factor may be an increase in dependency on social approval. In their verbal comments the older children expressed their concern that adults might scold them if they intervened, because they were not explicitly permitted to enter the other room. Longitudinal data indicate that orientation to others' approval continually increases in the age range 7–14 (Eisenberg et al., 1991) supporting the interpretation in terms of social approval.

Anxieties about social disapproval are plausible if it is true that the older children followed an implicit rule not to leave the room. This interpretation of the results was confirmed in a second study (Staub,

1971). In this study children from the 7th grade were divided into three groups: either they were explicitly permitted to enter the next room, or they were explicitly asked not to enter the next room, or they received no instruction. Only children who were explicitly allowed to enter the next room showed higher levels of prosocial behaviour.

Trivial prohibitions are sufficient to substantially reduce prosocial behaviour. In addition, the no-instruction condition is equivalent to an explicit prohibition. This may be explained by assuming that there is an overemphasis on the learning of prohibitions during social-isation. As a consequence, rigid adherence to the instructions without considering the situational requirement is acquired. A study with adults (Staub, 1971) showed that the experimental condition without an explicit instruction was functionally equivalent to the condition with the explicit permission to enter the next room. Therefore, in this age group the requirements of the situation are better understood. Nevertheless, even adults were inhibited from helping if it was explicitly forbidden to enter the next room.

Beyond adolescence

Little is known about the development of prosocial behaviour during adulthood and old age. But at least one cross-sectional study has been conducted on this issue which shows that the level of prosocial behaviour is likely to remain high in midlife and old age (Midlarsky, 1991). In this study donations were solicited to help infants with birth defects. Data were collected at weekends in order to avoid con-founding effects of retirement and available leisure time. In the 25–34 age group the level of donors was 60%. In the 35–44 group 73% gave to charity. This high level of donations was stable between 45 and 64 years. Older people were even more generous, with 91% donating. These results strongly indicate that helpfulness tends to increase—not decrease—depending on age. Additional results of a study on volun-teerism indicate that the motives of younger and older volunteers may differ, with older volunteers being more altruistically motivated (Omoto, Snyder & Martino, 2000).

Learning of prosocial behaviour 8

Most research on the learning of prosocial behaviour was conducted in the 1960s and 1970s. Two major mechanisms are relevant: reinforcement learning and modelling.

Prosocial modelling

Which characteristics of models increase the impact of those models on observers? Are video presentations of models as effective as real-life presentations? Additional questions refer to the comparison between explicit instructions and concrete modelling in behaviour. Do instructions have similar effects as the observation of behaviour? Finally, how do models who preach altruism but act egoistically influence the prosocial behaviour of children?

The term "modelling" is used as a generic term for observational learning, identification, and imitation (Bandura, 1971). In general, three effects of models on observers are distinguished:

- Acquisition of new behaviour patterns by matching the behaviour of others. This occurs when an observer imitates a model in his or her behaviour and the behaviour was not previously in the repertoire of the observer. An example: A child observes that an adult holds a door open while someone who is carrying a parcel enters the room. The child repeats this behaviour sequence on a similar occasion at a later time.
- Strengthening or weakening the inhibition of a response that was learned previously. Strengthening an inhibition of behaviour occurs when an observer perceives that a model is punished for a certain behaviour. This learning is relevant for the development of self-control in temptation situations. An example for prosocial behaviour: A pupil helps another pupil during an examination

and is punished by his or her teacher in the presence of the other pupils. This punishment contributes to the inhibition of prosocial behaviour in the other pupils. On the other hand, models may have disinhibiting effects, increasing the likelihood of certain behaviour patterns that are observed in models. Such a disinhibition is expected to occur in the area of deviant behaviour. An example: A pedestrian who is waiting at a red light sees another pedestrian cross the street. As a result, the likelihood increases that the observer will violate traffic rules (Lefkowitz, Blake, & Mouton, 1955).

- Facilitation of performance of responses by informing the person about the appropriate behaviour in the situation. In this case no new behaviour patterns are learned nor is there reduction in inhibition of learned responses. Instead the model functions as a releaser for the performance of certain learned response sequences (Bandura & Walters, 1963). This is relevant in many areas of neutral and socially approved behaviour patterns. An example for prosocial behaviour: A student observes that many other students volunteer to take part in a psychological experiment and decides to do the same (Rosenbaum, 1956; Rosenbaum & Blake, 1955). In this way behaviour patterns that comply with social norms are facilitated. One function of models is that they legitimise the behaviour that is modelled (Hoffman, 2000). They inform the child about what is appropriate in a given situation.

Modelling is a social process of the acquisition and transmission of simple and complex behaviour patterns. The basic principle has been demonstrated in studies on aggression, studies on the acquisition of self-reinforcement, and studies on delay of gratification. Such modelling effects have also been confirmed for prosocial behaviour in children. Many prosocial activities are under the control of models. Models frequently function as releasers that contribute to the performance of prosocial behaviour in children and adults. After relevant behaviour patterns have been learned, the performance of prosocial behaviour depends on facilitating situational circumstances. Modelling effects on prosocial behaviour are not limited to children— they have also been observed in adults.

Models may also reduce the likelihood of prosocial behaviour. When a model shows passivity in an emergency situation he or she suggests to observers that prosocial behaviour is inappropriate (see Chapter 15). In both cases—when models facilitate and when they inhibit prosocial behaviour—modelling includes information about what is legitimate, what is appropriate, and what is in accordance with social rules of conduct.

Social learning theory (Bandura, 1978, 1986) seems to offer the most comprehensive explanation of social modelling. A central assumption is that observers acquire symbolic representations of perceived behaviour sequences. Modelling includes a social comparison with others. Such social comparisons are usually directed towards persons who have a similar background as the observer (Buunk, VanYperen, Taylor, & Collins, 1991; Gorenflo & Crano, 1989). Social comparison implies that people infer what is appropriate behaviour in a situation where they are uncertain how to act (Buunk, Collins, Taylor, VanYperen, & Dakof, 1990).

An example is a study in which an emergency was simulated. A victim fell from a ladder, while a bookshelf crashed over on him. It is no surprise that observers of such an emergency show an initial "startle response" when they hear the rumbling and uproar. The startle response includes an orientation towards the source of the noise and facial expressions of concern (Darley, Teger, & Lewis, 1973). When the observers face each other, they immediately recognise that the others have had a fright and correctly infer that an accident has taken place. In contrast, when the observers sit back to back and cannot see the facial expression of the other bystander, social comparisons are impossible, and the presence of the other bystander induces social inhibition.

In the experiment three conditions of the accident were compared: students were alone; two students were facing each other; and two students were seated back to back. In correspondence with the theoretical assumption, results indicated that intervention rates were as high in the alone condition (90%) as in the face-to-face condition (80%). In contrast, willingness to intervene was very low (20%) in the nonfacing condition. It is likely that the startle response is interpreted as a valid sign of alarm in the face-to-face condition. In addition, efficacy beliefs in observers are strengthened if other people who are similar to them master comparable situations (Bandura, 1997). If the observer sees that others are able to overcome their uncertainty, they may infer that they themselves possess the capabilities to act successfully. In the same vein, the observation of passive bystanders in the nonfacing condition reduces the likelihood that the observer will respond positively.

Beliefs in personal efficacy are strengthened if similar others perform actions successfully. As a consequence, the judgements of one's own capabilities are increased. This is especially likely if the observer has little information in advance about how to respond in a specific situation. In this case the behaviour of models is especially relevant:

> Modelling that conveys effective coping strategies can boost the self-efficacy of individuals who have undergone countless experiences confirming their personal inefficacy. Even those who are highly self-assured will raise their self-efficacy beliefs if models teach them even better ways of doing things (Bandura, 1997, p. 87).

The information that is transmitted by models includes the illustration of specific competencies, knowledge and skills for dealing with tasks, and aspirations that may be appropriate in a certain situation. Therefore, models not only have an informational function but also exert a motivational influence. They transmit performance standards of what is possible in the face of specific difficulties in environmental tasks. The success or failure of models is taken as an indication of the difficulty or easiness of a task. In addition, successful strategies of models may be copied by observers who integrate them into their own coping repertoire.

The process of observational learning was broken down into four subprocesses by Bandura (1986). These include attentional processes, retention processes, production processes, and motivational processes. The four subprocesses of observational learning are immediately relevant for prosocial behaviour. For example, attentional processes are involved if models have characteristics that increase the attention devoted to them. Models who have a reputation of being powerful and influential will draw more attention to themselves than models who are less powerful and influential. As a result, powerful models exert more influence on prosocial behaviour than less powerful models (Grusec, 1971). The factors that direct the selective attention of the observer are highly relevant for observational learning, because in everyday situations many influences compete for his or her attention simultaneously.

Retention processes refer to the cognitive representational system. For example, social values may guide prosocial behaviour when they are activated from memory. Values of benevolence may elicit prosocial behaviour under appropriate circumstances when they are pre-activated by priming (Macrae & Johnston, 1998). The powerful effects of priming have been demonstrated with respect to memory processes and decision making, leading to the conclusion that much of social behaviour is under the control of retention processes (Macrae & Bodenhausen, 2000).

Production processes are facilitated if all components of the response are available in the response repertoire of the actor. In a study in which a breakdown of a car was simulated and helping consisted of changing a tyre, it was found that many more males intervened than females. The assumption is plausible that female drivers were less capable of changing the tyre than male drivers— females did not possess an important component of the response that was necessary to solve the problem. As a result, they were unable to produce the skills that were necessary for helping (Bryan & Test, 1967).

Motivational processes are relevant because actors consider the consequences of their behaviour. These may include tangible rewards of social approval on the one hand, but also self-reinforcements on the other hand (Bandura, 1997; Rosenhan, 1972). For example, an observer of an altruistic model may infer that such behaviour is a good deed (Grusec & Skubiski, 1970).

Performance of learned behaviour is under the control of three types of incentives: direct incentives such as rewards; vicarious incentives which are observed; and self-produced incentives which are the result of self-evaluation. Self-evaluations are triggered by comparison with a code of conduct. "The important issue is that, with the reification of a code of conduct, individuals can not only behave selfishly or unselfishly, they can feel that they have or have not met their own internalised standards" (Hinde, 2001, p. 27).

Such codes of conduct are especially accessible when the observer is in a state of high self-focus (Scheier & Carver, 1988). Because individuals tend to avoid the elicitation of guilt feelings, and support a positive self-image of which they can be proud, they are inclined to maintain a prosocial orientation (Hinde, 2001). The conformity with internalised standards is a self-protection against feelings of shame and guilt which are anticipated in the event of transgression (see Chapter 10). If a discrepancy emerges between codes of conduct and actual behaviour, the person tries to reduce it. This effort is increased if self-attention is high. As a consequence, the consistency between attitude and behaviour is higher in a state of high self-focus. Behaviour is more in correspondence with personal standards if private self-focus is high (manipulated by a mirror) and more in correspondence with societal standards if public self-focus is high (manipulated by the presence of an audience; Froming et al., 1982). High situational or dispositional self-focus intensifies matching-to-standards behaviour (Scheier & Carver, 1983).

Matching-to-standard effort depends on outcome expectancies, which refer to the likelihood that the person will be able to achieve the standard. If positive outcome expectancies prevail, the matching-to-standard process is repeated until the goal is reached. If negative outcome expectancies arise, withdrawal and disengagement occur. For example, if a negative action cannot be reversed under high self-focus, withdrawal is intensified (Scheier & Carver, 1988). An example is the individual who considers himself/herself to be a responsible person. Refusal to help another student who needs some notes does not fulfil the prevailing code of conduct. Therefore, it is likely that the individual will consider his/her behaviour in light of the self-image of a responsible person, and attempt to improve the behaviour so that it will conform with the standard of responsibility. This is especially likely if high self-focus prevails.

The process of matching-to-standard is represented as a hierarchy of responses (Carver & Scheier, 1990). At the most abstract level is the cognition of being a responsible person, which is identified as a system concept. Next, the principle is derived to follow through on commitments. On the next level of abstraction a behavioural program is activated that depends on the demands of the task. For example, if a student is asked to help another student in preparing for an examination, the program is described as "drive over and lend the notes". In even more concrete terms, the act of driving is executed, which is composed of different actions and finally may be described on the level of muscle tensions.

The expectation of successful performance of prosocial behaviour may be elicited primarily by models of self-evaluation. Memories of oneself performing successfully at a similar task may enhance feelings of competence and willingness to act accordingly. This is described as successful self-modelling, which increases self-efficacy in a given situation (Bandura, 1997).

Modelling works at all ages. Adolescents and adults are able to rehearse complex behaviour sequences and imitate them if needed; even young children take the behaviour of models into account and are able to listen to instructions that employ modelling cues. One developmental advantage of older children and adolescents is that they are better able to understand the meaning of social comparisons. Young children seem to be overtaxed if they have to represent the performance of others and compare it with their own results. Empirical research shows that children in the age range 3–6 have an incomplete understanding of social comparison information, whereas 3rd and 4th graders fully understand the implications of social comparisons (Boggiano & Ruble, 1979).

Modelling is not an all-or-none variable. Amount of prosocial modelling was varied in a study of sharing behaviour (Rushton & Littlefield, 1979, cited in Rushton, 1982) by a model who donated either 0, 2, or 8 tokens. Children who saw the selfish model donated fewer tokens than children who saw the very generous model. The moderately generous model elicited a level of sharing that fell in between these two conditions. The same pattern of results was evident in a retest 2 weeks later.

Model characteristics

Adults may act as prosocial models for children. Some 4th and 5th graders played a bowling game which included a mechanism that activated the numbers 5, 10, 15, or 20 respectively (Rosenhan & White, 1967). The children were instructed that each time the 20 came up they would earn two certificates worth 50 cents, which they could redeem for a toy in a shop if their parents agreed. Each round consisted of 20 trials in which earnings were pre-programmed. After winning two certificates, the children had to decide if they wanted to use the certificates for themselves or to donate one or both of them to orphans. Next to the pile of 20 certificates there was a box depicting poor children, which served as a collection box for the certificates to be donated to an orphanage. Each child played two rounds, the first one in the presence of a student and the second one alone. In one condition 120 children took turns in the first round with the student. The student behaved altruistically, donating one certificate in each of the two trials in which he won.

The results show that boys and girls demonstrate a significant amount of internalisation of the model's behaviour even if the modelling phase is brief. The fact that nearly 50% of the children donated gift certificates to charity even when the model was not present (although the base rate for such donations was very low) indicates that prosocial behaviour can be acquired quite rapidly from the observation of models. Other studies have also proved that adults transmit prosocial response patterns by modelling. The modelling of prosocial behaviour is facilitated if the children have an opportunity to exercise the appropriate behaviour and if the meaning of the good deed is explained to them.

In the study by Rosenhan and White (1967) the question of whether the model initiated a positive or negative relationship with the child did not exert any influence on the willingness to imitate the model's behaviour. Similar results were obtained by Grusec and Skubiski (1970). Other studies even found that models who gave negative reinforcement were imitated more than models giving positive reinforcement (Bandura, Grusec, & Menlove, 1967; Grusec, 1971).

In contrast, some researchers report a positive influence of models' nurturance on imitation (Bandura & Huston, 1961; Mussen & Parker, 1965). In these studies the imitation concerned neutral behaviour that did not have any negative consequences for the child. This may be contrasted with the sacrifices that were demanded in the studies on modelling of prosocial behaviour. For example, the donation of gift certificates means that the child loses a part of his or her gains. If the model provides an example of giving something away, a nurturant model is not more effective than a neutral or negative model. The same pattern of results was found for the acquisition of high standards of self-reinforcement and the willingness to delay gratification.

These results may be interpreted on the basis of two hypotheses. On the one hand, the possibility exists that a child interprets a nurturant model as both generous and lenient. Therefore, the children may interpret the friendly behaviour of the model as permission to set low standards for themselves. The second hypothesis assumes that the imitation of a friendly model is not rewarding if the behaviour involved leads to aversive consequences. Therefore, behaviour that is associated with aversive consequences and which is shown by a friendly model is not likely to be imitated by observers.

It must be pointed out that these results are based on studies in which the interaction period between model and child was rather short. Such limited friendliness of a stranger must be distinguished from the long-term friendliness of a person who has continuous contact to the child (Yarrow, Scott, & Waxler, 1973). The long-term warmth of a model is likely to induce trust and security in the child. It contributes to the development of a secure attachment style. Friendliness of parents is a positive correlate of prosocial behaviour (Mussen, Harris, Rutherford, & Keasey, 1970).

Whereas the evidence on the effects of a model's nurturance is mixed, another model characteristic seems to be quite influential on prosocial behaviour: the power of the model (Grusec, 1971). In a study children saw a powerful model who was described as a person who could distribute large rewards (in this case organising a visit to an airport) or a model who was not able to offer large rewards (low power). Once again donation to charity after winning in a bowling game was the dependent variable. The prosocial behaviour of a powerful model was imitated to a greater extent than that of a less powerful model.

In the natural environment of the child, warmth and power are frequently positively correlated. For example, many parents act in a friendly way towards their children and at the same time have a powerful position in the sense that they may distribute large rewards. Therefore, power and friendliness of a model are frequently confounded in field studies of the modelling of prosocial behaviour.

Live and video models

Live and video models seem to exert similar effects. For example, video models may transmit the performance of aggressive behaviour (Bandura, Ross, & Ross, 1963). Video models are also effective in the transmission of standards of self-control in temptation situations (Walters, Parke, & Cane, 1965). Therefore, it is likely that video models should also be effective in the transmission of prosocial behaviour. This suggestion was supported in a series of studies by Bryan and Walbek (1970; see also Bryan & Schwartz, 1971). Later research focused on the prosocial effects of public television programmes for children (Coates, Pusser, & Goodman, 1976; Friedrich & Stein, 1973, 1975). The evidence supports the conclusion that prosocial television models exert a positive influence on children's prosocial orientation (Huston & Wright, 1998).

Saying and doing

Do verbal admonitions and explanations have similar effects to concrete examples of behaviour? The socialisation process encompasses verbal instructions and behaviour examples: On the one hand, children are asked to adhere to certain rules; on the other hand, children observe the behaviour of adults who either act in accordance with these rules or violate them. A comparison of the effectiveness of verbal instructions and behaviour examples is difficult because it assumes that both communication channels are equally informative. If the behaviour example contains more information than the admonition, it may be more effective. In addition, if the admonition is more abstract than the behaviour example, instructions and examples may activate different cognitive processes.

In a series of studies (Grusec, 1972; Grusec & Skubiski, 1970; Rice & Grusec, 1975) children observed a model who either gave a behaviour example of altruism or recommended altruism verbally. In a bowling game children were given the opportunity to donate their earnings for children in need in an anonymous situation where they were not observed by others.

In the first study, type of modelling cues and nurturance of the model were varied systematically. In one condition 3rd and 5th graders saw a model who donated half of his/her earnings to poor children (performance condition). In the verbalisation condition the model explained before playing that he/she intended to donate part of his/her earnings (Grusec & Skubiski, 1970). The model's statement was quite elaborate in order to match the amount of information given in the performance condition. In the verbalisation condition the model left the room immediately after making the statement because he/she was called by his/her boss. Therefore, he/she was not able to act in accordance with expressed intentions. In addition, the model's nurturance was manipulated. In one condition the model and the child played together for 10 minutes with toys. In the other condition the model read a book for 10 minutes, ignoring the child.

With the exception of girls who played with a nurturant model, the verbalisation was almost without effect. In contrast, the behaviour example generally led to an increase in altruism compared to an additional control group in which no model was introduced. The conclusion is that the performing model exerts a much stronger influence than the verbalisation. The actual performance of sharing was a reliable method of teaching self-control, which led to internalisation of sharing behaviour independent of the warmth and nurturance of the model.

These results were reinterpreted after a second study which followed the same procedure (Grusec, 1972). Some 7- and 11-year-old children took part in this study. Among the 11-year-olds, the verbalisation was as effective as the behaviour example. The performing model elicited higher donations than the verbalising model only among the 7-year-old boys. This result leads to the conclusion that—at least among older children—verbalisation and altruistic performance are similarly effective as modelling cues. In contrast, the effectiveness of behaviour examples seems to be higher among younger children. It is possible that younger children have more problems in translating the verbalisation into their behaviour repertoire because description is less concrete and vivid than performance. Older children seem to be in a better position to understand the normative appeal of the statement.

In a later study (Rice & Grusec, 1975) with 3rd and 4th graders, long-term effects of performance and verbalisation, respectively, were measured. In this study much emphasis was placed on the creation of a similar context in which performing and verbalising models were observed. In the verbalisation condition the model played the bowling game and, after winning, explained his or her intention to donate to poor children. After that the experimenter knocked on the door and said the model's boss wanted to talk to him/her. Then the model left and the experimenter said the child could start bowling. In contrast, the performing model actually did donate some of his or her winnings.

The results indicated that verbalisation and performance equally elicited more donations compared to a control group in which no model was observed. This is remarkable as the children were 9–10 years old (cf. Grusec & Skubiski, 1970). Figure 8.1 summarises the results based on a post-test after 4 months which involved the children playing bowling without any further modelling. Both the immediate test and the follow-up showed that verbalisation and behaviour example were equally effective. In addition, gender differences emerged in the follow-up because girls shared more than boys. Only boys showed a decrement in sharing from immediate test to follow-up. In summary, a verbalisation that occurred in an appropriate context was as effective as a behaviour example. If the appropriateness of behaviour in a novel situation is at issue, performing models and verbalising models seem to be equally effective. Here saying is as effective as doing.

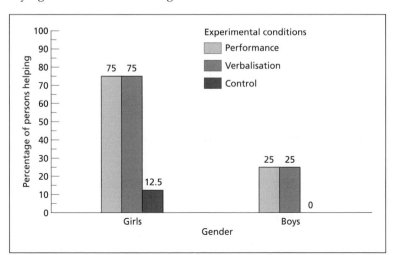

FIG. 8.1.
Percentage of children donating marbles depending on method of presentation and gender (based on data from Rice & Grusec, 1975, p. 587).

Inconsistency between practising and preaching

The fact that performing and verbalising models are equally effective in promoting children's prosocial behaviour under certain circumstances leads to an interesting question. What happens if saying and doing are inconsistent? We are all aware of examples in everyday life where individuals describe themselves as moral persons but seem to follow a selfish script in their decisions and actions. It might well be that people tend to emphasise their altruistic intentions in discourse, whereas egoism is the standard of behaviour in terms of what people do. It is not too far-fetched to assume that a person who insists verbally on a certain ideal while he or she does not live up to that ideal in his/her behaviour loses credibility. Therefore, an altruistic verbalisation that is followed by egoistic behaviour is not likely to elicit altruism among observers.

This speculation is not supported by empirical results with children. Bryan and Walbek (1970) report on a series of experiments in which they attempted to measure the competing effects of verbalisation and performance. Once again a bowling game was used. In these studies the model either donated part of the winnings or retained all the winnings. In addition, the verbalisation of the model was varied. The model either recommended a generous attitude, recommended selfishness, or made neutral statements. The results, which are summarised in Figure 8.2, indicate that selfish behaviour was generally accompanied by a lower frequency of donation. A dampening effect of the inconsistency between saying and doing did

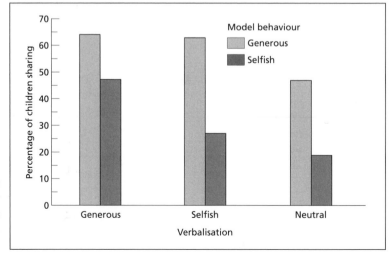

FIG. 8.2.
Percentage of children who donated for poor children (based on data from Bryan & Walbek, 1970, p. 334).

not occur. Finally, the results indicate that the behaviour example was effective in transmitting prosocial behaviour patterns, whereas the verbalisation was less effective.

In two additional experiments (Bryan & Walbek, 1970) the effect of behaviour examples was replicated. Verbalisation of a generous attitude had no influence on children's sharing. It only influenced the model's estimated attractiveness: The model was evaluated more positively when he/she supported verbally generosity instead of selfishness.

A weakness of these studies is that the model acted altruistically when he/she won and preached altruism when a no-win trial occurred. An improved procedure was used in a study with 7–11-year-olds who were able to earn tokens while bowling (Rushton, 1975). These tokens could be exchanged for attractive prizes. Before starting the game, the children met an adult who was introduced as a possible future teacher. This model played 20 trials in which eight winnings of two tokens were pre-programmed (cf. Rosenhan & White, 1967). Donations, which were invited by a "Save the Children Fund" poster showing a poor child ("Bobby"), were possible by putting tokens into a special bowl. In one condition the model donated one token on each winning trial. In another condition the model retained all the tokens for himself or herself. In addition, the verbalisation of the model was varied. After winning the model either preached generosity (e.g., "It's good to give to kids like him"), preached selfishness (e.g., "It's not good to give to kids like him"), or made a neutral statement (e.g., "I like this game").

After the model had left the room, the child played 20 trials alone of which 8 were pre-programmed as winning trials. Figure 8.3 depicts the mean number of tokens that were donated by the children in each condition of the experiment. This study once again reveals that modelling is a strong determinant of prosocial behaviour. Whereas the verbalisation did not have a main effect, the interaction between verbalisation and behaviour example was significant: An altruistic model who recommended selfishness was less influential than an altruistic model who recommended generous behaviour or who made a neutral comment. In addition, the verbalisation of a selfish model was less influential on children's prosocial behaviour than the verbalisation of an altruistic model.

The combined effect of verbalisation and performance was replicated in a follow-up test. Once again the children played the bowling game in which eight winning trials were pre-programmed. The results indicated that after 2 months the behaviour example was still

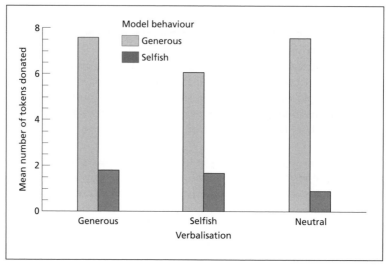

FIG. 8.3.
Mean number of
tokens donated (based
on data from Rushton,
1975, p. 463).

an important determinant of sharing behaviour. In addition, a selfish verbalisation led to less sharing than a neutral or generous verbalisation. This effect was more pronounced in the altruistic-model condition than in the selfish-model condition.

In summary, model inconsistencies such as those that were present in the reported experiments exert only little negative influence on prosocial behaviour. Children's insensitivity with respect to inconsistencies may depend on their level of cognitive development, which may preclude a sufficient analysis of the inconsistency between performance and verbalisation. Such an interpretation of the results is supported by the fact that children who are exposed to inconsistent models whose verbalisations do not correspond to their actual sharing behaviour frequently have incorrect recollections of the behaviour example or the verbalisation (Bryan & Walbek, 1970).

The possibility remains that stronger inconsistencies between verbalisation and performance may reduce the model's credibility. One example of such a strong inconsistency is if a model who acts selfishly praises the child for good deeds. An experiment that simulated such a sequence showed that a selfish model's praise resulted in a reduction in children's sharing (compared with a condition in which the selfish model did not comment about what was appropriate; Midlarsky, Bryan, & Brickman, 1973). Loss of socialisation agents' credibility which leads to a boomerang effect on children's behaviour is the worst case in the context of socialisation. The results show that adults may lose their credibility by thoughtless statements.

A field study with members of the civil rights movements in the USA (Rosenhan, 1970) revealed that inconsistency between verbalisation and performance inhibits strong involvement in civil rights. Interviews were carried out with people who were involved in the civil rights movement. These interviewees were either fully committed, supporting the movement for a year or longer, or partially committed, supporting one or two projects. The interview focused on personal development and activities with respect to the civil rights movement.

Results showed that learning experiences in childhood are related to prosocial behaviour of adults. For example, the interviewees were asked whether their parents showed consistency between saying and doing. Partially committed activists frequently reported a discrepancy between what parents said and what they did. In contrast, individuals who were fully involved only rarely reported about discrepancies of this kind. The typical answer of a fully committed activist was that "My father carried me on his shoulders during the Sacco-Vanzetti parades" (Rosenhan, 1970, p. 262). For the fully committed activists, parents were primarily characterised by active involvement in actions against injustice and by warmth and affection. In contrast, the reports of partially committed activists frequently referred to parental hypocrisy elicited by parents' inconsistency between verbal expression of ideals and behaviour that fell short of the ideals.

The partially committed activists are called normative altruists, whereas the fully committed activists are described as autonomous altruists (Clary & Miller, 1986). Parental hypocrisy was greater among volunteers at a telephone crisis-counselling agency who were identified by interview results as normative activists than among those who were identified as autonomous altruists. In addition, autonomous altruists described their parents as warmer and more affectionate. Whereas autonomous altruists did not depend so much on the group atmosphere, normative altruists maintained their involvement depending on whether they felt good in the group and experienced high cohesiveness.

Social reinforcement

Learning theories assume that principles of learning control social behaviour. These laws of learning have two basic assumptions in common (Rushton, 1982):

- Principles of learning are applicable to observable behaviour. Therefore, issues such as the sampling of behaviour, taxonomic systems of observation, and objectivity of measurement are of high importance to them.
- Laws of learning explain the acquisition, maintenance, and extinction of behaviour. The principles of learning differ from one theory to another. The principles include classical conditioning (Midlarsky & Bryan, 1967), instrumental conditioning (Weiss, Boyer, Lombardo, & Stich, 1973), and cognitive structuring (Kuczynski, 1983).

Social reinforcement is based on either reward or punishment. Whereas social approval encourages prosocial behaviour, social disapproval is expected to lead to a reduction in the likelihood that the target activity will be shown. This hypothesis was confirmed in a study with 8–11-year-olds (Rushton & Teachman, 1978). The first part of the modelling procedure closely followed that of Rushton (1975). After having modelled sharing in the context of the bowling game, the model stayed in the room while the child played the game and had several opportunities to donate tokens for poor children. The observation by the model led to high compliance by the children. Each time the child shared his/her winnings, the model either encouraged or discouraged the child by saying something like "Good for you" or "That's kind of silly for you to give to Bobby. Now you will have less tokens for yourself" (p. 323). In addition, in the positive reinforcement condition some of the children were told "So the reason you shared was because you are a generous kid" (self-attribution), whereas others were told "If you keep sharing with Bobby, I'll let you have a turn with me on this basketball game when you're finished" (external attribution; p. 323). Finally, a no-reinforcement condition was run in which the experimenter modelled prosocial behaviour but neither approved nor disapproved it in the second round.

Two weeks later children were tested for sharing in a follow-up study. Results indicated that sharing was highest in the positive reinforcement condition (independent of attribution), intermediate in the neutral condition, and lowest in the negative reinforcement condition. Whereas the approval or disapproval was quite influential, attributions had no effect on sharing. A reason for this failure may be that the attribution was always combined with positive reinforcement, which may have suggested to the child that he/she was a generous person anyway (Rushton & Teachman, 1978).

room. In the other-oriented condition the amount of work did not decline across the three phases of the work session. In contrast, a substantial decline of compliance over time was observed in the two other conditions to an equal degree.

The same pattern of results was observed in a second study (Kuczynski, 1982), in so far as in the other-oriented condition compliance with the instruction of the experimenter stayed on a high level during three 200-second intervals. The amount of time spent working on the task was generally very high (in the range of 170 seconds). In the self-oriented condition, amount of time spent on the task decreased from the first to the second interval and remained at that level in the third interval.

In the second study intensity of argument was varied as low (for example: you'll be a little bit unhappy), medium (for example: you'll be unhappy), and high (for example: you'll be very, very unhappy). It was expected that higher intensity would lead to more compliance. Intensity of the rationale did not interact with orientation of rationale. Higher intensity led to more compliance, especially for girls. The effect of low-intensity rationales did not differ much among boys and girls. These results show that giving explanations has an affective component which complements the cognitive component and that girls responded more strongly to the affective message than boys.

In summary, an explanation for helpful behaviour that refers to the well-being of another person was more effective in eliciting compliance with a request than a self-oriented rationale. Children's work on behalf of the experimenter may be interpreted as prosocial behaviour because children had to make a sacrifice (not playing with the toys) in order to help the experimenter (Hoffman, 2000).

These results confirm the assumption that children derive social rules about the appropriate behaviour in a given situation from the available information which is used as a behavioural guide. If the rule represents a prosocial script, prosocial behaviour is more likely than if the rule represents an egoistic script (Hoffman, 2000). In addition, prosocial justifications of compliance, victim-centred discipline, and appeals to the child's guilt potential, which are summarised under the term "induction" by Hoffman (2000), may contribute to the cognitive component of empathy.

What kind of parental discipline technique promotes prosocial behaviour in children? To answer this question, children's altruistic behaviour was measured in their natural environment and related to parents' values, discipline, and affection (Hoffman, 1975). The prosocial measure was based on sociometric assessments by classmates.

In addition, structured interviews were carried out separately with fathers and mothers. The parents assessed the importance of 18 values, 2 of which were relevant for altruism: "showing consideration of other people's feelings" and "going out of one's way to help other people" (p. 940). Then they ranked the three most important ones. The ranks of the two altruistic values (if any were assigned) were summed and used as an index of the parent's altruistic values.

A subcategory of induction was also taken into account because victim-oriented socialisation techniques were obtained on the basis of answers to three scenarios. The scenarios described a child who injures or insults others. The parents were asked to describe what they would do in these situations. Victim-centred discipline was assessed on the basis of parents' evaluation of three scenarios in which the misbehaviour of a child was portrayed. An example is: "The child and his friends are making fun of another child" (p. 940). The parent described what they would do if their child did what was illustrated in the scenarios. A content analysis of these open responses led to the assignment of a score of victim-centredness—it was high (3) if the parent explicitly suggested an act of reparation, intermediate (2) if the parent suggested apologising, and low (1) if the parent was concerned about the victim's feelings. Finally, measures of warmth and affection were obtained. Parents were asked to estimate the frequency with which they showed behaviours towards the child like hugging, kissing, and smiling at him/her. The responses were summed across five items.

The correlations between the variables obtained from the parents and altruistic behaviour were analysed separately for boys and girls (see Table 8.1). For girls the highest correlation between prosocial behaviour and parents' measures was obtained for victim-centredness of father. For boys the highest correlation was obtained for victim-centredness of mother. The pattern of results shows that parents' attitudes and their children's behaviour are interrelated in complex ways. In general, there is some evidence for cross-gender effects, although—in addition—same-gender effects also emerge. For example, altruistic values of mothers were associated with girls' altruism, whereas altruistic values of fathers correlated with boys' altruism.

Although the results are complex, they show that socialisation practices are important contributors to prosocial behaviour. Among the three antecedent conditions, altruistic values and victim-centredness seem to be most important. The correlation with warmth and affection is lower, except for mothers' warmth and

TABLE 8.1

Correlations of children's altruistic behaviour with parents' attitudes

Parental attitudes	Girls	Boys
Mother		
Altruistic values	.37	.05
Victim centredness	.01	.50
Affection	.18	.29
Father		
Alruistic values	.34	.35
Victim centredness	.53	.12
Affection	.12	.08

Correlations are based on the data of 5th graders and their parents.

Source: Modified from Hoffman, M.L. (1975). Altruistic behavior and the parent–child relationship. *Journal of Personality and Social Psychology, 31,* 937–943. Copyright © (1975) by the American Psychological Association. Adapted with permission.

affection and boys' altruism. Note that in a field study on members of the civil rights movement, full activists reported warmth and affection in the relationship with at least one of their parents (Rosenhan, 1970; see earlier). In Hoffman's study each of the three parental attitudes contributes to the development of prosocial behaviour, showing that it is multidetermined.

The use of inductive discipline may be contrasted with power-assertive discipline which encompasses physical punishment, material and social deprivation, and threats (Hoffman & Saltzstein, 1967). In a study with boys and girls aged between 11 and 14 years both forms of parental discipline were scored from scenarios that present the misbehaviour of a child (Krevans & Gibbs, 1996). They were correlated with five scores of children's prosocial behaviour which were provided by teachers (e.g., assessment of children's helpfulness) and by the children themselves, who had the opportunity to donate to UNICEF money that they had received as a bonus. Because the prosocial measures were highly correlated (Cronbach's alpha = .85), they were combined into an index of prosocial behaviour. In addition, measures of empathy and guilt were obtained. In this study four hypothesis were tested:

- Inductive discipline is positively related to prosocial behaviour, and power-assertive discipline is negatively correlated.
- Empathy is positively associated with prosocial behaviour.

- The relationship between inductive discipline and prosocial behaviour is mediated by empathy (empathy-mediation hypothesis).
- Empathy-based guilt feelings are positively associated with prosocial behaviour.

All four hypotheses were confirmed (Krevans & Gibbs, 1996). More specifically, inductive discipline correlated positively with empathy and prosocial behaviour. After controlling for empathy, inductive discipline was no longer significant as a predictor of prosocial behaviour, indicating that a mediation effect occurred. Power assertion was a negative predictor of prosocial behaviour. A difference score was formed by subtracting the power assertion score from the induction score. This score, which indicates relative preference for induction over power assertion, correlated $r = .34$ with the global prosocial behaviour scale. Finally, guilt feelings were highly associated with prosocial behaviour ($r = .60$) among children who scored high on empathy, but not among children in the intermediate or low range of empathy. In addition, the correlation between empathy and guilt was significant only if the parents expressed a relative preference for induction over power assertion. These results fit with those of other studies on parenting which show that supportive parenting and inductive discipline contribute to the child's prosocial orientation (Carlo et al., 1999; Eisenberg & Murphy, 1995).

Altruistic self-scheme

In many experiments on the acquisition of prosocial behaviour, children share something, or help in other ways. Social approval of such responses is a communication that operates on a highly specific level. How can a communication that confirms children's generosity be formulated on a more abstract level? One possibility would be to tell the child that he/she is the kind of person who acts responsibly. Such an abstract communication (e.g., "You are a helpful person") contributes to the development of an altruistic self-concept, which may function as an internalised standard of prosocial behaviour that is activated in a broad spectrum of social situations.

One of the first examples of the success of character attributions is a study on tidiness. Pupils in a classroom were described as orderly and tidy by their teachers (Miller, Brickman, & Bolen, 1975). This attribution led to more tidiness in the classroom. Pupils threw their rubbish into wastepaper baskets instead of letting it fall on the ground. The same principle led to more prosocial behaviour (Batson, Harris, McCaul, Davis, & Schmidt, 1979). Students responded more prosocially if their altruistic behaviour was explained by empathy instead of compliance with external pressure.

In a study with 7–10-year-olds (Grusec, Kuczynski, Rushton, & Simutis, 1978) three conditions were compared: The model donated for poor children (modelling); the model instructed the child to donate for poor children (instruction); or the model both shared with the poor and instructed the child to do the same (modelling plus instruction). When the child played the bowling game the model stayed and commented on the child's prosocial behaviour. In the external-attribution condition, the comment indicated that the child shared because of social pressure by the model. In the internal-attribution condition, the comment indicated that the child was "the kind of person who likes to help other people". In the no-attribution condition, no explanation was offered.

In summary, the 3 × 3 design contrasted modelling and instruction on the one hand and external and internal attribution on the other hand. After the first phase the child played the game alone (inter-nalisation test). In the modelling condition, internal attribution led to more sharing than external or no attribution. In the two other con-ditions, the level of sharing was as high as in the modelling condition and did not differ depending on attribution. An interpretation of this pattern of results is that direct instruction makes the reason why the child donated so clear that attributional feedback was irrelevant in this context. The high level of internalisation that was achieved by direct instruction shows that the children responded with a high level of compliance.

A generalisation test of prosocial behaviour was also conducted. Children were given 12 coloured pencils for attending. They were told that they could give some of the pencils to other schoolchildren who were not able to participate in the study. More pencils were shared in the self-attribution condition than in the other two condi-tions. An explanation is that self-attribution made it easier for the children to generalise their prosocial behaviour to new situations.

Additional research indicates that attributions that use the label "altruistic person" foster the self-schema of an altruistic person, which in turn heightens prosocial behaviour (Grusec & Redler, 1980). Such attributional techniques seem to work best with 7–8-year-olds. They were instructed by an adult to share their winnings in a bowling

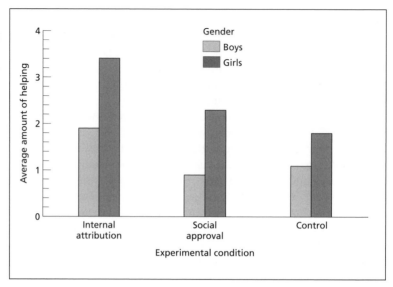

FIG. 8.5. Number of pictures drawn by children depending on experimental condition (based on data from Grusec & Redler, 1980, p. 528).

game with poor children. Internalisation of altruistic responses was compared across three conditions: In the first condition the adult explained the children's donations by their personality (that he/she is an altruistic person). In the second condition the adult merely praised the children. No feedback was given in the control condition.

Several weeks later the same children were asked to draw pictures for children who were in hospital. Results indicated that feedback that contained internal attributions (you are the kind of person who acts altruistically) generalised to new situations. Children drew more pictures in the attribution condition than in the other two conditions. The social approval and control conditions did not differ from each other (Figure 8.5). The higher level of prosocial behaviour in the attribution condition may be taken as strong evidence that internalisation is more likely after attributional feedback than after reinforcement feedback. In fact, no evidence of internalisation in the social-reinforcement condition was obtained after the time interval, leading to a certain scepticism with respect to possible positive consequences of social reinforcement on the development of prosocial behaviour.

In addition, a gender difference emerged which was independent of the experimental condition: Girls painted more pictures than boys. In summary, socialisation techniques that build on the positive decisions of a child should focus on the child as a person instead of on the specific decision made. In contrast, socialisation techniques that reduce the likelihood of negative decisions are more viable if they focus on the specific decision (Grusec & Redler, 1980). A further consideration is important from a practical perspective: The success of internally focused attributions depends on the age of the children. Attributional feedback is designed to change the self-schema of the target person. This is achieved when two preconditions are fulfilled: (1) the child has developed the cognitive capacity to understand the consistency between internal attribution and action, and (2) the child has not yet developed a stable self-schema that is resistant against attributional feedback. The first condition is not fulfilled in younger children (e.g., 5–6-year-olds), whereas the second condition is not fulfilled in 10–11-year-olds. Therefore, the age range that allows the modification of self-schema by internally focused feedback is quite limited. In correspondence with this analysis, it was shown that attributional feedback did not lead to higher levels of prosocial behaviour in 11–12-year-olds (Grusec & Redler, 1980) indicating that no internalisation occurred in this age group.

Foot-in-the-door technique

Why is internally focused attribution successful as a socialisation technique? The use of trait labels seems to work because it gives rise to a self-perception process that follows the script "I am a helpful person because I help needy people". Self-perception processes of this kind are likely when the person is searching for an explanation of what happened (Bem, 1972).

The same principle seems to operate in the foot-in-the-door technique. As the term suggests, prior prosocial behaviour may promote later prosocial behaviour. In general, a modest request that elicits a high rate of compliance will lead to a larger amount of compliance when a substantial request follows (compared to a control group, in which only the substantial request is used; DeJong, 1979). Freedman and Fraser (1966) were the first to demonstrate that the foot-in-the-door effect offered the explanation that the person who complies with the first request may infer that he/she generally is the kind of person who helps others in need. This self-perception explanation has found some support in later research (DeJong, 1979).

Eisenberg et al. (1987) combined the self-perception explanation of the foot-in-the-door effect with the assumption that self-inferences of being an altruistic person only occur in children who are able to infer consistency between self-attribution and behaviour, in other words at age 7 or older. The study included kindergartners, 2nd graders, and 5th graders. Whereas the foot-in-the-door effect was not observed in kindergartners and was only weak for 2nd graders, it was significant for 5th graders. In addition, a consistency scale that measured the preference for consistent behaviour was positively correlated with helping in the foot-in-the-door condition but not in the control condition. This indicates that the foot-in-the-door effect is facilitated by the preference for consistency, a result that was replicated only for girls in a second study (Eisenberg, Cialdini, McCreath, & Shell, 1989). This empirical evidence supports the self-attribution explanation of the foot-in-the-door effect.

Role-identity model

From an applied perspective, the issue of blood donation is of special significance in modern societies. According to statistical data, it is estimated that 95% of Americans will need a blood transfusion during their lifetime (Piliavin & Callero, 1991, p. 1). "Blood drives", which are conducted in many countries, may be based on quite different strategies because there are many reasons for donating blood:

Sri Lankan nurses chat with students as they donate blood in Colombo in April 2000, following a government appeal to help soldiers wounded during recent heavy fighting. Credit: Popperfoto/Reuters.

> We can divide reasons for donation into two basic categories. There are intrinsic motives, reasons that come from inside the person and have to do with values, interests and one's sense of responsibility, and there are extrinsic motives, reasons that are based in the actions of others and the structure of the social world (Piliavin & Callero, 1991, p. 12).

For example, blood donors may contribute to blood collections because they expect payment or because they feel a responsibility for the community in which they live. As a consequence, the people who are actually involved in blood donation may be quite different depending on which collection policy is used by official authorities. For instance, if blood drives are primarily based on payment, the demographic structure of the donors will be completely different from that of donors participating in drives that appeal to the responsibility of the individual to his or her community. Therefore, blood donors may have different motives depending on the social context (Piliavin & Callero, 1991).

In a social system that emphasises community responsibility, a basic principle is "from each according to his ability, to each according to his needs" (Piliavin & Callero, 1991). In the context of community responsibility, regular blood donations may be the result of the self-identity of the donor that he/she is the kind of person who donates blood for the well-being of other members of the community. The development of a salient blood donor role is associated with the definition of the self as a regular donor. In correspondence with the foot-in-the-door effect and principles of self-perception, it was assumed that continued prosocial activity increases self-commitment to the activity and changes the self-schema (Piliavin & Callero, 1991). As a result of increasing self-commitment, attitudes and traits that are in correspondence with regular blood donation become part of the personal identity. Finally, an altruistic identity is acquired.

The role identity model of blood donation attempts to explain why a group of individuals who donate blood regularly without payment come to define themselves as blood donors. The model explicitly focuses on repeated donors and their "altruistic career". It attempts to explain how consistency in blood-donation behaviour develops over time, and it assumes that the merging of the blood donor role with the self is the factor that leads to a consistent self-commitment as a blood donor. Further analyses indicate that role merger and role salience as a blood donor explain additional variance in intentions to donate blood over and above that which is explained by the theory of reasoned action (Fishbein & Ajzen, 1975; see Chapter 15).

The applied question is whether to base campaigns to increase willingness to donate blood on material reward or attributional principles. To address this question and to investigate the psychological consequences of different campaigning systems, three systems were compared (Piliavin, 1989):

- The United States "community responsibility" system, in which donors freely decide about donating blood and are not offered any material reward.
- The Polish volunteer system, in which participants are not paid although they receive other privileges (e.g., a day off from work with pay).
- The Polish payment system, in which participants are paid for blood donation.

Results indicate that the psychological determinants of intention to donate blood are quite similar for the American system and the Polish voluntary system. For example, self-definition as a regular donor and motivation to give were significant predictors of the intention to donate blood in the next 6 months for participants in those systems that do not focus on incentives. In addition, self-salience of the blood donor role identity was measured. An example is the item "To me, being a blood donor means more than just giving blood". People who agreed with such statements also expressed higher intentions to donate blood in the future.

In contrast, the pattern of results for participants within the Polish payment system was quite different. These persons emphasised external motives to a greater extent including social pressure and social approval. In addition, another important difference emerged between the payment and the volunteer system. The motives of Polish and American voluntary donors were classified as more internal as number of prior donations increased, whereas the motives of paid donors became more external with higher number of prior donations.

What do these results tell us about the planning of campaigns for blood donation? In general the development of an internal motivation of blood donors supports their feeling of competence and mastery and leads to strong internal control expectancies (Skinner, 1996). Therefore, systems that offer no payment function well. In addition, blood donation might be fostered by attributional feedback which focuses on the self-concept of the blood donor.

The payment system is also effective in increasing willingness to be a blood donor. But the willingness to contribute to blood donations comes more and more under the control of material incentives. In addition, in such a system the quality of collected blood is unsatisfactory (Piliavin & Callero, 1991). Under such a system, blood donors are likely to reduce their internal control expectancies, feeling more like a pawn than a responsible citizen. They simply donate blood in order to earn money.

The example of the Polish voluntary system shows that indirect incentives that facilitate becoming a blood donor in the first place may be combined with a volunteer system which focuses on the development of the role identity of a blood donor. In general, results on blood donations and especially on regular blood donors show that stable intentions to donate blood are linked to commitment to the role of blood donor and the development of a corresponding self-identity.

2000) to assume that several modes of empathic arousal exist, which may operate individually or in combination. This assumption implies that empathy may be aroused in quite different circumstances. Therefore, a broad spectrum of situations is likely to elicit empathic distress.

Automatic imitation plus afferent feedback

A first mode of empathy arousal is based on a mimicry response to another's expression of sadness. It is assumed that an observer automatically experiences the same emotion that another person expresses (cf. McDougall, 1908). An automatic imitation of components of the facial expression and posture movements observed in another person occurs, and via afferent feedback these imitative responses elicit the same emotion in the observer. This assumed process is in agreement with the hypothesis that the experience of emotion is the result of feedback that derives from visceral and facial muscles. This body reaction theory was developed by James (1890/1950) who wrote:

> Common sense says we lose our fortune, are sorry, and weep; we meet a bear, are frightened, and run; we are insulted by a rival, are angry, and strike. . . . The more rational statement is that we feel sorry because we cry, angry because we strike, afraid because we tremble and not that we cry, strike, or tremble because we are sorry, angry or fearful, as the case may be (pp. 449–450; quoted from Leventhal, 1974, p. 9).

The theory assumes that different feeling states are the result of different patterns of bodily reactions. In the case of empathy, the additional assumption is needed that an automatic imitation of the expressive and visceral responses of others is elicited by observing them in a given situation (Lipps, 1906, cited in Hoffman, 1977). Although the body reaction theory places too much emphasis on visceral responses, which are unlikely to mediate emotional responses (Leventhal, 1974), evidence shows that facial expressions may elicit specific emotions. For example, the facial feedback hypothesis, which states that emotions depend on feedback from facial expressions, has been supported in several experiments (e.g., Zuckerman, Klorman, Larrance, & Spiegel, 1981).

In one experimental demonstration, students were asked to hold a pen with their lips, whereas others were asked to hold the pen with their front teeth (Strack, Stepper, & Martin, 1988). In the lips condition the activation of muscles associated with smiling was inhibited. In contrast, in the teeth condition the activation of muscles associated with smiling was facilitated. In agreement with the facial feedback hypothesis, results indicated that cartoons were rated as more funny in the teeth than in the lips condition (see Stepper & Strack, 1993, for corroborative results). The advantage of this procedure is that facial expressions are manipulated unobtrusively without mentioning smiling. Therefore, the results add some credence to the assumption that emotions are related to proprioceptive feedback.

Direct association

People compare their own experiences with the experiences of others. This is the basic assumption of social comparison theory (Festinger, 1954). While comparing themselves with others, people register the situational cues that are associated with the sadness or joy of other people. These cues tend to be the same cues that were present when the observers themselves experienced sadness or joy. On the basis of the classical conditioning paradigm it is assumed that the cues observed when others suffer elicit sad feelings in the observer via classical conditioning.

Another way of expressing this assumption is that the situational cues remind the observer that specific situations elicit sadness and, as a consequence, the feeling of sadness is evoked. Individuals acquire implicit anticipatory responses to pain and frustration (Lott, Lott, & Walsh, 1970). The pain-eliciting situation of another person functions as a cue which resembles the observer's own pain-eliciting situations from the past, leading to empathic feelings of distress. When the cues that are related to the suffering of the other resemble similar pain cues which have elicited suffering in the observer, they simultaneously elicit negative affect in the other and in the observer. An example is a boy who has cut himself and experiences pain in his bleeding finger. When he sees another child who has cut himself, his own experience of pain becomes associated with this observation.

Classical conditioning

A special case of direct association occurs when the victim and the observer experience the same affect simultaneously. In this case, the cues that impinge on the victim elicit vicarious feelings in the observer at the same time. For example, empathic conditioning occurs when a mother is startled by a loud noise and responds with fright while handling her child. The startle response of the mother is transferred to the child by physical contact, signalling that something bad has happened.

The process of classical conditioning of vicarious feelings is based on a learning paradigm in which a direct association between feeling states of others and one's own feelings is established. This association may be based on the cognitive representation of the effect of a pro-social response associated with positive feelings (Aronfreed, 1976). The learning paradigm that is based on positive feelings consists of two steps:

- In the first step an association is established between the feelings of the donor-to-be (elicited by positive feedback) and the visible signs of another person's joy. The temporal contiguity of the other person's signs of joy and the positive feelings are a prerequisite for establishing the association. If this association is formed on the basis of conditioning, the signs of joy of the receiver-to-be elicit a positive feeling state in the donor. The other person's joy is a secondary reinforcer which continues to exert an influence after the primary reinforcer (positive feedback) is no longer available.
- The instrumental value of prosocial responses for the elicitation of joy in the receiver of the help is learned. The receiver's positive consequences function as a reinforcer which makes altruistic responses of the donor more likely.

This learning process is only initially dependent on direct observation of the other person's affective responses (Aronfreed, 1976). With growing ability to cognitively represent the consequences of actions for other persons, the association between prosocial behaviour and receiver's affect is anticipated without really having to observe the positive response.

Training of generosity is based on affective arousal of the donor and expressions of joy of the receiver which serve as secondary reinforcers after training has been successfully conducted (Midlarsky & Bryan, 1967). A total of 160 girls from the 1st to 4th grades parti-cipated in the experiment. In the first phase, five different training programmes were used. The female experimenter demonstrated the operation of an apparatus that had two levers. Pushing one lever released small sweets, whereas pushing the other lever activated a red light. The experimenter responded to the activation of the red light in the five experimental conditions in the following ways:

- EH condition: first, expressions of joy, then hugging the child (forward conditioning).
- HE condition: first, hugging the child, then expressions of joy (backward conditioning).
- E condition: only expressions of joy.
- H condition: only hugging the child.
- 0 condition: neither expressions of joy nor hugging the child.

Signs of joy were shown by the experimenter by saying something like "Oh, good, I see the red light." Note that in the conditioning trials positive feelings of the experimenter were associated with positive feelings of the child. The hypothesis is that conditioning has the effect that the receiver's expressions of joy become elicitors of positive feelings in the donor. As a consequence, prosocial behaviour is rewarding and is performed even if it means giving up one's own rewards (i.e., the sweets).

In the second phase of the experiment the girls operated the apparatus over 40 trials. During this phase, a second variable was added: Either the experimenter responded with expressions of joy when the red light was activated, or she showed no such response. The dependent variable was how often the lever that activated the red light was used (meaning that the child made sacrifices). The results in the 10 experimental conditions are depicted in Figure 9.1, and indicate that forward conditioning and backward conditioning were equally effective in promoting the self-sacrifice response. In addition, conditioning was most effective if the expressions of joy

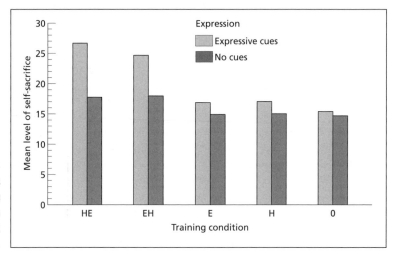

FIG. 9.1. Self-sacrifice as a function of learning condition (based on data from Midlarsky & Bryan, 1967, p. 410).

were continued in the second phase of the study. In this condition the red light was activated in about 25 trials, whereas self-reinforcement with sweets was preferred in only 15 trials.

After the second phase the earnings of all the children were equated. In the third phase of the experiment the children were asked to donate some of the sweets to poor children. The number of donated sweets was highest after forward or backward conditioning. Obviously, the success of the training programme generalised to sharing in the third phase of the experiment. These results indicate that the acquisition of altruistic responses is facilitated by the indirect elicitation of the helper's positive feelings (see also Bryan, 1972).

The two-step learning process is as follows: (1) Expressions of joy are associated with the helper's positive feelings on the basis of empathy-mediated altruism. (2) Signs of joy of a model who shows prosocial behaviour facilitate imitation of the prosocial behaviour by observers. This constitutes a positive feedback loop in which positive feelings and memories lead to the performance of positive activities (such as helpfulness), and such activities contribute to the maintenance of positive feelings (see Baron, 1987; Isen, Shalker, Clark, & Karp, 1978). Temporal coincidence of positive experiences frequently happens in everyday life. For example, shared joy between parents and children occurs regularly and is a basis of empathy-mediated altruism. In summary, vicarious feelings are an important basis of the child's prosocial responses. A positive atmosphere contributes to prosocial behaviour. On the other hand, a negative atmosphere creates readiness to respond aggressively (Berkowitz & Heimer, 1989).

Language-mediated association

Direct association is broadened when verbal descriptions of the suffering of others are used (e.g., "I am very depressed", "I feel so sorry"). Symbolic reference may trigger a direct association because the observer himself or herself uses such verbalisations when he or she is suffering. Whereas the classical conditioning arousal mode is restricted to the actual observation of the suffering of the victim, which allows the registration of situational cues, this extended mode of association is much more flexible. For example, when people describe their experience of disasters in the media, these descriptions may elicit empathic concern via symbolic association. In this way, it is possible to experience empathic distress with people in other countries, without ever having been there. It is likely that language-mediated association elicits less intense empathic distress than direct association, although no data on this issue seem to be available.

Role taking

An effective way of increasing empathic distress seems to be direct instruction, which asks the observer to imagine how he or she would feel if exposed to the same stressful event that is experienced by another person (e.g., an electric shock). This instruction was first used by Stotland (1969), who found that it increased empathic distress in the observer. Later studies (e.g., Toi & Batson, 1982) have shown that the "imagine-other" instruction is a reliable manipulation for inducing empathy in observers. The "imagine-other" instruction was compared with an "observe" instruction which is assumed to reduce perspective taking. Empathy was measured by an index that was calculated from the responses to three adjectives (sympathetic, moved, and compassionate). Results indicated that the imagine-other set led to greater empathic emotion (M = 4.67) than the observe-set (3.88) on a 7-point scale.

In this study students heard a tape-recording of an interview with a traffic accident victim, Carol Marcy, who had broken both legs. As a consequence, Carol had missed a whole month of school and so she was behind in her studies, particularly in introductory psychology. Therefore it was very important for her to find another student in the introductory psychology class who would go over the lecture notes with her. An excerpt from the instructions in the observe-set condition was: "While you are listening to the broadcast, try to listen carefully to the information presented. Try to be as objective as possible, carefully attending to all the information presented about the situation and about the person who is being interviewed" (Toi & Batson, 1982, p. 285). An excerpt from the imagine-other-set condition was: "While you are listening to the broadcast try to imagine how the person in the news feels. Try to take the perspective of the person who is being interviewed, imagining how he or she feels about what has happened and how it has affected his or her life" (Toi & Batson, 1982, p. 285).

The existence of several modes of empathy arousal has the implication that empathy is a robust phenomenon which is reliably observed in situations in which victims are confronted with their bad fate. It is an overdetermined response (Hoffman, 1984, p. 107). The role of situational cues is most obvious in the case of direct association and classical conditioning. Symbols are decisive for the occurrence of language-mediated association. Expressive cues are important for automatic imitation plus afferent feedback. It is likely that in specific situations, cues combine to elicit empathy via several channels. In such cases the empathy response is expected to have a short response latency and to be quite intense.

Self–other differentiation and the development of empathy

One obvious difference between the empathy of a 2-year-old and an adult is that only the adult is able to describe his or her feeling state in detail, give a name to it, and think about causes and consequences. This semantic processing of empathic arousal gives the perceived distress of others meaning by putting it into a network of ideas about justice, responsibility, and compensation.

Related to this difference in linguistic competence is the difference in the flexibility of information integration. Whereas the 2-year-old focuses on visual and verbal cues that express the plight of another person, the mature empathiser integrates several sources of information about the incident, including visual and verbal cues from the victim, biographic information about the victim, information about the situation, and reports by others. This broad information base leads to a better understanding of the incident but it also has a problem: When several sources of information are available, the chances increase that contradictory information will be obtained, which either leads to a neutral impression following information integration or evokes derogation of the victim by emphasising those pieces of information that point to the victim as the cause of his/her bad fate.

These ideas are derived from the theory of empathic arousal that combines affective and cognitive processes in explaining the development of concern for others (Hoffman, 1984). The theory assumes that cognitive and affective processes develop independently and constantly interact in producing the subjective experience of empathic concern for others. Although this experience is unitary and emotionally charged, it is based on several underlying constituents including cognitive processing of verbal and nonverbal cues, vicarious emotional responding, and reasoning about the causes of what has happened (i.e., attribution processes).

The cognitive component is closely linked with cognitive development as described by Piaget (1932; Piaget & Inhelder, 1947), specifically the development of object and person permanence, cognitive perspective taking, and the acquisition of an understanding of person identity. Two general comments apply to this development: The child seems to reach these different levels of cognitive development at an earlier age than assumed by Piaget, largely because of specifics of the methods he used (e.g., the quite complex three-mountain landscape task as a measure of perceptual perspective taking, with which even adults have problems). Furthermore, developmental progress occurs gradually, oscillating between levels, so that an earlier and a later level of development can co-exist during a transitional phase.

In the first year of life, children confuse their own emotions with the emotions of other children. This phase of self–other fusion sets the stage for the development of cognitive competencies that lead to higher cognitive achievements. The level of object permanence is reached when the child is able to imagine an object even when it is out of sight. Persons may be understood as a special class of objects. Learning that a person who is outside the child's view still exists is important for the development of social attachment (Bowlby, 1969). Person permanence and object permanence are understood in the second year of life, although the mastering of these tasks is a gradual process. This has the consequence that the other person is sometimes fused with the self (e.g., in an arousing situation) and sometimes seen as distinct from the self (Hoffman, 1984). After this transitional phase a stable self–other differentiation emerges.

The level of perspective taking includes perceptual, cognitive, and affective perceptual change (cf. Neuf, 1997, Table 9.2). Early indications of perspective taking are observed in 3–4-year-olds. In addition, 4–5-year-olds are able to infer the intentions of others. Rudiments of perspective taking are even observed in 2-year-olds (Hoffman, 1984). Note that perspective taking (as well as person permanence and person identity) does not guarantee that the person who has command over it will follow a prosocial course of action. Perspective taking is a cognitive tool that serves different motives. It may be used in order to exploit the good intentions of another person or to blame the other person by insinuating bad intentions. Perspective taking is positively related to deception and impression management, if a person is highly motivated to secure personal success (Gangestad & Snyder, 2000). Be that as it may, the results of meta-analysis show that perspective taking is positively related to sharing and helping in children.

1962), affiliative tendency and sensitivity to rejection (Mehrabian, 1970), and approval-seeking tendency (Crowne & Marlowe, 1960). The only significant predictor of amount of helping was empathic tendency, confirming the construct validity of the scale.

Bryant (1982) modified the Mehrabian and Epstein questionnaire to develop an empathy scale for children and adolescents. In correspondence with studies of adults, a gender difference was found with girls scoring higher than boys. In 13–14-year-olds empathy as measured by this scale was positively related to prosocial behaviour (Eisenberg et al., 1991). In a meta-analysis of studies that test the relationship between questionnaire measures of empathy and pro-social behaviour, a positive relationship was found. The overall correlation was $r = .17$, which is significant (Eisenberg & Miller, 1987). Many of the studies that show a positive relationship were based on the Emotional Empathy Scale (e.g., Archer, Diaz-Loving, Gollwitzer, Davis, & Foushee, 1981).

Another finding was that empathic tendency correlated positively with the arousal scale of the semantic differential (Mehrabian & Russell, 1974). The arousal scale includes adjective pairs like "stimulated–relaxed" and "excited–calm". Note that arousal represents a pancultural dimension of emotions which is found in languages as different as Croatian, English, and Japanese (Russell, 1983). Two other dimensions of the semantic differential which were labelled "pleasure" and "dominance" by Mehrabian and Russell (1974) did not explain any variance in empathic tendency over and above arousal. Therefore, students who scored high on arousal tendency, which may be considered a basic feeling dimension, tended to express more empathy. In retrospect, Mehrabian et al. (1988) interpreted emotional empathy as an indicator of emotional arousability in general.

One attribute of questionnaires is face validity. In general, high face validity, which is shown by the correspondence of item content and definition of the construct, is considered important (Cronbach, 1990). With respect to the questionnaires by Hogan (1969) and Mehrabian and Epstein (1972), as well as with respect to the scales by Sherman and Stotland (1978) and Davis (1983a) that will be discussed later, research has considered whether the items represent the content of empathy (Holz-Ebeling & Steinmetz, 1995), which was defined as the comprehension (recognition or understanding of feelings) of the conscious experiences of another person (thoughts, feelings, and/or needs) in a specific episode. This definition encompasses both "cognitive" and "affective" empathy.

Additionally, several other related terms were included in the analysis of the content of empathy items. Among these terms was sympathy, which was defined as a feeling of pity for another person connected with concern over his/her well-being (cf. Wispé, 1986; see Chapter 9). Another emotion that was contrasted with empathy was personal distress defined as a feeling of discomfort based on excessive concern about one's own well-being.

In an empirical study, judges who were familiar with these definitions decided whether each item of the questionnaire corresponded to the definition of each of the three emotions (empathy, sympathy, and personal distress, respectively). In addition, 10 further categories were used (e.g., nonverbal sensitivity, identification, projection, and envy). The criterion of the suitability of an item to represent each of the categories was agreement of two thirds of the judges.

Results indicate that only two items of the questionnaire by Hogan (1969) and two items of the questionnaire by Mehrabian and Epstein (1972) fulfilled this criterion of referring to empathy as defined. One of the items of the Emotional Empathy Scale fulfilled the criterion of measuring sympathy (Holz-Ebeling & Steinmetz, 1995). This result is less surprising with respect to the questionnaire by Hogan (1969), which is only minimally based on manifest item content, but is unexpected with respect to the questionnaire of Mehrabian and Epstein (1972), which is based on items that are assumed to reflect their definition of "affective" empathy. However, items such as "I like to watch people open presents" and "Lonely people are probably unfriendly" (reverse scoring; p. 528) are quite unspecific in their reference to the concept of empathy.

The situation is no different if the "cognitive" empathy definition of Hogan (1969) is used as a criterion to assess the suitability of his items and if the "affective" empathy definition of Mehrabian and Epstein (1972) is the criterion for the assessment of the suitability of their items. Only in a few items of these questionnaires does the content correspond to the proposed definitions.

Clearly, a validity problem exists with respect to dispositional empathy. The majority of the items in the questionnaires by Hogan (1969) and Mehrabian and Epstein (1972) are categorised differently by different judges with no general trend evident. This is unfortunate because content validity is a matter of concern in test theory, indicating how relevant the items are given the theoretical concept (Cronbach, 1990). It is remarkable that the item of the Empathy Scale that is best in representing face validity ("As a rule I have little difficulty in 'putting myself into other people's shoes'") did not load heavily on even one of the factors extracted from the items of the Empathy Scale by Johnson et al. (1983).

It is unlikely that an intelligence test would be widely used if it contained items that seem to be unrelated to intelligence, and therefore not face valid. Such indirect measures of a construct might be valuable as a supplement to more direct measures. They allow the measurement of a construct without the participant being aware of what is being measured. However, it is usually considered unsatisfactory if only indirect measures of a construct are available.

Multidimensional approaches

Somewhat better evaluations with reference to content validity are given to the questionnaires developed by Sherman and Stotland (1978) and Davis (1983a; Holz-Ebeling & Steinmetz, 1995). Sherman and Stotland (1978) started with the definition of empathy as "the individual's capacity for emotional or affective experience, that is, with the transfer of emotion from the perceived to the perceiver" (p. 28). On the basis of this "affective" definition they developed five scales to measure empathy. Their approach was based on a systematic mapping of situations of empathy on the basis of four dimensions:

- Quality of emotion (positive, negative).
- Similar or contrasting response (i.e., the emotion of the observer corresponds with that of the observed person vs the observer experiences a different emotion, such as envy).
- Relationship between observer and the observed (similarity, liking, and dependency).
- Perceived cause of the emotion of the observed (physical, achievement, social success).

A factor analysis of the 48 items that were formulated on the basis of this classification scheme led to six factors. Because the first factor was interpreted as response bias, only the remaining factors were used as the basis for the development of scales (Sherman & Stotland, 1978, pp. 140–144):

- Denial–avoidance as resistance against empathy ("I seldom get deeply involved in the problems and experiences of others").
- Involvement–concern ("When I see a retarded child, I try to imagine how he feels about things").

- Hostility–empathy as contrast experience ("Sometimes I am not at all pleased when I hear about a person who got top grades").
- Friend–empathy ("When a friend becomes engaged or gets married, I am very happy").
- Fantasy–empathy referring to involvement with an actor in a play or character in a story ("When I am reading an interesting story or novel, I imagine how I would feel if the events in the story were happening to me").

The factors contrast empathy vs empathy avoidance and similar empathy vs contrast empathy, respectively. The positive–negative quality of empathy is not reflected in the scales, suggesting that the tendency to share positive emotions is positively related to the tendency to share negative emotions. On all scales, females scored higher than males, with the smallest differences emerging on the involvement–concern scale and the fantasy–empathy scale. Additional results indicated that the fantasy–empathy scale was systematically related to physiological arousal that was elicited as a response to another's pain (Mitchell, Stotland, & Mathews, 1978).

In the content analysis of Holz-Ebeling and Steinmetz (1995) 11 items were identified as measuring empathy and 4 as measuring envy (contrast empathy in the terminology of Sherman & Stotland, 1978). Examples for empathy items are "When I see strangers, I almost never try to imagine what they are thinking" (reverse scoring) or the items quoted earlier to illustrate involvement–concern and fantasy–empathy. The hostility–empathy item described earlier represents the category of envy, which corresponds to contrast empathy.

The Interpersonal Reactivity Index (Davis, 1983a, 1994) is based on a broad definition of empathy as "a set of constructs having to do with the responses of one individual to the experiences of another" (Davis, 1994, p. 12). This definition says nothing about the similarity of the emotional responses of observer and observed, accurate knowledge of another's thoughts and feelings, the contrast between cognitive role taking and affective reactivity, and the contrast between passive experience and active attempt to understand. Instead, in a theoretical model these forms of empathy are identified as processes and intrapersonal outcomes (Davis, 1994). It is assumed that antecedents (e.g., observer/target similarity and individual differences) influence processes, intrapersonal outcomes, and, finally, interpersonal outcomes.

Following Hoffman (1984), processes include motor mimicry, direct association, language-mediated associations, and role taking.

Intrapersonal outcomes include affective outcomes (e.g., empathic concern and personal distress) and non-affective outcomes (e.g., interpersonal accuracy; see later). Finally, interpersonal outcomes (e.g., helping) are assumed to be a joint function of antecedents, processes, and intrapersonal outcomes.

The multidimensional approach of Davis (1994) is based in part on the integration of sympathy and empathy (cf. Wispé, 1986; see Table 9.1) by assuming that both constructs are separate but related. The common element is the reference to the experience of another person. In the Interpersonal Reactivity Index (Davis, 1983a, 1994) empathy is measured by the perspective-taking scale. Sympathy is reflected in the empathic-concern scale. Two further scales are included in the Interpersonal Reactivity Index: personal distress and fantasy. Whereas personal distress refers to an unpleasant emotion that is aroused by observing the plight of another person, fantasy refers to the tendency to imagine what actors, characters, and other fictional persons experience in literature, on stage, or in movies. The scales are illustrated by the following items (Davis, 1994, p. 56):

- Perspective taking: "I sometimes find it difficult to see things from the 'other guy's' point of view" (reverse scoring).
- Empathic concern: "I often have tender, concerned feelings for people less fortunate than me".
- Personal distress: "In emergency situations, I feel apprehensive and ill-at-ease".
- Fantasy: "I really get involved with the feelings of the characters in a novel".

The two items that refer to perspective taking and fantasy are suitable as measures of empathy from the viewpoint of content validity. The item of the empathic concern scale fulfils the criterion of measuring sympathy. The item of the personal distress scale is an appropriate measure of personal distress (Holz-Ebeling & Steinmetz, 1995). Each subscale of the Interpersonal Reactivity Index consists of seven items. Of the 14 items of the scales for perspective taking and fantasy, 7 refer to empathy; of the 7 items of the empathic concern subscale, 3 refer to sympathy; and of the 7 items of the personal distress scale, 5 measure what they are intended to measure. In sum, a comparison of the four questionnaires shows that the Interpersonal Reactivity Index is superior with respect to content validity (Holz-Ebeling & Steinmetz, 1995).

The correlations of the subscales of the Interpersonal Reactivity Index with personality scales support the validity of the subscales (Davis, 1983a). Perspective taking and empathic concern were positively related to sensitivity to others (as measured by the expressiveness scale of the Extended Personal Attribute Questionnaire; Spence et al., 1979). Both subscales correlated positively with predispositional empathy (see later; Batson, Bolen, Cross, & Neuringer-Benefiel, 1986). In the same study empathic concern was positively correlated with prosocial behaviour, but only in the difficult-escape condition (not in the easy-escape condition; see Chapter 13). Empathic concern was also positively related to the Social Responsibility Scale by Berkowitz and Lutterman (1968; Omoto & Snyder, 1995). In addition, fantasy was positively related to prosocial behaviour (Fultz, Batson, Fortenbach, McCarthy, & Varney, 1986). Finally, personal distress correlated positively with shyness, social anxiety, and audience anxiety, indicating that the personal distress scale is related to a lack of social competence. Of the four scales, empathic concern and fantasy were reliably related to prosocial behaviour (see also Davis, 1983b).

Predispositional empathy

The challenge of measuring situation-specific empathy has led to two quite different experimental approaches: one for adults using adjective lists and one for children based on nonverbal indicators. These approaches have in common that they consider empathy a state variable that is measured on the basis of specific episodes.

Emotional Response Questionnaire

An example of the experimental approach is a study by Coke, Batson, and McDavis (1978, Exp. 2) in which respondents heard about a student who was looking for participants for her master's thesis research. She had difficulties in finding volunteers and was not able to pay for participation. In this experiment the Emotional Response Questionnaire was employed as a measure of empathic concern. Eight adjectives were used, which a priori were assumed to be possible indicators of empathy: moved, *soft-hearted*, sorrowed, touched, *empathic*, *warm*, *concerned*, and *compassionate*. Ratings were obtained on a 7-point scale ranging from 1 (not at all) to 7 (extremely). Respondents expressed how much they had experienced each emotional state. In a factor analysis the five adjectives shown in italics which loaded highly (> .60) on the empathy factor were included in the index of empathy.

In addition, an index of a second emotional dimension was created, which was termed personal distress. Whereas empathic distress refers to other-oriented emotions, personal distress refers to concern about one's own well-being (cf. Holz-Ebeling & Steinmetz, 1995). The following adjectives were assumed to tap personal distress: *alarmed*, perturbed, disconcerted, bothered, irritated, disturbed, worried, uneasy, distressed, *troubled*, *upset*, anxious, and grieved. On the basis of a factor analysis the three adjectives in italics were selected as representing personal distress. The personal distress factor and the empathic concern factor were orthogonal to each other. Scores on the personal distress scale and the empathic distress scale correlate positively ($r = .55$ in Experiment 1 by Cialdini et al., 1987).

Batson et al. (1987) summarised the factor-analytic results of six studies using adjective lists as measures of personal distress and empathic concern. In later studies two additional adjectives were included as measures of empathic distress: sympathetic and tender. Across the studies the following six emotions were found to represent empathic concern: sympathetic, moved, compassionate, tender, warm, and soft-hearted. The following eight emotions represent personal distress: alarmed, grieved, upset, worried, disturbed, perturbed, distressed, and troubled. These adjective lists have several advantages. They are easy to comprehend, short in exposition, and proven as measures of emotional states (cf. Watson, Clark, & Tellegen, 1988).

To indicate the relative dominance of empathic concern and personal distress, a difference score was calculated by subtracting the average personal distress score from the average empathic concern score. Respondents who have positive values on this index are more motivated by empathic concern than by personal distress. By splitting the difference score at the median it was possible to compare respondents who are predominantly motivated by empathic concern with those who are predominantly motivated by personal distress. It is assumed that persons who are high on empathic concern are altruistically motivated, whereas persons who are high on personal distress are egoistically motivated (see Chapter 13).

The distinction between empathic concern and personal distress is not only related to the issue of altruism as an independent motive system but is also relevant with respect to Hoffman's (1984, 2000) assumption that empathy originates in toddlers on the basis of personal distress (see earlier). On the basis of this reasoning, positive correlations between empathic concern and personal distress are expected, which are indeed reported by Batson et al. (1987). This positive relationship may also be explained by the fact that both personal distress and empathic concern are dependent on the perception of a need situation of another person. In addition, individual differences in emotionality and response sets that distort responses on rating scales may explain the positive correlation.

In several experiments it was shown that personal distress and empathic concern relate differently to prosocial behaviour, adding support to the assumption that both emotions are qualitatively different (Batson et al., 1987). Whereas empathic concern motivates prosocial behaviour independently of the availability of an escape alternative that allows the person to ignore the need situation of another person by leaving the situation, personal distress motivates prosocial behaviour as long as no escape alternative is available (see Chapter 13).

Furthermore, correlations between empathic concern and prosocial behaviour depend on the condition (Toi & Batson, 1982). In the easy-escape condition a positive correlation was obtained, whereas the correlation was insignificant in the difficult-escape condition (see also Batson, O'Quinn, Fultz, Vanderplas, & Isen, 1983). Unfortunately, the pattern of correlations was reversed in a later study (Batson et al., 1986). Only after conducting a complex partial-correlation analysis, the expected pattern with higher correlation in the easy-escape condition was obtained, and zero correlation in the difficult-escape condition a result that was corroborated in a later study (Carlo, Eisenberg, Troyer, Switzer, & Speer, 1991a).

These results are interpreted as indicating that empathic concern reflects altruistic motivation. It is assumed that if prosocial personality reflects egoistic motivation, a significant positive correlation with prosocial behaviour will be found in the difficult-escape condition (but not in the easy-escape condition). The argument is that egoistic prosocial motivation is based on self-censure (Am I acting according to my values?). If the person cannot ignore the needs of another person, higher egoistic prosocial motivation (and therefore higher self-censure because of threat to self-image) leads to more helping. If it is easy to ignore the plight of the other person, the egoistically motivated person has no problem with his/her credibility as a prosocial person and does not act according to the prosocial self-scheme. In contrast, altruistic motivation, which is presumably measured by situation-specific empathic concern, is expected to influence prosocial behaviour when situational pressure to act prosocially is absent (that is, in the easy-escape condition).

This reasoning is also supported by a partial-correlation analysis, in which situation-specific empathic concern and personal distress were considered as predictors of prosocial behaviour (Batson, 1987). Based on the data of three studies, the partial correlations between empathy and helping (partialling out personal distress) are positive in the easy-escape condition and tend to be negative in the difficult-escape condition. In contrast, the partial correlations between personal distress and helping (partialling out empathy) tend to be negative in the easy-escape condition and positive in the difficult-escape condition. These results indicate that *empathic concern* that is *free of personal distress* is positively correlated with prosocial behaviour in the easy-escape condition. This positive relationship does not occur in the difficult-escape condition. In contrast, in the latter condition *personal distress* that is free of *empathic concern* tends to be positively correlated with prosocial behaviour, although the data are inconsistent on this point. These results demonstrate that empathic concern and personal distress are functionally different and that empathic concern is less "egoistic" than personal distress.

Television programmes aimed at raising money for charity, such as the UK's Comic Relief, rely on high levels of personal-distress-free empathic concern among viewers. Credit: Popperfoto/Reuters.

Nonverbal indicators of empathy

A second procedure for the measurement of empathic concern (and personal distress) is based on nonverbal responses (Eisenberg, McCreath, & Ahn, 1988). In correspondence with the assumption that self-report measures may be influenced by response bias, vicarious emotions were derived from facial/gestural expressions. The basic procedure is that children watch an emotionally arousing film which shows other children suffering (for example, because of an accident in a playground). Using a one-way mirror the children's facial affect is recorded unobtrusively on a videotape. Although several emotions may be coded from facial expressions, the main interest is to obtain measures that are equivalent to empathic concern and personal distress. Whereas a sad/concerned expression refers to empathic concern, an anxious expression reveals something about personal distress. The coding of emotions from facial clues is based on criteria developed by Ekman and Friesen (1975).

In another experiment 6–9-year-olds encountered a "baby-cry helping task" which gave them the opportunity to talk with a baby in distress (Eisenberg et al., 1993). Empathic concern was indirectly assessed through tone of voice. Coders rated whether the children talked in a comforting manner with the baby in need. In addition, they gave a rating for irritation in the tone of voice. A difference score (comforting versus irritated tone of voice) represented the predominance of empathic concern derived from the tone of voice.

Personal distress in facial expression was coded on the basis of videotapes using the criteria developed by Ekman and Friesen (1975). Indicators were raised eyebrows and eyebrows pulled together as well as nervous mouth and chin movements (e.g., biting the lips). Personal distress was negatively correlated with talking to the baby in the baby-cry episode. Because talking to the baby is a mode of prosocial behaviour in this context, the results indicate that higher personal distress was associated with less prosocial behaviour. In contrast, comforting tone of voice did not predict prosocial behaviour.

The results on personal distress were not replicated in a second study with kindergartners and 2nd graders (Fabes et al., 1994b). In this study physiological measures were obtained. High heart rate variability (HRV) in the baseline period was used as an index of emotion regulation. HRV was positively correlated with comforting tone of voice in the baby-cry episode. In addition, heart rate deceleration/acceleration in the baby-cry episode served as an index of self- vs other-oriented responding of the child, because heart rate deceleration was related to more comforting in children's tone of voice. Therefore, heart rate deceleration may serve as a marker of vicarious emotional responding.

Further data reported by Eisenberg et al. (1993) support the validity of the personal distress measure derived from facial expression and the validity of the index of comforting versus irritated tone of voice, but only for girls. Mothers' scores on three subscales of the Interpersonal Reactivity Index (Davis, 1983a) were correlated with facial distress of their daughters in the baby-cry episode. Mothers' perspective taking was negatively correlated ($r = -.43$) with personal distress of the daughters and positively correlated ($r = .35$) with a predominance of comforting tone of voice. This result agrees with the social learning perspective on socialisation of prosocial behaviour, because mothers who easily take the perspective of others are presumably good in communicating interest in others in general and "cognitive" empathy in particular. In addition, this finding shows that nonverbal variables have some validity as indicators of vicari- ously experienced emotions (see also Holmgren, Eisenberg, & Fabes, 1998).

Although the results of these two studies are not completely consistent, and although gender differences exist in the pattern of results (see for a summary Eisenberg, 2000), this research points to new directions in the measurement of vicarious emotions. The use of facial distress cues and comforting tone of voice is an important innovation. In addition, HRV and heart rate deceleration were shown to be related to prosocial behaviour in the baby-cry episode and might be interpreted as indicators of emotion regulation and vicarious emotional responding.

Empathic accuracy

From the "cognitive" definition of empathy, inferences concerning the thoughts, feelings, and intentions of others are of central import- ance (Neuf, 1997). The question is whether these inferences are accurate or inaccurate. In Davis's (1994) process model of empathy, interpersonal accuracy is understood as an intrapersonal outcome. In this section two instruments for the measurement of these intra- personal outcomes of empathy are considered: empathic accuracy and perspective change. Both instruments focus on matters of accur- acy, although they differ with respect to standardisation of materials.

Ickes and his co-workers developed a procedure for the meas- urement of empathic accuracy which is minimally standardised (Ickes, Stinson, Bissonnette, & Garcia, 1990; Stinson & Ickes, 1992; see also Ickes, 1997). A typical experiment on empathic accuracy focuses on social interaction in a dyad. For example, strangers or friends are left alone in a waiting room. While they "wait" for the experiment to begin they are videotaped. When the experimenter returns he/she explains that a videotape of the waiting situation was made and asks for permission to use the tape for research purposes.

The index of empathic accuracy is based on the degree of corre- spondence between assumed and true thoughts and feelings of another person. Each member of the dyad views the videotape by himself or herself. Participants are instructed to stop the videotape each time they remember a specific thought or feeling that they had in the situation, and to write down each thought or feeling. In addition, they indicate the time interval during which each event occurred, whether it was a thought or feeling, and whether its emotional tone was positive, neutral, or negative. In the final step of the procedure, participants view the videotape again, this time with markers indicating where the other person has made an entry. The task of the participant is to infer what the other person thought or felt and to indicate whether the entry was a thought or a feeling. Finally, participants infer the emotional tone of the entry as positive, neutral, or negative.

Empathic accuracy is high if the observer infers a content that is similar to that of the entry the target person has written down. Accuracy is derived from subjective content similarity. The measure of empathic accuracy is constructed on the basis of the assessments of coders who compare the actual thoughts and feelings with the inferred thoughts and feelings with respect to similarity. For each actual–inferred entry pair the coder decides whether the content is essentially different, somewhat similar but not the same, or essentially the same. The ratings are coded as 0, 1, or 2. The scores are summed, and the sum is divided by the highest score that would be possible if each actual entry matched the inferred entry. This procedure leads to scores that are normalised with respect to number of entries; they range between 0.00 and 1.00.

The procedure for measuring empathic accuracy is highly flexible because it may be applied to many dyadic relationships. It combines elements of subjectivity and objectivity. Whereas the establishment of the time frame and the content of experienced and inferred thoughts and feelings are subjective, the coding of content similarity is based on a high degree of objectivity. In a study that compared empathic accuracy of male friends and male strangers, content accuracy was significantly higher for friends than for strangers (Stinson & Ickes, 1992). In addition, convergence of accuracy scores occurred across dyads, resulting in a substantial intraclass correlation for friends. This convergence of empathic accuracy in pairs of friends did not occur among strangers.

The measurement of empathic accuracy was also applied to pairs of romantic partners (Simpson, Ickes, & Grich, 1999) who were videotaped in a threatening situation. The threatening situation involved partners evaluating male and female stimulus people in the presence of the partner. The stimulus people, who were shown as slides, were evaluated with respect to physical attractiveness and sexual appeal. The instruction stressed that the participants were expected to provide accurate ratings of the target people. One question was: "How physically attractive do you find this person to

witness of the misfortune of another person. A number of empirical differences exist in responses to witnessed and caused distress (Zahn-Waxler et al., 1992a):

- Children show more self-distress in situations where they have caused the distress (compared with witnessed distress).
- They show less empathic concern when they cause the distress themselves than when they are bystanders.
- They engage less in hypothesis testing in situations of caused distress.
- In addition, caused distress is accompanied by more aggression, especially from boys, and positive affect is lower than in bystander situations.

The psychological meaning of empathy and guilt is quite different, which is well illustrated by increased self-distress in guilt situations. In addition, caused distress is accompanied by more aggression, especially in boys, and positive affect is lower than in bystander situations. The response to caused distress may be an early expression of conscience development, whereas the response to witnessed distress resembles empathy and compassion (Zahn-Waxler et al., 1992a).

The difference between caused and witnessed distress is also relevant in adults. In an experimental study with students, a condition of caused distress was contrasted with a condition of witnessed distress (Regan, 1971). The hypothesis was that caused distress elicits guilt feelings, whereas witnessed distress threatens just-world beliefs. The students received the information that there had been a breakdown in an animal experiment. They were led to believe either that they had made the mistake that caused the failure, or that they were the innocent witnesses of the breakdown of the experiment.

Afterwards the students were interviewed with respect to their reactions to psychological experiments. Half of the students were allowed to verbalise their feelings during the experiment, whereas the other half responded to neutral questions which were irrelevant to the malfunction of the experiment that they had observed. This variation was introduced to compare a condition in which guilt feelings could be reduced by verbalisation with a condition in which no such confessions were possible. Finally, the students were offered the opportunity to donate money for a research project.

Without the relieving interview, the percentage of students who donated money was equally high in the witnessed and caused

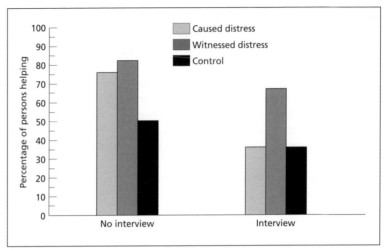

FIG. 10.1. Donations as a function of witnessed and caused distress (based on data from Regan, 1971, p. 129).

distress conditions, respectively. When the relieving interview was held, donations were more frequent in the witnessed distress than in the caused distress condition (Figure 10.1). These results confirm the hypothesis that the prosocial motivation that occurs in caused distress situations is different from that which occurs in witnessed distress situations. Additional data indicate that in the caused distress situation those students who felt more guilty donated more money.

In correspondence with the assumption of an innate component of guilt, twin research shows that guilt displays a heritability component in 1-year-olds (Zahn-Waxler & Robinson, 1995). This genetic influence on guilt is accompanied by a systematic environmental influence. In general, the genetic influence on guilt is less than that on shame, fear, and anger. In 2-year-olds, the environmental component of guilt was much stronger, indicating that socialisation influences on the development of guilt feelings are strong. In this age group, genetic influences on guilt are no longer detectable. These results support the conclusion that guilt feelings represent innate emotions, which are open to environmental influences operating in the second year of life. The development of guilt is closely linked to the development of conscience. In generalising from guilt feelings to moral internalisation, the proposal is justified that in the first years of life conscience development comes under the control of environmental factors (e.g., socialisation experiences) more and more, although the precursors of conscience seem to be influenced by innate factors.

Early indications of the development of guilt are found in the second year of life. From 13–15 months to 23–25 months of age an increase in prosocial responses in natural settings is observed (Zahn-Waxler et al., 1992a). Whereas in the youngest age group the proportion of prosocial responses in caused distress situations was .07, the proportion increased to .52 among the oldest age group investigated, indicating that more than half of the incidents elicited attempts at reparation. The frequency of guilt feelings also increased when comparing children aged 5–6 years with children aged 7–9 years (Zahn-Waxler et al., 1990). Therefore, early socialisation and conscience development seem to foster feelings of guilt.

Toddlers' response to caused distress may be an early expression of conscience development, whereas the response to witnessed distress resembles empathy and compassion (Zahn-Waxler et al., 1992a). Responsible conduct is regulated by guilt feelings. Guilt plays an important role in the process of moral internalisation because it is linked to conscience development (Barrett, 1998). A perceived mismatch between own behaviour and moral standards leads to feelings of guilt (Hoffman, 1998). Conscience development is important in several respects. For example, guilt facilitates the performance of moral behaviour that is in accordance with values and social norms. In addition, it contributes to the maintenance of a positive interpersonal bond because interpersonal transgressions are compensated for. Therefore, guilt contributes to the maintenance of close relationships which are threatened by moral transgressions (Baumeister, 1998a). Guilt counteracts self-centredness and egoism which constantly threaten the continuity of good interpersonal relationships. Rather, guilt is an adaptive emotion that motivates moral conduct (Tangney, 1998) and contributes to the stability of personal relationships as well as to the availability of social support. In fact, guilt is an emotion which has high importance in personal relationships (e.g., more important than fear and anxiety; Baumeister, Reis, & Delespaul, 1995a).

Guilt in social life

Baumeister (1998a) emphasises the positive aspects of guilt in social life. Guilt is understood as an emotional mechanism that protects threatened interpersonal relationships (Baumeister, Stillwell & Heatherton, 1994, 1995b). Guilt is primarily aroused after hurting a relationship partner (e.g., parent, romantic partner). It functions like a warning signal which indicates that the person must do something good if there is a likelihood that his/her interpersonal relationship will deteriorate because he/she has hurt a relationship partner. Guilt signals the existence of an interpersonal disturbance. It is an emotional response to harming a person (or to anticipation of harming a person) with whom a positive relationship has been established. If the person harms another, there is a high likelihood that the victim will retaliate, leading to an escalation of the conflict. Guilt feelings contribute to the preservation of the threatened relationship, because they motivate actions that are likely to lead to reconciliation (e.g., reparation, apologies, compensation; see also Alexander, 1987).

Research indicates that guilt feelings arise if a personal failure led to the deterioration of an interpersonal relationship (Baumeister et al., 1994, 1995b). Guilt originates in personal relationships that are characterised by mutual concern. The personal failure that is most likely to lead to feelings of guilt is interpersonal neglect. Guilt contributes to the avoidance of continued neglect of the partner in personal relationships, which most probably would jeopardise the future of the relationship. By inducing the person to compensate for past neglect, the threatened relationship is kept going. Therefore, guilt is a prosocial emotion. "At the extreme, the absence of the sense of guilt is one defining feature of the psychopath, who preys on other people and often ends up in various forms of trouble, ranging from unsatisfying intimate relationships to prison" (Baumeister, 1998a, p. 136).

In his provocative analysis Baumeister (1998a) contrasts guilt and (exaggerated) self-esteem. Whereas guilt as a prosocial emotion facilitates the compensation of harm done to others, leading to the maintenance of valued personal relationships, high self-esteem is linked to feelings of superiority and demonstrations of arrogance which are hard for people in the social network to tolerate. Therefore, the strong emphasis on inflated self-evaluations of children found in many families today (using messages like "you are a hero", "you are something special") is likely to produce negative interpersonal side-effects. Because people are social beings who need secure social attachments, mechanisms that foster beneficial relationships are very adaptive, whereas tendencies that interfere with interpersonal harmony are problematic. Because belongingness is a fundamental human need, the forming and maintenance of social bonds has high priority in everyday social life (Baumeister & Leary, 1995; Bowlby, 1969; Shaver, Hazan, & Bradshaw, 1988). Guilt contributes considerably to this goal because it is positively related to empathy and achievement and negatively to aggression (Bybee & Quiles, 1998). In contrast, shame correlates positively with anger, aggression, and externalisation of blame (Tangney, Wagner, Fletcher, & Gramzow, 1992).

Shame vs guilt

Empirical data indicate that shame and guilt are not linked to different situations or standards of comparison (Tangney, 1998; Tangney, Niedenthal, Covert, & Barlow, 1998) but are the result of different interpretations of failure, either as a threat to the self with reference to one's core identity or as remorse over the wrongdoing. If the focus is on one's failure and its consequences, guilt dominates. If the focus of disapproval is on oneself as a person who is unworthy, shame is more likely (Lewis, 1971; Tangney, 1998). Whereas guilt is limited in the sense that it refers to specific events, shame tends to be more self-threatening, because the transgression is interpreted as a personal defeat which is observed by a real or imagined audience. Shame results from perceived discrepancies between actual self and moral standards of what ought to be or ideally should be (Tangney et al., 1998). As a consequence, shame leads to the wish to make oneself invisible to avoid the scorn of others. In contrast, guilt as the more moral emotion leads to the intention to repair the damage that has occurred.

The differences between shame and guilt summarised by Tangney (1998) show that both self-relevant emotions are related to distinct patterns of experience, including behavioural tendencies, with shame leading to a desire to escape or to retaliate and guilt leading to reparations and confessions. Therefore, shame makes prosocial behaviour unlikely, whereas it is facilitated by guilt (see Figure 10.2).

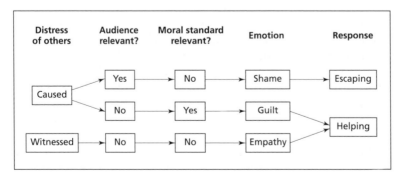

FIG. 10.2. Empathy, guilt, and shame: Critical comparisons.

Measures of guilt

In the presentation of measures of guilt I will closely follow the excellent analysis of Ferguson and Stegge (1998) who have evaluated available measures of guilt and shame in children (and adults). Several questionnaire measures are available which tap predispositional and chronic guilt respectively. The distinction between predispositional and chronic guilt has heuristic value and contributes to the elimination of apparent contradictions of results in the relevant literature (see also Bybee & Quiles, 1998). It is also reflected in different formats of instruments that purport to measure guilt:

- Predispositional guilt refers to feelings that are aroused by specific incidents. For example, after deceiving one's parents about poor performance in school, predispositional guilt may be aroused.
- Chronic guilt refers to a stable trait that characterises the continuing existence of guilt feelings without a concrete cause. For example, a father may be constantly ruminating about treating his grown up daughter unjustly when she had been a child.

Chronic guilt is defined as "an ongoing condition of guiltiness, regret, and remorse unattached to an immediate precipitating event" (Bybee & Quiles, 1998, p. 272). In contrast, predispositional guilt, which is defined as "a personality proclivity for experiencing guilt in response to specific, cirumscribed, eliciting situations" (Bybee & Quiles, 1998, p. 272), represents situationally appropriate responses (Ferguson & Stegge, 1998). The distinction between chronic and predispositional guilt is supported by low correlations between measures that tap both constructs. Quiles and Bybee (1997) report that chronic and predisposional guilt load on separate factors in factor analysis.

Predispositional guilt

First, I will describe two instruments that were constructed as measures of incident-specific guilt. The Test of Self-Conscious Affect (TOSCA; Tangney, Wagner, & Gramzow, 1989, cited in Ferguson & Stegge, 1998) describes several scenarios that are negative in content and offers four alternative responses that indicate guilt, shame, externalisation, or detachment. Respondents assess how much they agree with each response alternative. The TOSCA-C (Tangney, Wagner, Burggraf, Gramzow, & Fletcher, 1991, cited in Ferguson & Stegge, 1998) is especially adapted for children between 8 and 12 years. Like the adult version, the responses refer to 10 negative and 5 positive scenarios. The scenarios describe situations that can be found in the everyday experience of children.

Across the 10 negative scenarios, a satisfactory internal consistency was obtained for guilt- and shame-proneness in children (based on the TOSCA-C) and adults (based on the TOSCA). Shame- and guilt-proneness correlate positively (between .40 and .50; Ferguson & Stegge, 1998). A related questionnaire, which is also based on scenarios, is the Child–Child Attribution and Reaction Survey (C–CARS) by Stegge and Ferguson (1990, cited in Ferguson & Stegge, 1998). One purpose of the C–CARS is to reduce, as far as possible, social desirability with respect to guilt-proneness. The scenarios include four situations of transgression and four situations of failure. Three response dimensions are represented: guilt, shame, and defensive externalisation. In addition, an open question was included, namely "Why would you feel that way?" to tap the reasons for the feeling. The C–CARS was developed for children between 5 and 12 years.

Chronic guilt

Other guilt questionnaires have the format of a trait measure. The Conscience Measure (Kochanska, DeVet, Goldman, Murray, & Putnam, 1994) which is also referred to as the My Child measure (Hastings et al., 2000) consists of 100 items that refer to 10 scales. The categories of the Conscience Measure were derived from a literature review on conscience and personality development as well as from interviews with mothers. The focus of the scale is response to violations of rules, which is treated in 10 aspects: guilt and remorse; concern over good feelings with parents after wrongdoing; confession; apology; reparation; concern occasioned by others' transgressions; internalised conduct; empathy; symbolic reproduction of wrongdoing (e.g., in play); and sensitivity to flawed or damaged objects (Kochanska et al., 1994, pp. 864–866).

The questionnaire is directed towards parents, and items refer to their child. An example item from the confession scale is "May confess to doing something naughty even if unlikely to be found out" (Kochanska et al., 1994, p. 865). Fathers and mothers showed substantial agreement in their rating of the items. Internal consistencies of the scales were very good or good with the exception of sensitivity to flawed or damaged objects, which was alpha = .59 (this pattern of results was replicated by Hastings et al., 2000).

The results of factor analysis indicated that the items of the conscience measure load on two orthogonal factors that are considered two dimensions of conscience: affective discomfort and active moral regulation/vigilance (see also Hastings et al., 2000). Affective discomfort is represented by guilt; concern over good feelings with parent; empathic response; and apology. Active moral regulation/vigilance refers to confession; internalised conduct; reparation; and concern occasioned by others' transgressions. The facets of conscience measured by the questionnaire were already found in 3-year-olds. For example, 100% of mothers reported that their 3-year-olds showed reparation. Affective discomfort and active moral regulation/vigilance represent two quite distinct conscience dimensions. Whereas affective discomfort refers to knowledge of rules and emotional involvement when they are violated, active moral regulation/vigilance refers to the adherence to the rules and their implementation in the child's social setting (see Chapter 11).

The Guilt Inventory (Jones & Kugler, 1990, cited in Kugler & Jones, 1992) includes three scales: trait guilt, state guilt, and moral standards. State and trait items have different temporal anchors with state items referring to current feelings (e.g., "At the moment, I don't feel particularly guilty about anything I have done") and trait items referring to a large time frame (e.g., "Guilt and remorse have been a part of my life for as long as I can recall"). Items of the moral standards scale (e.g., "I believe in a strict interpretation of right and wrong") tap the adherence to social norms and values. Trait and state items were highly correlated ($r = .56$). In addition, state items and moral standards correlated negatively ($r = -.34$), whereas trait guilt and moral standards were unrelated.

In a sample of students, the correlations of the Guilt Inventory with several other guilt questionnaires were positive. State and trait guilt showed the same pattern of correlations (Kugler & Jones, 1992). These results support the construct validity of the guilt questionnaires. A factor analysis of items of several inventories that measure trait guilt led to four factors: regret, self-hate, guilt-experience, and conscience. Although these factors indicate an internal differentiation of the guilt items, all four factors were positively correlated with guilt ratings of the Differential Emotions Scale (Izard, 1977). In addition, the correlation of the overall guilt score with other negative emotions (shame, fear, sadness, anger) was consistently positive (see also Watson & Clark, 1992).

Guilt and mental health

Guilt is an adaptive response to transgressions and personal failures which threaten the stability of personal relationships. By motivating compensation and reparation, guilt fulfils the need to belong (Baumeister & Leary, 1995), to strengthen social bonds, and to be a member of a group. In general, emotions are functional in regulating the adaptation of the individual to the ongoing interaction (Barrett, 1998). Like all emotions, guilt feelings (and the lack thereof) may be maladaptive under certain circumstances. On the one hand, excessive guilt that is experienced over a long time is maladaptive (Bybee & Quiles, 1998). On the other hand, lack of guilt feelings after transgressions may constitute a social problem (Baumeister, 1998a).

Bybee and Quiles (1998) assume that predispositional (short-lived) and chronic (unalleviated) guilt are fundamentally different. Predispositional guilt, which is measured by instruments like the TOSCA and C–CARS, is related to prosocial behaviour (Estrada-Hollenbeck & Heatherton, 1998). Chronic guilt, which is measured by instruments like the Guilt Inventory, is maladaptive and is related to several psychopathological symptoms.

Predispositional guilt is not related to depression and other psychopathological symptoms, but it is positively related to trustworthiness and consideration as perceived by classmates. In addition, predispositional guilt is positively related to volunteer work and prosocial behaviour. By reparation and other reconciliatory responses (e.g., excuses, confessions), a constructive solution to transgression problems is achieved. In addition, guilt-proneness is negatively related to antisocial behaviour in general and criminality in particular (Bybee & Quiles, 1998).

The pattern for chronic guilt is different, showing positive correlations with depression and eating disorders (Bybee, Zigler, Berliner, & Merisca, 1996). Chronic guilt is associated with a self-concept of resentfulness, anger, and suspicion (Kugler & Jones, 1992). It is associated with several psychopathological symptoms: obsessive-compulsive disorder, depression, anxiety, and psychoticism (Bybee & Quiles, 1998).

Transgression, guilt, and reparation

The effects of guilt on reparation were studied in experiments in which a transgression was induced, after which the participants were offered the chance to do something good. Transgressions are defined as "situations in which one harms someone or is about to act in a way that might harm someone" (Hoffman, 1998). Studies using the transgression paradigm have shown that guilt is a prosocial emotion.

In one experiment students were informed that a rat that was difficult to control because of brain damage was the test animal. The student was asked to apply electric shocks to the rat, which was in the next room where the "victim" (a confederate) was sitting as an observer. After several shocks a crash was heard and the victim called out, "What happened? The rat escaped! What happened? . . . I'm scared, it bites!" This was the neutral witnessed distress condition. In two other conditions the mistake was blamed either on the victim or on the student. In the caused-distress condition, the victim called out, "What did you do? The rat escaped! What did you do?" In the witnessed-distress, victim-responsible condition, the victim called out, "What did I do? The rat escaped! What did I do?" (Schwartz & Ben David, 1976).

Blaming the student increased helpfulness, whereas blaming the victim decreased it (compared with the neutral witnessed distress condition). The blame manipulation explained 13.7% of variance in helping. The results demonstrate two things:

- Caused distress motivates compensation, which leads to more intervention than neutral witnessed distress.
- Victims who are assumed to be responsible for their unfortunate situation (and who in fact blamed themselves for causing the problem) received less help than innocent victims.

Across all conditions 72% of students attempted to help. This high intervention level attests to the strong social influence that was exerted by the experimental situation which made the emergency very dramatic. The high intervention rate is especially impressive because students who intervened had to expect a direct confrontation with the dangerous rat. In this dramatic situation, the effect of the attribution of guilt was quite strong: In the caused-distress situation, average response latency was about 1 minute. In contrast, in the witnessed-distress, victim-responsible condition, average response rate was about 2 minutes (Schwartz & Ben-David, 1976).

The strong effects of guilt on prosocial behaviour in adults were confirmed in several studies during the 1960s and 1970s (Carlsmith & Gross, 1969; Freedman et al., 1967; Regan, 1971). In these studies transgressions were induced which apparently caused some damage.

For example, electrical equipment was damaged, students were induced to lie, or ordered index cards fell from a table. In all these transgression experiments, the participants were objectively not responsible for the damage caused, but subjectively they had the feeling that they had caused the damage or had behaved wrongly (because of rigged procedures).

Guilt feelings motivate a broad spectrum of prosocial responses: blood donation (Darlington & Macker, 1966); willingness to participate in an unpleasant shock experiment (Freedman et al., 1967); willingness to make phone calls for an ecological campaign (Carlsmith & Gross, 1969); and willingness to donate money for a student research project (Regan, 1971). The guilt hypothesis (Freedman, 1970) assumes that guilt is an internal feeling state which elicits self-distress. Therefore, motivation to reduce the unpleasant feeling state is aroused. In general, several techniques for the reduction of self-distress are available, including compensation, confession, expiation, denial of responsibility, rationalisation, and minimising the severity of the damage, which are assumed to reduce the guilt feelings that were aroused by the transgression (Bybee & Quiles, 1998).

An elegant demonstration of the effectiveness of confessions for the reduction of self-distress is a study in which Catholics were offered the opportunity to donate money to charity before or after their confession in church (Harris, Benson, & Hall, 1975). The true believers donated more money before than after their confession. The interpretation is that the confession reduced the self-distress of the true believers, also reducing their prosocial motivation.

In the case of negative consequences for a victim, the person who has caused the damage is motivated to act prosocially (either on behalf of the victim or on behalf of a third party who is not involved in the transgression; Carlsmith & Gross, 1969; Konecni, 1972). This prosocial tendency seems to be quite general and is not limited to direct compensation for the damage caused. The guilt hypothesis is supplemented by two additional hypothesis which explain the link between transgression and prosocial behaviour: The negative state relief hypothesis and the fairness hypothesis, which is derived from equity theory.

Negative state relief hypothesis

One explanation of the effects of transgression on prosocial behaviour focuses on mood effects. The negative state relief hypothesis is based on the following reasoning (Cialdini, Kenrick, & Baumann, 1982): A transgression induces a negative feeling state in the transgressor. Several techniques are available to reduce the unpleasant state, each of which is sufficient to improve the bad mood of the transgressor. If, for example, the transgressor's mood is improved by achieving a success, he or she is no longer motivated to compensate for the damage. Prosocial behaviour is one technique, among others, which helps the transgressor to feel better because it is self-rewarding. It drives away the sadness that the harm-doer feels. Prosocial behaviour as a self-reinforcing response improves negative mood in general.

Why is prosocial behaviour rewarding? The answer is that it acquires a rewarding quality because it was associated with rewarding events in the past (Cialdini et al., 1982). People learn as children that prosocial behaviour is socially desirable and that it is good to fulfil society's expectation of a responsible citizen. They are praised when they do something good and correctly recognise that good deeds are expected from them.

A test of the negative state relief hypothesis includes the inducement of a negative and a positive mood (Cialdini, Darby, & Vincent, 1973). The idea is that the negative mood, which is induced by harming others, is improved by prosocial behaviour or by rewards that occur. In the experiment prosocial behaviour was enhanced after a transgression (compared with a neutral control condition), except when the transgressor was praised or received a small amount of money. It is well known that social approval and small gifts are mood-improving events (Bierhoff, 1988; Isen, 1987). The results confirmed the assumption that prosocial behaviour could be an attempt to overcome the negative mood that arises after harming another person, which is effective because altruism has self-reinforcing qualities (cf. Weiss et al., 1973).

Such a replacement of prosocial behaviour by other mood-management methods did not work for 6–8-year-olds (but it worked for 10–12-year-olds and 15–18-year-olds; Cialdini & Kenrick, 1976), supporting the assumption that prosocial behaviour acquires a mood-improving quality only after children's socialisation has been completed. After children learn that prosocial behaviour has reinforcing qualities they can use prosocial behaviour as a technique for mood management when they feel bad. The negative state relief hypothesis considers the transgressor as a person who is primarily interested in mood management. Prosocial behaviour is only a side-effect, which is not the result of altruistic intentions but of the fact that doing good expels bad mood.

Transgression and the violation of standards of fairness

What about justice and caused distress? Equity theory, which is based on the assumption that people tend to reduce any inequity that they perceive in their social relations, may offer an answer to this question (Walster, Walster, & Berscheid, 1978). A transgression contributes to inequity. Therefore, equity theory leads to the prediction that transgressors are motivated to undo the violation of standards of fairness.

From the viewpoint of equity theory, the transgressor has two options which contribute to the reduction of unpleasant feelings resulting from perceived inequity: compensation or rationalisation. Compensation means that the transgressor provides for reparation. Rationalisation means that the transgressor justifies the inequity by derogating the victim or minimising the damage. The most important question, then, is when will the transgressor prefer reparation and when rationalisation? The simple answer is that choice of strategy for the termination of inequity depends on its efficiency in reducing felt inequity. That strategy will be chosen which reduces inequity most completely (Berscheid & Walster, 1967).

This prediction has straightforward implications. For example, transgressors will choose reparation over rationalisation if they have resources available that compensate for the damage completely. If damage is extensive and resources are limited, rationalisation is more likely than reparation. For example, after World War II, Germans did not do much to provide reparation for victims of the Nazis. Why did they hesitate although economic prosperity was high? The answer may lie in the sheer magnitude of destruction that the Nazis had caused. Total reparation was an unreachable goal. Thus, it was simpler to suppress the past. Motivated forgetting seems to be another strategy for avoiding the perception of continued inequity.

In addition, the negative state relief hypothesis leads to the assumption that the economic prosperity of the 1950s and 1960s contributed to general good mood among Germans, with the result that they no longer felt the strong personal distress associated with guilt. Instead, they were able to congratulate themselves for their diligence and competence. As this historic example shows, both equity theory and negative state relief theory may apply in instances of failed reparation.

Survivor guilt

The only passenger who survived after a plane crash in Peru was a teenager named Juliane Köpcke. Many years later she confessed on a

German talk show (*The Johannes B. Kerner Show* on 17 August 2000) that she felt some guilt at being the only survivor. Why did she feel badly after having survived the disaster?

This is a real-life example of survivor guilt, which is often the result of competing tendencies to feel joy and guilt over survival simultaneously. Survivor guilt is not necessarily linked to events in which the person is directly involved. People who hear about a catastrophe occurring in a different part of the world may start to wonder if their egoistic concerns are really as important as they believe them to be, when they compare their situation with the tragic fate of others (Hoffman, 2000). Whereas this attenuated survivor guilt may occur in many people, strong survivor guilt typically emerges when the person has survived a disaster in which family members were killed (as in the case of Juliane Köpcke; Lifton, 1968).

Hoffman (2000) speculates that survivor guilt has something to do with fairness considerations. In a social world where the equality principle is usually applied to decide issues of fairness (Bierhoff, Klein, & Kramp, 1986), the extreme discrepancy of fates between survivors and non-survivors is simply unjust. Whereas justification of differences in outcomes works quite well as long as the differences are small or moderate, this mechanism no longer functions when the discrepancy is apparently gigantic.

Strong survivor guilt typically emerges when the person has survived a disaster in which others were killed. These ethnic Albanian women and children survived an attack on their village by Serbian forces during the war in Kosovo, but have to live with feelings of guilt for having survived. Credit: Popperfoto.

Survivor guilt may motivate prosocial behaviour. Hoffman (2000) gives real-life examples that point in this direction. From what we know about the dynamics of guilt, including the close link between guilt feelings and reparation, it is quite likely that survivor guilt is a prosocial emotion. However, the distinction between chronic and predispositional guilt (Bybee & Quiles, 1998) may be relevant here. In so far as survivor guilt is an example of unalleviated guilt that is chronically experienced over years, it may contribute to helplessness and depression because the survivor sees no way out. Survivor guilt that corresponds to predispositional guilt may well motivate involvement in volunteer work and other prosocial activities.

Guilt over affluence

Society is full of examples of underprivileged people. Although many individuals ignore the social inequality that is frequently correlated with social status, highly empathetic persons are aware of the general living conditions of disadvantaged people. Hoffman (2000, pp. 184–187) coined the term "guilt over affluence". Are the underprivileged people victims of prejudice? Are they systematically discriminated against? Has the discrimination been going on for several decades or even centuries? People may develop a tendency towards generalised empathic distress when they recognise that the suffering of under-privileged people is the result of societal problems. Guilt over affluence is not a common phenomenon. There are several pre-requisites for the arousal of guilt over affluence (Montada, Schmitt, & Dalbert, 1986): perceived interconnection of own advantages and discrimination of others; doubts with respect to the justness of the discrimination; and compassion with and felt responsibility for the disadvantaged.

At this point another insight is relevant: The distance between empathy and guilt is quite small. For example, a bystander who does not intervene on behalf of an accident victim may feel compassion for the victim. A short time later he or she may feel guilty because of the realisation that he or she could have offered help. "The line between empathic distress and guilt thus becomes very fine, and being an innocent bystander is a matter of degree. To the degree that one realises that one could have acted to help but did not, one may never feel totally innocent" (Hoffman, 1984, p. 126).

People who live in privileged conditions may come to the realisation that they profit from the fact that underprivileged people are suffering. For example, the prices of coffee and tea are so low because plantation workers have such low wages. Therefore, the insight may develop that one's own advantages are linked to the disadvantages of others. Such an insight is likely to intensify feelings of guilt over affluence (Hoffman, 2000). In addition, if the divergence between one's own privileges and discrimination against others is attributed to one's failure to reduce the difference, guilt over afflu-ence is aroused. Psychological justifications of the status quo may contribute to the reduction of the resulting tension. Empirical results show that psychological justifications (e.g., denial of the discrepancy between own prosperity and that of underprivileged groups; justi-fying one's own privileges and justifying the fate of the disadvan-taged) reduce guilt over affluence. Those individuals who do not deny the existing discrepancy, who do not think that they have earned what they have achieved, and who do not blame under-privileged people for their fate, are most likely to express guilt over affluence (Montada et al., 1986).

If justice and guilt over affluence are linked, which kinds of justice considerations are associated with guilt feelings? The results of multiple regressions show that guilt over affluence is connected with emphasis on the need principle, rejection of the equity principle, and high control beliefs (the assumption of a high degree of control over redistribution of rewards; Montada et al., 1986). In contrast, individuals who emphasise the equity principle, reject the need principle, and believe in high control over redistribution tend to feel less guilt over affluence. Note that perceived control intensifies or minimises guilt feelings depending on the emphasis on the need principle or the equity principle, respectively.

Responsibility 11

Social responsibility means two things: ensuring the welfare of others in everyday life (concern for others component) and progressing towards one's goal attainment without violating the justified expectations of others (interpersonal harmony component). Whereas the first component is related to empathy, the second component is related to guilt. Empathy and guilt are considered the "quintessential prosocial motives" (Hoffman, 1982, p. 304). Responsibility does not emerge in adolescents out of nowhere. Feelings of responsibility are derived from empathy and guilt feelings which develop much earlier, in the first years of life (Zahn-Waxler & Robinson, 1995). Here responsibility is not considered the third quintessential prosocial motive, rather it is seen as the moral structure that develops in children on the basis of empathy and guilt, and which guides prosocial and environmental behaviour in adolescence and adulthood. Not only are several dimensions of empathy as measured by the Interpersonal Reactivity Index (Davis, 1994) and guilt positively correlated (Tangney, 1991), but both emotions are also linked to social responsibility (Bierhoff et al., 1991; Hastings et al., 2000; Omoto & Snyder, 1995; Penner & Finkelstein, 1998).

The meaning of responsibility: Voluntariness and controllability

What does responsibility mean? One colleague whom I asked this question told me it means taking care of one's children. Another colleague responded that she felt responsible for foreign refugees in Germany by offering them advice and guidance. In addition, responsibility reminds us that we may make mistakes that cause damage to others and—even worse—that we may be blamed for our failures by these others. Given the close relationship between responsibility and blameworthiness (Fincham & Jaspars, 1980; Fincham & Roberts, 1985; Shaver, 1985), it is not too far-fetched to assume that guilt is an important precursor of responsibility because the anticipation of guilt feelings may be a strong reminder in many situations to take the interests of others into account. But empathy too is likely to substantially contribute to the development of moral obligation because responsibility is based on perspective taking and feelings of compassion and sympathy with others.

Responsibility contributes to a meaningful life where people pursue personal goals, interrelate with significant others in a mature way, and live in harmony and solidarity in their community (Auhagen, 2000). Although responsibility is based on self-control at the individual level, it is understood as a mechanism of social control at the societal level (Schlenker, Britt, Bennington, Murphy, & Doherty, 1994). When a person accepts responsibility for what he or she will do or has done, such a stance is evaluated positively by most members of society. In contrast, a person who does not want to accept responsibility is not regarded positively by others. "Ascription of responsibility to people for their actions means that the actions are considered as their personal 'products'. If these are good, the people deserve praise and reward. If they are bad, they deserve blame and punishment" (Montada, 2001a, p. 81).

Responsibility is—at least in part—based on moral decisions that are the ultimate justifications for what is considered good or bad. In correspondence with this viewpoint, Shaver and Schutte (2001) state that the terms "responsibility" and "moral responsibility" are not clearly distinguishable in their meaning. In two empirical studies on the meaning of "responsible" and related terms (e.g., controllable, caused, blameworthy, obligated), multidimensional scaling revealed a basic dimension with the endpoints "voluntary" and "coerced" underlying similarity judgements of attribution experts as well as of students (Shaver, 1985). Interestingly enough, "responsible" was not located that far towards the endpoint "voluntary", but was located in the middle of the voluntary–coerced dimension in the neighbourhood of "blameworthy", "morally accountable", "morally responsible", "culpable", and "guilty". The second dimension underlying the similarity judgements was labelled "controllable–punishable". "Controllable" refers to characteristics of acts that are "intended" and "foreseeable", whereas "punishable" refers to characteristics of persons who are "at fault" and "liable".

The origin of social responsibility

Another approach asks why responsibility has emerged as a human phenomenon. Why is it that people go beyond reinforcement learning and consider the question of responsibility in their lives? A possible answer is that responsibility is a precondition for the development of autonomy, which gives the person the choice of self-realisation (cf. Erikson, 1963, 1968). In a complex society it may turn out that individuals who develop autonomy, and follow goals and intentions that are derived from their subjective construction of reality, are more successful than people who simply subordinate themselves to the principles of conditioning. Success is not guaranteed by simply following win–stay–lose–change rules. Individual capabilities may be applied more effectively if the person operates on the basis of a system of self-control and responsibility attributions.

In correspondence with this line of reasoning, Hinde (2001) argues that responsible behaviour is the product of human nature (see Chapter 5). Responsibility is realised in parent–child relationships, between friends and neighbours, and within members of the in-group, but not so much in in-group–out-group relationships (Lilli & Luber, 2001). Moral codes of responsibility seem to be a universal characteristic of human societies although they differ to a limited extent, the limits being set by biological predispositions.

Social responsibility seems to be an innate property of human beings which serves basic human needs. In accordance with this, both empathy and guilt displayed reliable genetic influence in 14-month-olds (Zahn-Waxler & Robinson, 1995; Zahn-Waxler et al., 1992b). In addition, at 24 months, the environmental influence on both emotions had increased (while the genetic influence had decreased), which is interpreted as the result of a growing influence of socialisation.

The genetic influence on responsibility is documented in a study of adolescents (Neiderhiser et al., 1996). However, at the same time the data indicate that changes in responsibility over 3 years were better predicted by environmental factors. In summary, although responsibility has a genetic basis, environmental factors play an important role in modifying children's and adolescents' adherence to the norm of social responsibility.

Cultural differences in the understanding of social responsibility were found in a comparison of the moral reasoning of people in India and the United States (Miller, Bersoff, & Harwood, 1990). Participants read scenarios that described a refusal to help another person. The need of the other person was either life-threatening, moderate, or minor. In addition, the relationship between the hypothetical persons was varied as either parent–child, best same-sex friend, or stranger. Indians perceived responsibility as a more encompassing orientation which was routinely extended to family members, friends, and strangers, whereas Americans were more restrictive in their understanding of situations in which the norm of social responsibility applies, focusing on family relationships and serious incidents (e.g., life-threatening emergencies).

Responsibility and social conduct

Responsibility is a strong predictor of prosocial behaviour (Weiner, 1980, 1995, 2001). Everyday experience shows that people are reluctant to help others who have caused their own misfortune. An example is a student who urgently needs lecture notes because he did not attend a class. If the cause of this dependency is attributed to the student's negligence (e.g., because he or she went to the beach to enjoy the beautiful summer day), level of helpfulness is lower than if it is assumed that the student is not responsible for his/her predicament (e.g., because of an illness; Ickes & Kidd, 1976; Reisenzein, 1986). In the first case, the cause of the predicament is perceived as controllable and, as a consequence, anger is aroused in the observer, whereas in the second case the cause is perceived as uncontrollable and, as a consequence, sympathy with the victim is elicited.

Willingness to help is expected only when sympathy dominates. The attribution–affect model of helping behaviour (Weiner, 1980) which was later extended as a responsibility-based theory of social conduct (Weiner, 2001), is based on the assumption that attributed responsibility triggers affective reactions which are the proximal causes of prosocial behaviour. Affective reactions that are included in the model are sympathy and anger, with sympathy presumably leading to helping and anger leading to neglect, condemnation, and retaliation.

In one study, the subway emergency that was staged by Piliavin et al. (1969) in a "drunk" and an "ill" condition (see Chapter 12) was described in a written scenario (Reisenzein, 1986). Respondents indicated their level of helpfulness (on items like "How likely is it that you would help that person?"). Furthermore, they rated perceived controllability and gave responsibility attributions; these variables were highly correlated ($r = .75$) and were therefore combined as

of prediction of use of public transport, the contrast between internal and external attribution of responsibility is emphasised.

Meta-analytic results shed further light on the association between responsibility (as conceptualised in the two research traditions) and pro-environmental behaviour (Kaiser et al., 2001). External attribution of responsibility reduces the likelihood of ecological behaviour, whereas internal attribution of responsibility increases it. In addition, one's sense of moral obligation is a reliable predictor of pro-environmental behaviour. In fact, the link between responsibility and ecological behaviour is stronger if one's sense of moral obligation is used as an indicator of responsibility than if external/internal ascription of responsibility is used to represent the responsibility concept. In terms of explained variance the sense of moral obligation accounted for about 21% of variation in ecological behaviour. In contrast, internally ascribed responsibility explained 7.5% of ecological behaviour and externally ascribed responsibility explained about 12% (Kaiser et al., 2001).

In general, the level of methodological rigour is not completely satisfactory in the studies on the link between responsibility and pro-environmental behaviour. One reason is that the indicator of behaviour is based on self-report in nearly all studies, leaving viable the alternative interpretation that those who express more responsibility distort their reports of pro-environmental behaviour in the socially approved direction. The use of diaries as in the study by Hunecke et al. (2001) certainly reduces this methodological concern. However, the demonstration of a link between ecological responsibility and pro-environmental behaviour would be more convincing if more observational data were available supporting the link.

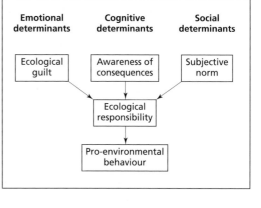

FIG. 11.1. Pro-environmental behaviour as a function of ecological responsibility.

Responsibility as a predictor of prosocial behaviour

Does social responsibility predict prosocial behaviour? Laboratory studies have found mixed evidence. The strength of the link between sense of personal obligation and prosocial behaviour seems to depend in part on the characteristics of the situation. For example, responsibility is a better predictor of prosocial behaviour when the potential helper has an easy escape route available and when the victim's need cues are strong (Carlo et al., 1991a). Another demonstration of the context-specificity of responsibility effects is the result that social responsibility and prosocial behaviour were positively correlated only if the social responsibility norm was salient (Berkowitz & Daniels, 1964).

Social situations that strongly elicit the norm of social responsibility are expected to produce higher correlations between social responsibility and prosocial behaviour than situations that are less relevant for the social responsibility norm. In accordance with this assumption, Staub (1974, p. 327) summarised his research by stating that prosocial orientation facilitated helping, especially in situations in which the circumstances supported an intervention.

The items of the Social Responsibility Scale refer to two dimensions (see later): fulfilment of justified expectations of others, and adherence to social rules. Results indicate that both dimensions of the sense of personal obligation are differentially related to prosocial behaviour. In a laboratory experiment, fulfilment of justified expectations of others correlated positively with helping. In a field study of helpers who offered their assistance to accident victims in Hanover, Germany, adherence to social rules correlated with emergency helping. In both studies the total score of the Social Responsibility Scale correlated positively with prosocial behaviour (Bierhoff, 2000a). In other studies too the Social Responsibility Scale was a significant predictor of prosocial behaviour (Eisenberg et al., 1989c; Oliner & Oliner, 1988).

Personal norms reflect people's assessment of responsibility in a specific situation on the basis of their moral values. Therefore, the prediction is warranted that personal norms predict prosocial behaviour. In correspondence with this prediction, the average correlation between personal norm and prosocial behaviour is $r = .29$ across six studies (Schwartz & Howard, 1984).

In addition to spontaneous helping, social responsibility is an important predictor of nonspontaneous helping as, for example, in volunteerism

The "meals-on-wheels" programme allows many elderly people in the UK to retain their independence, and relies largely on volunteers to keep it going. Credit: Photofusion/Wayne Tippetts.

(Benson et al., 1980; see Chapter 21). In a study of university students, social responsibility and prosocial behaviour (e.g., voluntarily working in orientation programmes for new students) were positively correlated (Witt & Silver, 1994). In summary, the results indicate that social responsibility predicts prosocial behaviour especially in socially significant settings.

Two dimensions of social responsibility

Interpersonal responsibility was empirically defined in a study of mothers of 6–7-year-olds averaging across scales of confession, apology, reparation, concern occasioned by others' transgressions, and internalised conduct (measured by the My Child Questionnaire; Hastings et al., 2000). The internal consistency of this scale of interpersonal responsibility was high (alpha = .82). It is similar to the factor active moral regulation/vigilance originally extracted by Kochanska et al. (1994) which contained four of the five subscales (with the exception of apology; see Chapter 10).

Kochanska et al. (1994) reported that a second factor, which they named affective discomfort, summarises maternal reports of guilt and remorse, concern over good feelings with parents after wrongdoing, empathy, and apology. The two-dimensional factor structure is interpreted on the basis of a conceptual model of conscience which contrasts affective discomfort with behavioural control (Kochanska, 1993). Affective discomfort refers to distress (anxiety and guilt after transgression) when a standard of behaviour is violated. It is presumably associated with individual differences in fearfulness and anxious arousal. Behavioural control is exemplified by self-control in situations in which a standard of conduct applies. High behavioural control is assumed to be linked to low impulsivity and high inhibitory control. These assumptions were supported at least in part by empirical results which were based on maternal reports (Kochanska et al., 1994). A relationship between fearfulness and affective discomfort was found for girls only, but the link between behavioural control and inhibitory control was confirmed for both boys and girls. In addition, both components of conscience were significantly related to resistance to temptation in a situation in which the children were forbidden to play with attractive toys.

The two-component model of conscience includes an important dichotomy: On the one hand, affective discomfort is experienced when rules are violated. On the other hand, behavioural control refers to concrete situations in which behaviour is monitored so that forbidden behaviour is inhibited. It is one thing to know what is wrong and to associate guilt feelings with transgressions and another thing to follow the social rules that apply in a given situation.

A similar distinction was suggested in the context of social responsibility (Berkowitz & Daniels, 1964; Bierhoff, 2000a) by delineating two dimensions of moral obligation: moral fulfilment of the justified expectations of others and adherence to social rules. Both components of social responsibility may serve as the basis of solidarity. Moral fulfilment of justified expectations of others focuses on being reliable and acting as a good member of society (e.g., "I would never let a friend down when he expects something of me"). Adherence to social rules refers to (non)compliance with social standards (e.g., "When given a task I stick to it even if things I like to do better come along").

The two components of conscience that were delineated by Kochanska et al. (1994) refer to facets of responsibility as distinguished by Bierhoff (2000a) on the basis of the Social Responsibility Scale (Berkowitz & Daniels, 1964) which is the classic instrument for the measurement of individual differences in social responsibility. Moral fulfilment of the justified expectations of others is closely related to the responsibility definition proposed by Schwartz (1977, see earlier) including feelings of obligations that are linked to the sense of connectedness with others in need, and refers to the strength of moral orientation. Adherence to social rules refers to the inclination to follow the moral rules that society dictates. The basic concern is adherence to social prescriptions (Hirschi, 1969; Oyserman & Markus, 1990). The first dimension refers to affective responses to the violation of social rules, and the second dimension is related to the issue of transformation of social standards into social behaviour. Whereas the first dimension means to act in accordance with the spirit of humanity, the second dimension refers to the inhibition of rule violations in concrete situations of temptation.

The similarities between the two components of conscience and the two dimensions of responsibility are intriguing. Fulfilment of the justified expectations of others is an analogue of affective discomfort. Both refer to recognition of what the standards of behaviour are. This is presumably accomplished by the elicitation of guilt and other forms of distress over wrongdoing and leads to the acceptance of the moral norms that guide interpersonal encounters. In addition, adherence to social rules resembles behavioural control. Both dimensions emphasise the willingness to follow social standards in temptation situations.

The distinction between two dimensions of social responsibility is based on conceptual as well as empirical grounds. Conceptually, two concerns of the socially responsible citizen are distinguished: to promote humanity in society and to follow social rules and regulations (e.g., obey the laws) which were both mentioned by Piaget (1932) in his writings on the moral development of the child. Empirically, the question is whether we know more about social reality if we distinguish between fulfilment of justified expectations of others and adherence to social rules than if we treat social responsibility as a unitary construct.

Are the correlates of the two dimensions of social responsibility different? To answer this empirical question more evidence is needed than is currently available. An example that points to the fruitfulness of distinguishing between two types of social responsibility is the explanation of the relationship between just-world belief and pro-social behaviour when the need of the victim is limited (Bierhoff et al., 1991; Miller, 1977). Just-world theory (Lerner, 1980) is based on the subjective belief that people get what they deserve. Such a belief is a continuation of what Piaget (1932) described as the moral realism of the child. Although moral realism decreases in older children and adolescence, residuals of the moral realism of the child may survive and continue to determine moral thinking in adults, although to a lesser degree than in children.

Belief in immanent justice may be understood as an individual-difference variable. Strong believers in a just world admire success more and derogate victims of failure more than do weak believers. Strong believers place high subjective importance on their social construction of the social world as fair and just. For them, everyday examples of injustice in general and of the undeserved suffering of victims in particular are threatening because such evidence shakes the fundaments of their view of the world. Therefore, strong believers in a just world attempt to defend their world view against contrary evidence on the basis of two strategies: They either contribute to the alleviation of the undeserved suffering, leading to the restoration of justice, or derogate the victims, so that their suffering appears to be justified because they deserve their bad fate. In correspondence with this analysis it was empirically demonstrated that belief in a just world correlates positively with helping victims of bad fate (e.g., victims of traffic accidents; Bierhoff et al., 1991). In contrast, strong belief in a just world is a negative predictor of helpfulness when the number of victims is large, because strong believers in a just world presumably doubt that the injustice that has occurred can be undone (Miller, 1977). The belief in a just world is measured by a questionnaire originally developed by Rubin and Peplau (1975). An item from a current version of the questionnaire is: "I believe that, by and large, people get what they deserve" (Dalbert, 1999, p. 84).

What are the similarities and differences between just-world belief and personal obligation to act altruistically as tapped by the Social Responsibility Scale? Both constructs explain responses of observers to the suffering of victims, and both predict prosocial responses. The just-world hypothesis predicts that undeserved suffering of others will lead to prosocial behaviour as long as the likelihood is high that the suffering will be completely alleviated by offering help. The social responsibility approach makes the prediction that help is offered to victims if the personal obligation to act altruistically is high.

Is there a conceptual overlap between just-world belief and social responsibility which may explain the partial correspondence of predictions with respect to prosocial behaviour? The distinction between two dimensions of social responsibility may lead to an answer (Bierhoff, 2002). Whereas fulfilment of the justified expectations of others and just-world belief have little in common, adherence to social rules and just-world belief have much in common. Both are based on the personal conviction that the social world is regulated by rules and that the adherence to these rules is natural. Both attitudes are based on the general expectation that people follow social norms of conduct and that such an approach to social life is good.

Based on this conceptual similarity the assumption is warranted that individual differences in just-world belief and in adherence to social rules (but not in fulfilment of the justified expectations of others) are positively correlated. This conclusion was confirmed in four studies (Bierhoff, 2002). For example, in a student sample the correlation between just-world belief and adherence to social rules was $r = .25$, but the correlation with fulfilment of the justified expectations of others was $r = .00$.

Another assumption was that the prediction of prosocial behaviour in real life on the basis of individual differences in just-world belief is mediated by individual differences in adherence to social rules. This second hypothesis was supported by a reanalysis of data that were originally reported by Bierhoff et al. (1991). Adherence to social rules as well as just-world belief were significant predictors of prosocial behaviour. But the influence of just-world belief was completely mediated by adherence to social rules. In contrast, fulfilment of the justified expectations of others did not function as a mediator, leaving the influence of just-world belief on prosocial behaviour undiminished.

In summary, just-world belief and adherence to social rules have some conceptual and empirical overlap. The common component of both constructs seems to be immediately relevant for the prediction of prosocial behaviour in everyday-life situations. Belief in a just world also refers to a genuine belief in justice which is not related to adherence to social rules. Social responsibility also comprises a dimension that is not related to belief in a just world: fulfilment of the justified expectations of others.

With respect to the distinction between two dimensions of social responsibility, these results are encouraging because they show that one component is related to attitudes and social behaviour in a way that is not true for the other component. This evidence on discriminant validity supports the view that moral obligations are at least two-dimensional, with one dimension based on attitude content and one dimension based on translating attitudes into actions.

Denial of responsibility

Acceptance, ascription, and denial of responsibility may go hand in hand. Sometimes, the person is tempted to deny responsibility in order to reduce the burden of self-control. Denial of responsibility is a ubiquitous phenomenon. Usually it is accompanied by justifications and excuses (Montada, 2001a). People feel that they should act in a responsible way, although they are tempted not to do so. One solution to this problem is to choose the easy alternative and justify this choice with excuses and altered priorities. Another solution is to vote for the alternative that agrees with standards of responsibility. High self-control leads to the expectation that the person will act in a responsible way.

Whereas the Social Responsibility Scale indicates prosocial orientation (Staub, 1974) and concern for others (Omoto & Snyder, 1995), responsibility denial, which was originally labelled "ascription of responsibility" (Schwartz, 1968), has the opposite implication. It was defined as "the individual tendency to deny that one is responsible for the consequences of action and hence to neutralise moral obligation" (Schwartz, 1977, p. 257). The tendency to distort responsibility is measured by a questionnaire. A sample item is "I wouldn't feel badly about giving offence to someone if my intentions had been good" (Schwartz, 1977, p. 257).

The hypothesis is plausible that people who tend to deny responsibility are less helpful than people who tend to accept responsibility This hypothesis was investigated in the rat experiment on prosocial behaviour (Schwartz & Ben David, 1976; see Chapter 10). Responsibility denial was correlated $r = -.24$ with helping. The rationale for not helping the victim may be something like "This is only an experiment". Responsibility denial accounts for a small but significant amount in the variance of helping (see also Eisenberg et al., 1989c; Schwartz, 1973; Schwartz & Clausen, 1970). People who permanently tend to deny responsibility also seem to feel less demand for intervention in an emergency.

Denial of responsibility is based on at least four rationales (Montada, 2001a):

- Minimisation of the victim's need.
- Blaming the victim.
- Diffusion of responsibility, for example when other people have the duty to offer help as part of their profession.
- Emphasis on own privileges as deserved and justified.

Persons who use these rationales when they encounter a needy victim tend to be prejudiced against the people in need and tend to deny that they themselves are able to help. In addition, they experience less sympathy with the needy and feel less existential guilt (Bybee, Merisca, & Velasco, 1998). Responsibility denial is a technique that serves the maintenance of belief in a just world (cf. Montada & Lerner, 1998). By denying their responsibility to help, individuals manage not to help the needy and at the same time maintain their belief that people get what they deserve. The strategic function of responsibility-denial arguments is clear: to follow an egoistic orientation and at the same time to preserve the belief in a just and moral world (Batson, Thomson, Seuferling, Whitney, & Strongman, 1999).

Acceptance and denial of responsibility may be considered the endpoints of an internal–external dimension. The assignment of extreme positions will be an exception. Most people will place themselves somewhere in between the endpoints of the responsibility dimension. From this perspective it makes sense to speak of the strategic management of responsibility attributions (Montada, 2001a): People are motivated to place their responsibility between the internal and the external pole in such a way that it is functional for their well-being and facilitates their coping with critical life events. The evidence shows that recognition of multicausality and multiple responsibilities contributes to successful coping with serious personal crises. One-sidedness in attributions of responsibility (either on the victim or on others) has the disadvantage that negative emotions like guilt and anger are maximised, which may reduce the individual's ability to cope with problems. A strategic management of responsibility that is directed towards the attribution of co-responsibilities serves the regulation of these negative emotions.

Theories of prosocial behaviour IV

Theories of prosocial behaviour vary with respect to their emphasis on selfishness and selflessness. Whereas the arousal: cost–reward model of intervention, the theory of social inhibition of bystander intervention, and the threat × control model of responses of help-recipients start with the assumption that people are egoistically motivated, the empathy–altruism hypothesis, the notion of vicarious emotional responses to others' needs, and the hypothesis of the altruistic personality are based on the assumption that people are—at least sometimes—altruistically motivated. However, this sharp contrast is not always upheld. For example, the negative-state-relief theory offers an egoistic explanation for prosocial behaviour, which other theorists trace back to altruistic roots. Another example is the

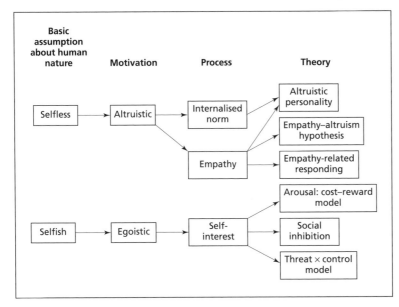

Six theories of prosocial behaviour.

focus on perspective taking, which is visible in the revised cost–reward model of intervention.

Moreover, the dichotomy between selfishness and selflessness oversimplifies matters because selflessness may result either from internalised norms (e.g., social responsibility) or from empathy. Therefore, prosocial behaviour can be traced back to three broad classes of prosocial motives (Eisenberg, 1986; Staub, 1978): self-interest, internalised norms and principles, and empathy (see Figure on previous page). Whereas the theory of the altruistic personality takes internalised norms and empathy into account, the other theories that emphasise altruistically motivated behaviour focus exclusively on empathy and contrast it with self-interest (e.g., personal distress).

Arousal: cost–reward model of intervention 12

The arousal: cost–reward model of bystander intervention starts with the assumption that the observers of an emergency are physiologically aroused and that the arousal is experienced as aversive (Piliavin, Dovidio, Gaertner, & Clark, 1981). Analogous to dissonance arousal and reduction, it is assumed that observers select those responses that presumably will reduce the experienced arousal. Possible responses that may change the arousal level are direct and indirect help and leaving the situation. Indirect help includes looking for someone who might offer help or informing the police or other institutions that an emergency has occurred.

Costs of helping and costs of not helping

The core of the arousal: cost–reward model of intervention is the matrix of most probable responses of bystanders depending on cost of direct help and cost of no help to victim. The four conditions of the matrix are derived from a 2 × 2 design in which costs of helping and costs of not helping are systematically crossed (Table 12.1). Costs of helping are associated with the process of intervention and include danger, effort, and time loss. Costs of not helping include empathic arousal as well as self-blame and self-esteem damage.

The prediction of helping on the basis of cost of help and cost of no help is based on the assumption that prosocial behaviour is egoistically motivated. Is there any evidence that indicates that prosocial behaviour is mainly influenced by people's self-interest and not by their moral sentiments? The answer is yes. In an experiment in which students could either choose a task that served their self-interest or a task that provided an advantage to another person while they themselves had to work more, a strong effect of self-interest was

TABLE 12.1

Prediction of bystander responses in emergencies depending on cost of direct help and cost of no help to victim

Cost of no help to victim	Cost of direct help	
	Low	High
High	(a) Direct intervention	(c) Indirect intervention or Redefinition of situation, disparagement of victim, etc.*
Low	(b) Variable (largely a function of perceived norms in situation)	(d) Leaving scene, ignoring, denial, etc.

Source: Modified from Piliavin, I.M., Piliavin, J.A. & Rodin, J. (1975). Costs, diffusion, and the stigmatized victim. *Journal of Personality and Social Psychology, 32*, 429–438. Copyright © (1975) by the American Psychological Association. Adapted with permission.

* This lowers the cost of not helping, leading to (d).

revealed, whereas moral obligations had no effect (Epley & Dunning, 2000). When self-interest was high, willingness to give up the short task (giving it to another person) and work on a long task instead was very low. Only when self-interest was low did a substantial number of students behave prosocially. In contrast, level of moral sentiment did not influence the results. Finally, in a prediction condition other students predicted they would be influenced by level of moral sentiment, but not by self-interest. These results in combination indicate that people who have a personal interest at stake choose quite selfishly in reality, although they assumed, in a condition in which they were instructed to imagine what they would do, that they would choose quite selflessly.

The model in Table 12.1 predicts that when costs of helping are high, direct help is unlikely. Instead, indirect help or leaving the situation are expected as typical bystander responses. When costs of helping are low, direct intervention is likely. These predictions become more complex when costs of not helping are additionally considered. They are higher when the person takes the perspective of the victim and empathises with the victim. In general, high costs of not helping tend to increase willingness to intervene.

The arousal: cost–reward model of intervention may be understood as predicting a chain of successive events in which the elicitation of arousal is the precondition for responding to the emergency (see Figure 12.1).

1972). Compared with a neutral control condition, the unfriendly condition elicited less prosocial behaviour, whereas the level of helpfulness was similar in the friendly and neutral conditions.

When impending danger reduces feelings of bystander safety, costs of helping increase. In a field experiment in a New York subway (Allen, 1972), danger was induced by a threat stemming from the ill-mannered behaviour of a confederate. This confederate was reading a body-building magazine. When a passenger (a second confederate) tripped over his legs, he threatened him physically, adding "Watch out, buddy, you want to get hurt?". Shortly afterwards, a subway passenger (third confederate) asking for directions was misinformed by the first confederate. This physical threat condition may be considered as a high-cost condition of helping because correcting the giver of the wrong information might lead to a physical assault on the helper. In the control condition, 52% corrections were given. In contrast, in the physical threat condition corrections occurred in only 16% of the trials. Finally, when the misinformer showed no prior history of aggressiveness and indicated that he was uncertain about the correct directions (adding "I think so"), corrections were offered in 82% of the trials.

These results indicate that high costs of helping reduce bystanders' willingness to intervene and that physical threat is very effective in suppressing any tendencies to help the recipient of wrong directions. Whereas costs of helping tend to reduce prosocial behaviour, it is assumed that costs of not helping will increase willingness to help. The data in the following studies tend to support this prediction.

The loss of postcards was arranged in a field experiment (Deaux, 1974). The postcard either gave the impression that the information was very important for the recipient or that the information was not so terribly important. Important news had a higher chance of being sent to the recipient than unimportant news.

In two field experiments (Bickman & Kamzan, 1973; Harris & Samerotte, 1976, Exp. 1) the participants could give money to buy a nutritious drink (e.g., milk) or a less nutritious drink (e.g., cola). People responded more generously when the money was used to purchase the nutritious drink.

A person asked for money to buy a tetanus injection. If the visible health risk was high, people gave more money than if the visible risk was low (West & Brown, 1975).

These results show that if the costs of not helping are high, helpfulness is higher than if the costs of not helping are low. The costs

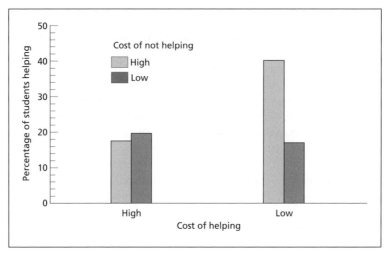

FIG. 12.3.
Helping as a function of
cost of helping and
cost of not helping
(based on data from
Clark, 1976, p. 326).

of not helping are not determined by an objective standard but by subjective assessments. It was shown that if objective standards and subjective estimates of costs of not helping diverge, only subjective estimates are important as determinants of donating money for charity (Wagner & Wheeler, 1969).

In several studies, costs of helping and costs of not helping were simultaneously manipulated. In the most convincing study (Clark, 1976) students were asked to read for 5 hours to a blind student who was either preparing for an important examination (high cost of not helping) or doing his normal learning programme (low cost of not helping). In addition, the distance between help-recipient and help-giver was either large (high cost of helping) or small (low cost of helping). A short distance combined with an important examination elicited a high willingness to help. In the other three conditions, helpfulness was much lower (see Figure 12.3). This pattern of results corresponds with the arousal: cost–reward model of intervention, which predicts a high level of help when costs of helping are low and costs of not helping are high.

A careful analysis of all the evidence on the interaction between costs of helping and costs of not helping leads to two generalisations (Piliavin et al., 1981):

- More costs of not helping lead to more helping, as long as costs of helping are low.
- More costs of helping lead to less helping, as long as costs of not helping are moderate or low.

Impulsive helping

Whereas in Table 12.1 prosocial behaviour is considered as a rational choice among several alternatives which serves to minimise net costs, experimental observations as well as everyday experience indicate that there are certain circumstances in which people will almost always intervene and that they do this very quickly—often within seconds of onset of the emergency. An example is a study in which nearly 100% of students helped when a technician received an electric shock while he was making repairs to a switchboard (Clark & Word, 1974, Exp. 1). Due to an apparent electrical malfunction, the victim fell on the floor while giving a sharp cry of pain. He collapsed next to the electrical equipment and seemed to have lost consciousness. Even if the victim fell down so that he was lying on several wires, the intervention rate was very high with 91% of the students in the alone condition helping. In a two-person condition, at least one student intervened in all simulations (as well as in the nondangerous condition).

Intervention rates were lower only when the emergency was characterised by a moderate or high level of ambiguity. For example, if the victim cried in pain but was lying in a corner of the laboratory not directly visible to students, intervention rates dropped to 36% in the alone condition and to 50% in the two-person condition. If, in addition, the cry was eliminated from the simulation and subjects only heard the noise of the overturning equipment, the response rate dropped to 18% in the alone condition, whereas it stayed at 50% in the two-person condition.

Another case of impulsive helping was observed in several studies that were conducted in the subway. A simple collapse of a victim who seemed to be ill elicited an intervention rate of 80–90% (Piliavin & Piliavin, 1972; Pilivian et al., 1975). In addition, interventions occurred within 40 seconds of the onset of the emergency. Impulsive helping is almost a reflexive response to an emergency. It is characterised by intuitive appraisal of the situation, holistic responding, and "irrational" decisions that ignore the cost–reward balance. Impulsive helping omits the phase of assessing and comparing net costs of several alternatives. Piliavin et al. (1981) predict impulsive helping depending on sudden onset of the emergency that is so urgent that the attention of the bystander is drawn to it. In addition, clarity of the emergency situation and sudden onset of the emergency facilitate a quick response, which is not the result of careful decision making but of strong cues inherent in the situation. The most important situational factor that promotes impulsive helping is clarity of the situation (e.g., victim is visible as the emergency occurs, victim calls for help, someone else defines the situation as an emergency). Other relevant factors are high reality of the emergency, which is found in field but not in laboratory settings, and prior contact between victim and bystander.

In contrast, a drunken person who suffered a collapse in an underground train received very little help (Piliavin et al., 1969). Only 20–30% of such collapses of drunken persons elicited an intervention by bystanders. Presumably, the bystanders attributed guilt to the victim and inferred that prosocial behaviour was inappropriate. Another factor that reduces the likelihood of intervention in emergencies is related to the cost of action. This was demonstrated in another study in which a person's collapse was simulated in a subway train (Piliavin & Piliavin, 1972). In one condition, a disabled person broke down (simple collapse). In the comparison condition, the disabled person broke down while blood was coming out of his mouth (high-cost collapse). In the simple collapse condition, about 90% of the bystanders intervened. This high level of intervention was reduced in the high-cost condition, where 60–70% of the victims received help. In addition, after the high-cost collapse there was a tendency to give indirect help (other people were contacted as potential helpers) which was not observed in the simple collapse condition.

Additional data show that diffusion of responsibility (see Chapter 15) primarily occurred in the high-cost condition. In a later study high cost of helping was induced by marring the victim's face with a "birthmark" which was created with make-up (Piliavin et al., 1975). The disfigured victim received less help than a neutral victim. Evidence for diffusion of responsibility was obtained only in the stigma condition. These field studies lead to the conclusion that diffusion of responsibility primarily occurs in situations in which an intervention causes high costs for the helper.

The revised theory

The revised version of the arousal: cost–reward model of intervention (Figure 12.4) gives more weight to arousal processes and their meaning for prosocial behaviour (Piliavin et al., 1981). Arousal is no longer considered an undifferentiated physiological response, but the

that most of the evidence on the empathy–altruism hypothesis was collected in collaboration with one single researcher, although there are a few other studies that support it (Dovidio, Allen, & Schroeder, 1990; Schroeder, Dovidio, Sibicky, Matthews, & Allen, 1988). From the point of view of meta-analysis such a situation is considered a restriction of generalisability (see, for example, Johnson & Eagly, 1989). In addition, data on cross-cultural research are missing, making it problematic to generalise the results to different cultures.

Another limitation is that the 1-versus-3 pattern was not observed when the costs of helping were high. In the Elaine scenario, cost of helping was varied by specifying different shock levels to create an aversive situation (Batson et al., 1983). Four shock levels were used ranging from 1 = minimally uncomfortable (lowest shock level that is perceived as aversive) to 4 = moderately painful (maximum level of shock; clearly painful but not harmful). When observers were informed that level-1 shocks were being used, the expected 1-versus-3 pattern was found: Students whose predominant emotional response was empathic concern were very helpful, independent of difficulty of escape, whereas students whose predominant emotional response was personal distress helped to a great extent only if it was not possible to stop having to watch Elaine receive the electric shocks in the rest of the trials. In another condition students were informed that level-4 shocks were going to be applied. This modification completely changed the pattern of results. Not only was the general level of helping much lower than in the level-1 shock condition, but also the 1-versus-3 pattern of results vanished. In addition, the difference in helping related to difficulty of escape, which was previously observed in students who were predominantly motivated by personal distress, was now found in the high-empathy condition: Students who were predominantly motivated by empathic concern helped less in the easy-escape condition than in the difficult-escape condition. The limitation of the 1-versus-3 pattern low-cost helping reduces the practical importance of the empathy–altruism hypothesis. Its generalisability to real life seems to be quite restricted (see Eysenck, 2000, p. 588).

Further tests of the empathy–altruism hypothesis

Because social psychologists are by and large convinced that people are basically egoistic, trying to maximise their own payoff (a conviction that social psychologists share with sociobiologists), the suggestion of an independent altruistic motive system (Batson, 1991) has elicited considerable controversy. This controversy concerns the question of whether the ultimate goal of prosocial behaviour is ever truly altruistic.

How did the empathy–altruism hypothesis fare in further tests? Some of the evidence is supportive and indeed very impressive from a scientific point of view. Other results are more problematic for the empathy–altruism hypothesis, pointing to the validity of a hedonistic approach to empathy which was originally proposed by Krebs (1975). In the following, both directions of research will be illustrated.

Empathy-specific rewards and punishments

The suffering of others may elicit indirect costs in the observer when he or she has taken the perspective of the other and empathises with his/her suffering. These indirect costs are integrated into the current cost–benefit balance of the observer. Batson (1991) labels these indirect costs as empathy-specific punishments. An example may illustrate the issue of vicarious costs: Television reports about catastrophic famines in Africa have touched many people deeply. While listening to the comments and seeing the pictures, observers may suffer because they become aware of how terrible it is to die of starvation. These negative consequences for the observer primarily occur if high empathy is aroused. They are empathy-specific. People who feel little empathy are unlikely to experience much of these vicarious costs. Therefore, vicarious costs are higher in a high-empathy condition than in a low-empathy condition (Krebs, 1975).

In addition, the fact that something is being done to alleviate the suffering of those who are starving elicts positive feelings in observers who empathise with these victims. These vicarious rewards occur only when people have taken the perspective of the needy, enabling them to better understand what such needy persons feel when their desolate situation improves. Therefore, empathy with the victims of bad fate may elicit vicarious rewards which increase the benefits of the observer (Krebs, 1975). For example, he or she may think that the world is not such a bad place after all, or the observer may be somewhat optimistic about the likelihood of finally eliminating the negative consequences of poverty and improving the survival chances of people in famine areas of the world. These considerations are summarised in Figure 13.4. Vicarious consequences are expected to be higher in a high-empathy condition than in a low-

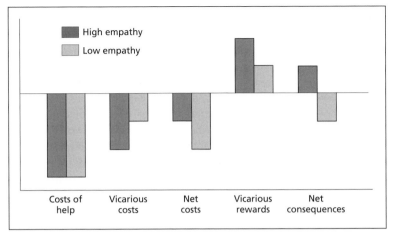

FIG. 13.4.
Consequences of helping as a function of level of empathy.

empathy condition. Therefore, Batson (1991) refers to these vicarious consequences as empathy-specific rewards and empathy-specific costs.

Empathy may exert an influence on the cost–benefit balance of the observer (Krebs, 1975). The costs that are incurred by helping (e.g., donating money) may be contrasted with the vicarious costs that occur as long as no help is given. When the vicarious costs are subtracted from the direct costs, the net costs of helping are obtained. In addition, helping in a high-empathy condition leads to vicarious rewards when the suffering of the victim is reduced. These empathy-specific rewards heighten the benefits for the high-empathy helper. Therefore, one can expect that the net benefits are positive in the high-empathy condition, whereas they are negative in the low-empathy condition. Figure 13.4 also illustrates the cost–benefit calculations if a low level of empathy is assumed. In this case vicarious costs and vicarious rewards are negligible and do not contribute significantly to the cost–benefit balance. As a consequence, helping appears to be costly, and a possible prediction is that people are less likely to intervene. Instead they might prefer to leave the situation.

The question is whether this analysis in terms of empathy-specific rewards and punishments is a viable alternative to the empathy–altruism hypothesis. Batson (1991) reports on several experiments that test specific versions of the hypothesis of empathy-specific rewards and the hypothesis of empathy-specific punishments.

Empathy-specific punishments may be socially mediated. An audience that is informed about a student's refusal to help a person in need is likely to evaluate the student negatively. In one study (Archer et al., 1981) the misattribution paradigm was used (see Coke et al., 1978, Exp. 2). False feedback led to the impression that students were either highly aroused or less aroused when they heard a newscast (supposedly produced by the university radio station) in which another student requested help because she needed volunteers for her research project. In addition, anonymity of the decision to help was manipulated. Whereas students in the anonymous condition thought that no one else in the laboratory would learn whether they had decided to help or not, students in the public condition expected that the experimenter would see how they had decided.

Before the experiment started, dispositional empathy was measured by the Questionnaire of Emotional Empathy (Mehrabian & Epstein, 1972). High dispositional empathy was associated with more helping. The results that were relevant for the empathy–altruism hypothesis were as follows: A high-empathy and a low-empathy group were formed. Situation-specific arousal motivated prosocial behaviour in students who were high on dispositional empathy and who expected that the experimenter would monitor their responses. In an anonymous condition the arousal of empathic concern was not effective in heightening the level of prosocial behaviour. These results, which contradict the empathy–altruism hypothesis, are instructive in showing what the focus of the hypothesis is: It is not the prediction that dispositional empathy is positively associated with prosocial behaviour (which was confirmed by the data), rather it is the association between predispositional empathy and prosocial behaviour.

The logic behind the study by Archer et al. (1981) is that expectation of negative social evaluation is a necessary precondition for the confirmation of the empathy–altruism hypothesis. A later study (Fultz et al., 1986, Study 2) did not support the social-evaluation interpretation of the empathy–altruism hypothesis. Empathy was varied by instruction (imagine-other vs observe). High manipulated empathy led to more helping than low empathy. The possibility of social evaluation did not increase helping among high-empathy students. In fact, level of helping was higher in the low-social-evaluation, high-empathy condition than in the high-social-evaluation, high-empathy condition. The opposite pattern of results was found in the low-empathy condition, with students in the anonymous condition helping somewhat less than in the public condition. In summary, studies on the empathy-specific-punishment hypothesis do not refute the empathy–altruism hypothesis, although the evidence is inconsistent.

Finally, dispositional empathy, which was measured by the Interpersonal Reactivity Index (Davis, 1983a), was positively correlated with prosocial behaviour, with the fantasy subscale being the only significant subscale ($r = .35$). Predispositional empathy measured by the adjective-list method also positively correlated with amount of prosocial behaviour ($r = .40$), whereas the association of personal distress and prosocial behaviour was not significant ($r = .21$; Fultz et al., 1986, Study 2).

In a series of experiments, Batson et al. (1988) contrasted the empathy–altruism hypothesis with the hypothesis of empathy-specific punishments that are self-administered. Three studies were reported in which justifications for not helping were offered to the participants. It was assumed that such justifications would reduce the tendency to self-administer empathy-specific punishments. The anticipation of guilt feelings might be stronger in high-empathy conditions, leading participants to help not so much because of concern for the victim, but out of their striving to avoid guilt feelings. Three kinds of justifications were employed in the experiments:

- Justification for not helping by consensus (others don't help either).
- Justification for not helping by offering a plausible alternative explanation for not helping (in addition to being an irresponsible person).
- Justification for not helping by setting a high standard for qualifying as a potential helper which is hard to meet.

The results of these three experiments support the empathy–altruism hypothesis. For example, students who were predominantly motivated by empathic concern were not influenced very much by the manipulated difficulty of helping, whereas students who were predominantly motivated by personal distress helped much less when they could excuse their indifference by the high performance standard that was set by the experimenter. In general, high justification for not helping reduced prosocial behaviour in low-empathy conditions but not in high-empathy conditions, confirming the 1-versus-3 pattern of results that supports the empathy–altruism hypothesis.

In another experiment (Batson et al., 1988, Study 1) a version of the hypothesis of specific empathy rewards was tested as an alternative to the empathy–altruism hypothesis. The starting point was the assumption that because high-empathy observers of the plight of another person are primarily interested in the well-being of the other, their empathic concern is effectively reduced not only by their prosocial behaviour, which reduces the plight of the other, but also by prosocial behaviour of others, which has the same effect. Therefore, high-empathy observers should feel good if the plight of the other is reduced—independently of the source of the help—whereas they should feel bad if the plight of the other continues.

Participants in the experiment were instructed that they would perform a task that had no consequences for themselves but would have positive consequences for another person, because he/she would not receive the electric shocks for wrong responses that would otherwise be applied. In addition they were instructed that possibly they would not have to perform the task at all. An analogy was drawn with understudies in the theatre who prepare for a role and only play it if they have to replace the regular actor.

To measure the emotional effects of alleviation of the plight of another, a mood scale was employed which consisted of seven items: bad mood–good mood; sad–happy; depressed–elated; dissatisfied–satisfied; gloomy–cheerful; displeased–pleased; and sorrowful–joyful. A mood index was constructed by averaging across the seven items. To control for individual differences in mood, the pretest was subtracted from the post-test that was filled out at the end of the experiment. By performing a median split, students were divided into high- and low-empathy groups on the basis of their scores on the predispositional empathy measure.

A 2 × 2 experimental design was used with prior relief of the victim's need (yes vs no) and opportunity to perform the prosocial task (yes vs no). Prior relief of the victim's need was accomplished by informing the students that the victim was reassigned to a neutral condition where he/she would no longer be a victim. Opportunity to help the victim was denied by simply informing students that they would not perform the task that would alleviate the suffering of the victim. The main dependent variable was the mood change between pretest and post-test. As expected, high-empathy students revealed a positive mood change in all those conditions in which the other person did not suffer (either because a neutral task was substituted or because the student performed the task that would alleviate the suffering of the other person). Only when the other person received no help and had to suffer, did a negative mood change occur. In contrast, low-empathy students displayed positive mood changes in all four conditions of the experiment.

Negative state relief vs empathy–altruism hypothesis

Imagining the plight of another person may elicit sadness in the observer. An alternative explanation of the empathy–altruism hypothesis focuses on whether mood management, which is connected with vicariously experiencing the suffering of a victim, may explain the 1-versus-3 pattern of results. Following this idea, the Elaine scenario (Batson et al., 1981) was replicated in a study by Cialdini et al. (1987). Their argument, which is derived from the negative state relief hypothesis (see Chapter 10), focuses on the high-empathy, easy-escape condition in which the empathy–altruism hypothesis predicts a high level of helping (see earlier). They argue that highly empathic persons feel very sad when they encounter another person who is suffering. A higher level of sadness predicts prosocial behaviour. Many studies of the effects of bad mood on helping have shown that bad mood motivates prosocial behaviour (Carlson & Miller, 1987). Therefore, it is not too far-fetched to assume that after being confronted with the Elaine scenario, sad persons show increased willingness to help and respond quite prosocially even if they are free to leave the situation.

The sadness–helping association is explained by assuming that sad people use prosocial behaviour as a mood-management technique, which contributes to the improvement of their mood. This explanation corresponds with the negative state relief hypothesis (Cialdini et al., 1973, 1982; see Chapter 10), which states that several techniques are available to improve a sad mood and that after the successful improvement of mood other techniques are no longer used. Prosocial behaviour is one such technique. It is rewarding because children and adolescents have learned that it is good to help. This socialisation contributes to the development of self-reinforcement for prosocial behaviour in adulthood. Other mood-improvement techniques include visiting a comedy show or receiving social approval. If these alternative techniques improve the mood state of a sad person, he or she is no longer interested in prosocial behaviour as a mood-management technique.

The negative state relief hypothesis was supported by experimental results that were reported by Batson et al. (1989, Exp. 1). Students who felt sad after thinking about an unhappy event in their past helped more than students who were in a neutral mood. The sadness–helping effect did not occur when students expected mood enhancement by viewing a funny video. Current sad mood only enhanced level of prosocial behaviour when no alternative mood-management technique was available. Note that up to this point the test of the negative state relief hypothesis does not consider empathy. Instead, the results show that the sadness–helping link is limited to persons who have no alternative mood-management technique available.

The alternative explanation of Cialdini et al. (1987) assumes that high-empathy observers of the plight of a suffering person act pro-socially because they want to improve their sad mood. Cialdini et al. (1987) included conditions in the experimental design of Batson et al. (1981) that were previously used in research on the negative state relief hypothesis. The students received money or were praised for their social abilities. In the no-reward conditions the 1-versus-3 pattern of results was marginally significant. Students in the high-empathy condition were less helpful if they received the additional financial incentive, which presumably improved their mood. An elevated level of helping was found only in the high-empathy, no-reward condition.

In the second study a misattribution paradigm was used in an easy-escape situation. Students were informed that the research was about a drug that influenced information processing. All students received a placebo. Some of them were later told that a side-effect of the drug was that it preserved the student's mood (mood-fixing condition). In the other condition the mood-fixing effect of the drug was not mentioned. The assumption was that only those students who did not believe that their mood had been influenced by the placebo would help in the high-empathy condition, because they could still expect prosocial behaviour to improve their mood state. Results supported the prediction of the negative state relief theory: In the four cells of the 2 (high vs low empathy) × 2 (fixed vs unstable mood) design only the students in the high-empathy, unstable-mood condition showed an elevated willingness to help.

The negative state relief hypothesis was not confirmed in an experiment reported by Batson et al. (1989, Exp. 2). The Elaine scenario was run in the easy-escape version. An alternative technique of mood improvement was made available to some students by telling them that a funny video would be shown. It was assumed that the announcement of the funny film would lead to the anticipation of mood enhancement. On the basis of their predominant emotional response in the Elaine scenario, which was measured by the adjective list, students were divided into a distress and an empathy group. Results indicated that the empathy-oriented students helped more than the distress-oriented students. Anticipated mood enhancement

Given the common roots of personal distress and empathic concern, it is not surprising that adults who encounter a victim of misfortune focus more on either personal uneasiness or the plight of the other (Batson et al., 1987). In addition, the sociobiological interpretation of predispositional empathy that was proposed by Cialdini et al. (1997) fits the general framework described by Hoffman (2000): Either the observer's focus of attention is more on self or more on the victim, but the observer's emotional responses are part of a biologically prewired behavioural system which unfolds from an undifferentiated egocentrism into a dichotomy of personal distress and empathic concern. After this dichotomy has been unfolded, it is reasonable to distinguish between egoistic and altruistic motivation on the basis of specification of ultimate goals. In the realm of pro-social behaviour—as well as in the closely related domain of solidarity—people primarily act either out of their own interest or out of concern for others. Although this difference is peripheral from the perspective of the help-recipient, who is more interested in the issue of whether help occurs or not, it communicates a basic lesson regarding human nature, which is neither so simple nor so straightforwardly egocentric as many assume.

Empathy-related responding and emotional regulation

14

An important lesson of the work on the empathy–altruism hypothesis is that empathic concern and personal distress relate differently to prosocial behaviour. Eisenberg and Fabes (1992) summarised empirical research with children which shows that it may be fruitful to consider empathic concern and personal distress as individual-difference variables that are closely linked to temperament and social integration. Children who tend to respond with empathic concern to the distress cues of others appear to be well regulated in their emotions and to be socially competent in their group of peers. In contrast, children who primarily respond with personal distress to the distress cues of others tend to respond with empathic overarousal which leads to a focus on the self. They seem to be less competent in their social interactions, tending towards a high level of compliance.

Differences between personal distress and empathic concern as correlates of prosocial behaviour were found in a study in which spontaneous prosocial behaviour and requested prosocial behaviour were contrasted with each other (Eisenberg et al., 1988). The situation was that two children had to get along with each other, although they only had one attractive toy to play with. In this context the spontaneous giving away of the toy to the other child was coded as spontaneous prosocial behaviour and the requested giving away (when the other child demanded the toy) as requested prosocial behaviour.

In addition, children saw films in which two children were hurt while playing in a playground. During the presentation of the film a videotape was made, which was later used for the coding of facial and gestural responses. Two types of responses that correspond to empathic concern and personal distress were coded: sad/concerned and anxious. Results indicated that spontaneous prosocial behaviour correlated significantly with sad/concerned affect, whereas requested prosocial behaviour was significantly correlated with anxious affect. In the experimental situation prosocial behaviour in response to a request is likely to indicate less social competence than spontaneous prosocial behaviour. Therefore, the facial indicator of empathic concern was correlated with the variable that represents the more advanced form of social integration. Personal distress, on the other hand, was a correlate of compliance with peers. In an earlier study (Eisenberg, Pasternack, Cameron, & Tryon, 1984) requested prosocial behaviour was correlated with low sociability and low assertiveness, supporting the interpretation of requested prosocial behaviour as yielding to peer pressure.

In the following, three examples of research on empathy-related responding are presented, which illustrate different experimental methods for evoking vicarious emotions in distress situations. In addition, a conceptual model is discussed, which connects basic emotional processes (e.g., regulation of emotion) with empathic concern, personal distress, and perspective taking.

Multimethod approach

In one study (Fabes et al., 1994a) mothers told two stories to their children, one about a child who fell from a tree and injured his head, and one about a child whose dog died. Later they saw a film about children who had been injured in an accident and were in hospital. The experimenter asked the children what they would rather do: help to fill crayon boxes for the children in the hospital or play with toys. The number of crayons the children put in boxes and the time spent on this task constituted the measure of helpfulness.

During the film skin conductance was measured, which is assumed to be a physiological indicator of personal distress. In addition, empathic concern and personal distress were measured with modified items from Batson's Emotional Empathy Questionnaire. Personal distress was measured by three items: feeling nervous, afraid, and uncomfortable; empathic concern was assessed by four items: feeling sorry, sad, bad for somebody, and concerned for others (Fabes et al., 1994a, p. 48). Facial distress and concerned attention of the child during the film were coded from a videotape which was made through a one-way mirror. In addition, several measures were obtained from the mothers (see later).

In both age groups skin conductance was negatively related to helpfulness. In addition, mothers' facial expressiveness (relative dominance of positive expressiveness over negative expressiveness)

(Eisenberg et al., 1994). Therefore, the complexity of the results of these comprehensive analyses of vicarious emotional responding is an expression of the complex determination of responses that are evoked by the distress of others.

Social inhibition of bystander intervention 15

Public interest in determinants of emergency intervention was elicited by an incident in New York in 1964 when 38 witnesses observed the attack by a man on Kitty Genovese, who was on her way home and only a few metres from her apartment. The police were finally called 35 minutes after her first scream and arrived after the man had already killed her. The tragic fate of Kitty Genovese suggests that bystanders tend to respond with apathy and indifference in such a situation. Indeed, during his interrogation the murderer said that he had expected such apathetic behaviour (Brown & Herrnstein, 1975).

What is behind the apparent apathy of bystanders? Is it that they don't care about what is happening because of an egoistic personality? Latané and Darley (1969) suggest a different explanation, one that focuses on situational factors—specifically, factors involving the immediate social environment. They consider explanations in terms of "apathy" or "alienation due to organisation" as too vague.

Failure of bystanders to intervene in emergencies may be better understood by knowing the relationship among bystanders, rather than that between bystander and victim. In a series of studies, witnesses of emergencies showed less willingness to intervene when several other witnesses were present at the scene than when they were alone. The results of various experiments have shown that social-inhibition effects in emergency situations are a robust finding. The presence of several bystanders reduces the likelihood of intervention compared to a single bystander (Latané & Darley, 1969, 1970).

The decision-making process: From bystander to actor

Before going into the details of the social processes that inhibit bystander intervention, I will examine the decision-making process of bystanders, which may turn them into prosocial actors. Emergency intervention is based on a problem-solving process and may be understood as a coping response (Schneider, 1988). Several models of the intervention process have been suggested which highlight different facets of the coping processes involved.

Latané and Darley (1970), the pioneers of empirical research on emergency intervention, were among the first to suggest a model of the intervention process. They distinguished between five steps in their model of the intervention process. Let us imagine that an emergency has taken place: A man walking down the street has a heart attack and collapses on the pavement. The question is how high is the likelihood that a bystander will come to his assistance? The answer to this question depends on the outcome of the decision-making process, which consists of five steps where each step is seen as a prerequisite for the following one. Before a bystander intervenes: he or she notices the incident; interprets it as an emergency; accepts some personal responsibility to intervene; weighs up which form of intervention is best; and decides how to implement the intervention.

Evidence from an experiment on emergency intervention is available which shows that recognition processes exert an early effect on likelihood of intervention—that is, these processes influence the bystander in the first 30 or 40 seconds after an emergency has taken place, whereas diffusion of responsibility and evaluation apprehension occur later (Schwartz & Gottlieb, 1976). Recognition of the needy person's distress is part of the interpretation of the emergency, diffusion of responsibility reduces felt responsibility, and evaluation apprehension influences preference for and implementation of an intervention strategy.

A more comprehensive model of the decision-making process in emergency situations was proposed by Schwartz and Howard (1981, 1982) and combines elements of the Latané and Darley model with norm activation processes (see Figure 15.1). Before a bystander intervenes he or she:

- attends to the emergency (subprocesses include recognition of the needy person's distress, search for and selection of an effective prosocial action, and evaluation of own ability as either high or low);
- is motivated to act (subprocesses include activation of social norms, construction of personal norms, and acceptance of personal responsibility);

responsibility, Schwartz and Howard (1981) refer to the interplay between ascription and denial of personal responsibility. The attitude approach (Pomazal & Jaccard, 1976) reveals another feature of the helping process: beliefs about consequences and about the approval of important referents. In addition, the importance of external control is emphasised, which is subjectively reflected in perceived behavioural control (Ajzen, 1988).

Finally, the coping model emphasises that intervention in emergencies is an adaptive response that reflects the resources of the person and the demands of the situation. Prosocial behaviour is often based on a difficult decision, the outcome of which is hard to predict on the basis of general assumptions about the nature of human beings. But coping successfully with the challenge by giving help to those who need it may not only alleviate the plight of the help-recipient, but also maintain the well-being of the helper (Luks & Payne, 1991; Midlarsky, 1991). Therefore, a person who encounters an emergency situation might cope with the personal challenge by helping, which in turn will increase his or her well-being. However, it is also possible that the challenge may be too much for the potential helper to handle, so that he/she does not have the chance to help. Bystander apathy is especially likely if the social situation is one that discourages potential helpers who are afraid of intervening.

Social inhibition: When the situation is difficult to handle

An emergency has been defined as "an event that involves or threatens to involve loss of or damage to life or limb and that requires some intervention to prevent or contain" (Piliavin et al., 1975, p. 429). From the outside it is easy to claim to be a helpful person in such a situation. However, in the situation itself, bystanders must overcome the inhibiting social influences they encounter.

The presence of witnesses leads to the reduction of individual willingness to intervene in emergency situations. This social-inhibition phenomenon was demonstrated in a study in which students worked on a questionnaire while smoke drifted into the room. Three conditions were compared (Latané & Darley, 1970; pp. 43–54): an alone condition in which a student worked on the questionnaire without company; a three-person condition in which three students simultaneously filled out the questionnaire; and a three-person condition in which a student and two passive confederates of the experimenter, who were instructed to ignore the smoke, filled out questionnaires.

Six minutes after the start of the experiment, the room was filled with smoke. In the alone condition 75% of the students reported the smoke incident to someone outside the waiting room. Compared with this baseline, the intervention rate was much lower in the three-person groups of naive students, where 38% intervention was recorded. Of the twenty-four students who were in the eight groups of the three-naive-students condition, only three reported the smoke within the experimental session.

This result shows that there is a strong inhibition of intervention in the group condition. Social inhibition is even stronger than the comparison between 75% in the alone condition and 38% in the three-person condition suggests at first sight. Calculated on the basis of the data from the alone condition, the expected proportion of groups in which at least one person intervenes is 98%. Based on the 75% who intervened in the alone condition, the expected intervention rate in the three-person group is higher, because there is a chance for each student in the group to report the smoke (for the derivation of the formula, see the Appendix at the end of this chapter).

Finally, in the condition with two passive confederates only 10% of the students intervened. This is clearly less than in the alone condition. (In both of these conditions only one person had to decide whether to report the smoke, so the intervention rates are directly comparable.) The smoke study demonstrated the global influence of social inhibition. Further studies have shown that three distinct processes contribute to the number effect, i.e., the inhibition of helping by the presence of other bystanders (see Figure 15.3). In the following, each of these processes will be discussed separately. After that, the interplay of different factors that contribute to social inhibition will be considered.

Diffusion of responsibility

If several bystanders are witnesses of an emergency, each bystander is aware that each of the other witnesses may intervene. This knowledge contributes to reduction of felt individual responsibility: Each witness divides the entire responsibility among the persons present. As a result, felt individual responsibility is lower in groups than when alone.

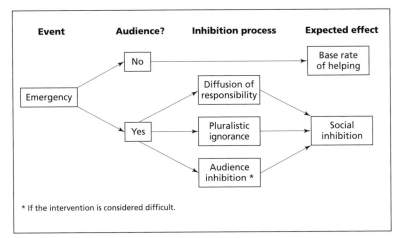

FIG. 15.3.
Social inhibition: Three
possible paths.

This hypothesis implies that witnesses of an emergency, who are aware that other witnesses are present although they have no direct contact with them, will be less willing to intervene the larger the number of potential helpers. If large numbers of witnesses are present, the amount of felt responsibility of each witness will be smaller than in an alone condition, and the willingness to intervene will be reduced.

Students took part in a discussion about personal problems related to college life (Darley & Latané, 1968). They sat in separate rooms and were connected with each other by an intercom system so that no face-to-face interaction was possible. During the discussion one of the participants simulated what appeared to be an epileptic attack. The dependent variable was whether the participants reported this emergency to the experimenter. In addition, the speed with which the participant reported this emergency was measured.

The discussion was performed in two-person, three-person, and six-person groups—actually, only one real discussant took part, and all other contributions were played from a tape recorder. The first discussant who was simulated by the tape recording mentioned that he suffered from epilepsy. When this person next spoke, he simulated a fit, which became clear after 70 seconds. The major independent variable was group size. It was expected that students in two-person groups would intervene more quickly than students in three- and six-person groups. In addition, it was assumed that intervention rates in six-person groups would be lowest.

The intercom connection with the victim was interrupted after 125 seconds. Results indicated that the intervention rate was highest in the two-person group in which the student was alone with the victim. The level of intervention was lower in the three-person groups and lowest in the six-person groups. At the end of the epileptic attack 85% had intervened in the alone condition, 62% in the three-person condition, and 31% in the six-person condition. Average response time was 52, 93, and 166 seconds in the three conditions. These results are explained by a diffusion of responsibility effect.

Diffusion of responsibility occurs in many contexts. For example, people give a smaller tip in a restaurant when they are in groups of four than when they are alone (Freeman, Walker, Borden, & Latané, 1975). Social impact theory is a general theory of social influence whose predictions may be applied in a broad spectrum of situations. One application is conformity (Latané & Wolf, 1981): People conform more with the unanimous vote of others who are members of a larger group (e.g., 12 persons) than a smaller group (e.g., 3 persons). Social impact is assumed to be a function of the strength, immediacy, and number of sources. Strength includes salience, power, and intensity. Immediacy refers to proximity. With respect to diffusion of responsibility the following "psychosocial law" may be applied, which only takes number of persons into account (Latané, 1981):

$$I = sN^t \quad t < 1.$$

In this power function I denotes impact and N number of persons. S and t are constants that are empirically estimated. The use of power functions is borrowed from Stevens' (1972) psychophysiological law which connects objective values on a stimulus dimension with subjective impressions of the stimuli.

Because the exponent t is assumed to be lower than 1, the social-impact function is negatively accelerated. The marginal impact of people in the social field decreases with larger N. The social impact of the Nth person is smaller than that of the $(N - 1)$th person. Whereas t determines the shape of the curve, s is a scaling constant.

The number of bystanders who respond with indifference in an emergency is systematically related to diffusion of responsibility, with higher diffusion connected with higher numbers (Latané, 1981). A group of bystanders may be conceptualised as a social force field in which, for example, the sixth passive bystander does not exert as much inhibiting influence on the target person as the third passive bystander. This prediction was confirmed in the Darley and Latané study described earlier, because intervention rate *decreased* with number of bystanders, with the first passive bystander (in the three-person discussion group) exerting more inhibiting influence than each of the four passive bystanders in the six-person discussion group. In contrast, response time *increased* as predicted as a root function (cube root of the number of bystanders; Latané, 1981).

This psychosocial law has a broad area of application. It also correctly predicts helping in nonserious situations, e.g., responses of bystanders in a lift who encounter a person who "accidentally" drops 8–10 pencils or coins. Such incidents were arranged by 145 experimenters who conducted about 1500 trials with almost 5000 bystanders (Latané & Dabbs, 1975). The number of bystanders ranged between one and six. Results indicated that the individual probability of helping (derived from formula A in the Appendix at the end of this chapter) decreased with the number of bystanders. The exponent t of the root function was −.55 (female bystanders) and −.45 (male bystanders), respectively. These results were explained by diffusion of responsibility. The functions explained 82% and 94% of the variance, indicating that the psychosocial law fitted the data very well.

Pluralistic ignorance

Besides diffusion of responsibility there is at least one further process that inhibits willingness to intervene in groups. The typical reaction of passers-by is characterised either by consistent helping or by persistent ignoring of the emergency (see Chapter 3). If two people approach the scene of an accident and one of them demonstratively ignores the incident, the passive model conveys the norm that an intervention is not appropriate. Because of this, the second person is easily tempted to act passively too and to ignore the accident (Latané & Darley, 1970).

Witnesses of emergencies are usually so surprised by the sudden event that most of them are unable to respond—they show passivity and signs of helplessness. As a consequence, other onlookers get the impression that each witness does not believe the event to be serious. Because people are afraid of embarrassing themselves, they do nothing rather than do something wrong, which is interpreted by others (who themselves show the same initial immobilisation) as evidence that no intervention is necessary.

When all witnesses show the same behavioural pattern, they infer from each other that the emergency is not serious and does not require intervention. Although each witness actually feels overwhelmed by the emergency and searches desperately for an appropriate response, he or she simultaneously infers that the other bystanders interpret the situation as harmless. As a consequence, a social definition of the situation arises which is far from what is actually going on in reality and also far from what is going on in the bystanders' heads. Such a divergence of what is to be seen on the surface and what lies beneath, between public actions and private insights, was named pluralistic ignorance by Allport (1933). This term is more formally defined as "the case in which virtually every member of a group or society privately rejects a belief, opinion, or practice, yet believes that virtually every other member privately accepts it" (Prentice & Miller, 1996, p. 161).

Pluralistic ignorance contributes a great deal to adherence to social norms that are controversial among group members, but nevertheless serve as standards of behaviour. Social norms are followed, although the individual feels that they are inappropriately applied to the given situation. The individual is aware that the normatively prescribed behaviour deviates from his/her preferences. At the same time, the individual erroneously assumes that the same norm-following behaviour of others is in correspondence with their attitudes (Prentice & Miller, 1996).

An example is the reluctance of many students to ask questions in seminars, even when they have not understood what was explained (Miller & McFarland, 1987). Such reluctance to ask questions is understandable given the possibility that the question might be regarded as stupid by other participants in the seminar. However, the conclusion that the other students have completely understood everything is unrealistic. No one asks a question because everyone is worried about looking stupid to the others—each person assumes that everybody except him- or herself has understood the lesson. This misunderstanding occurs in many public situations. People definitely want to avoid making a fool of themselves in public (Prentice & Miller, 1996), leading to the phenomenon of audience inhibition (see later). However, they do not ascribe to others their own motivation to look good in public.

Is there direct evidence for the effect of pluralistic ignorance on likelihood of intervention in emergencies? One study shows that witnesses who stand face-to-face when an emergency occurs, respond with more helping than witnesses who stand back-to-back (Darley et al., 1973). It is assumed that the effect of pluralistic ignorance is stronger in the back-to-back condition because the witnesses cannot see each other's facial reactions when the emergency occurs. These facial reactions include a startle response of initial surprise and signs of embarrassment. The startle response is usually correctly interpreted as an indication that the other witness considers the event to be an emergency which requires intervention. If the witnesses stand back-to-back this information channel is blocked, which facilitates the definition of the situation as not serious.

In situations that are new and in which no prior experience has been acquired, individuals tend to focus on other persons as models that they tend to imitate (Bandura, 1971). If the physical evidence is somewhat ambiguous, people look for a social comparison for the definition of the situation (Festinger, 1954). When they are uncertain about the appropriateness of applicable standards of behaviour, people tend to follow the example given by others.

If all witnesses respond with uncertainty and attempt to imitate the behaviour of others, it is quite likely that the result will be general apathy. Such apathy is increased if—as in our culture—there is a social rule that prescribes appearing cool and collected in public. By following this rule in the case of an emergency, people unintentionally give an example of passivity. They want to look cool and collected, although their inner feelings are characterised by uncertainty and anxiety. Here the goal of impression management leads to misunderstanding and misinterpretation of a situation that requires fast intervention.

Individuals engage in many forms of mental control for social purposes (Wegner & Erber, 1993), which serve the preparation of appropriate self-presentations in public. The answer to the question of which behaviours are appropriate in a given situation is largely dependent on social cues. In the absence of clear information about appropriate behaviour, people try to appear poised and collected (Erber, Wegner, & Therriault, 1996). Individuals apply regulatory processes, which guide their behaviour in the direction of neutrality. People are inclined to appear cool and collected in many situations—coolness is a value in itself which people attempt to maintain in order to demonstrate self-control (Lyman & Scott, 1968).

In summary, social comparisons are important when people are uncertain about what to do in a given situation. Many emergencies elicit strong uncertainty about the appropriate behavioural decision. This intensifies the need for social comparisons which, in turn, tend to increase the effects of pluralistic ignorance.

The role of social comparisons in emergency situations is made clear by the role of similarity among witnesses. A consistent finding in research on social comparisons is that similarity is a facilitating factor (Festinger, 1954; Goethals & Darley, 1977). If a passive witness is similar to the observer, there is a higher likelihood that his or her behaviour will be imitated by the observer. In agreement with this reasoning it was found that the passivity of a witness who is similar to oneself is imitated more than the passivity of a witness who is dissimilar (Smith, Smythe, & Lien, 1972). This result is further evidence for the importance of pluralistic ignorance in emergency situations.

Direct empirical evidence for the process of pluralistic ignorance is also found in emergency experiments, in which responses of groups of naive witnesses on the one hand and groups of passive confederates including a naive student on the other hand are compared. When confederates respond passively to an emergency, they activate the process of pluralistic ignorance because their behaviour is a strong behavioural example of apathy. On the other hand, if naive students are witnesses of an emergency, the chances are high that they will show some startle response and other signs of embarrassment which may be interpreted as an indication of a serious incident. Therefore, the likelihood that pluralistic ignorance will be elicited in naive students is higher if confederates are present than if a group of naive witnesses is present. In accordance with this analysis, results indicate that in groups of confederates prosocial responses of naive students are inhibited to a greater extent than in groups of naive witnesses (Latané & Darley, 1968; Latané & Rodin, 1969).

An important precondition for the operation of pluralistic ignorance is that the emergency has some ambiguity. Quite a high level of ambiguity is created in many experimental situations in which witnesses are not able to observe what is going on directly because the emergency is staged in a way that precludes the witnesses seeing the event. Typically they hear something happening in another room that is outside their range of vision. Thus, there is some ambiguity in the situation with respect to what has occurred. In contrast, social inhibition of intervention is reduced when an emergency is plainly visible (Piliavin & Piliavin, 1972; Piliavin et al., 1969). If it is perfectly clear that an emergency has happened, people do not need social comparisons to interpret the situation appropriately. Therefore, they tend to intervene immediately on the basis of their correct understanding of what has happened.

A demonstration of this principle is the fact that a cry for help reduces social inhibition effects (Clark & Word, 1972, 1974; Yakimovich & Saltz, 1971). A cry for help eliminates any uncertainty in witnesses with respect to whether an emergency has occurred and whether an intervention is needed. As a consequence, the witnesses immediately intervene and attempt to offer help. This result is of direct practical importance: Victims of emergencies are more likely to receive help from bystanders if they cry for help.

Pluralistic ignorance as an inhibiting influence on bystanders is limited to emergency situations in which there is a certain level of ambiguity about what is going on. In such situations the witnesses attempt to construct a social definition of the situation, derived from social cues. Under such circumstances striving to look calm may dominate over every other response tendency, while the heads of the bystanders, unknown to each other, are buzzing with questions about what they should do.

Social facilitation and the disentangling of three processes of social inhibition

Effects of an audience

Another factor that contributes to social inhibition is being under the observation of other bystanders. Observation by others may elicit a state of audience inhibition in the observed. This is especially likely if the observed are not very competent in the behaviour sequence required of them, and therefore feel some uncertainty about whether they will be able to perform the required actions. They are afraid that others may laugh at them and that they might look ridiculous. Under such social pressure many people prefer passivity over intervention because they want to avoid any chance of being seen as ridiculous. This phenomenon was mentioned earlier in the context of pluralistic ignorance, in connection with the example of students in a seminar, who do not have the nerve to ask a question. Whereas audience inhibition contributes to the emergence of pluralistic ignorance, it is also an inhibiting factor in itself, because in many situations people who feel observed hesitate to give up their anonymity.

In experimental studies audience inhibition was investigated by creating the impression that other participants are observing the actor. What is the difference between performing an intervention in public and in private? In 1897 Triplett was the first experimenter to investigate this issue. Since that time a large number of studies has been conducted, leading to contradictory results. In some studies the presence of others led to an increase in performance, whereas in other studies the presence of others reduced performance.

This inconsistent pattern of results was resolved by Zajonc's (1965) drive theory of social facilitation. The term social facilitation is a misnomer because it implies that the presence of others contributes to the facilitation of performance. Nevertheless, the theory explains the facilitation as well as the inhibition of performance depending on the presence of others. Zajonc (1965) assumes that the effect of other persons' presence depends on task characteristics: If the task is simple, a facilitative effect is expected, whereas for difficult tasks, a deterioration of performance is predicted. These predictions are based on the assumption that other persons' presence induces a physiological arousal which leads to the activation of responses that are dominant in the situation.

This social facilitation supports the performance of well-learned activities, for which the dominant response is the correct one. Therefore, the prediction is that other persons' presence will positively influence the performance of simple tasks. With complex tasks, the predictions are different. The dominant response is no longer the correct one. Therefore, the solving of such tasks might be impaired by high arousal in public situations. In agreement with social facilitation theory, a meta-analysis shows that other persons' presence enhances performance with simple tasks, whereas performance in complex tasks deteriorates (Guerin, 1986).

What does the theory of social facilitation imply for the likelihood of intervention in emergencies? In public situations, willingness to intervene is expected to be reduced if the intervention is considered difficult. Under such circumstances, which seem to be more the rule than the exception, an inhibition of intervention by other people's presence is expected. In contrast, if the behaviour necessary to carry out the intervention is well learned, other people's presence is expected to enhance willingness to intervene. Therefore, there is no simple prediction with respect to the effects of audience presence. If the situation is difficult to handle, intervention rates might decrease in public, compared to an alone situation in which only the witness is confronted with the emergency. In contrast, if members of an ambulance crew arrive at the scene of an accident, it is likely that the presence of other people will have a motivating effect on the crew members.

The theory of evaluation apprehension (Cottrell, 1972) goes one step further: it assumes that the mere presence of others induces social facilitation only if the other persons direct their attention to the task and observe the performance. This means that primarily observers who evaluate the performance elicit a social facilitation effect. The results generally agree with the prediction of evaluation apprehension theory. In the case of an emergency intervention, it is very likely that other witnesses focus on the scene of the accident and evaluate the helper's performance. Therefore, the conditions of high evaluation apprehension arise, and the predictions of social facilitation theory apply.

A third related theory is distraction conflict theory (Baron, 1986). The assumption of this theory is that the presence of others constitutes a distraction which leads to an attention conflict while performing the task. This conflict elicits an increase in physiological arousal. From this point on, distraction conflict theory makes the same predictions as social facilitation theory. An implication of distraction conflict theory is that besides social factors, nonsocial factors that elicit a distraction during performance may also lead to effects that are predicted by social facilitation theory. In the case of emergency intervention, distraction conflict theory considers the possibility that—in addition to witnesses—nonsocial factors may contribute to high physiological arousal of potential helpers (e.g., traffic noise). Therefore, social facilitation effects are presumed to be stronger in noisy situations than in quiet situations (independent of other people's presence).

Breaking down social inhibition into its subprocesses

Diffusion of responsibility arises from the awareness that other witnesses are present who are able to intervene. Pluralistic ignorance is the result of the passivity of other witnesses who act as models. Finally, audience effects are elicited by the awareness that other witnesses observe one's own actions. In general, if these processes are effective in combination, the reduction of helpfulness is stronger than if only one process (e.g., diffusion of responsibility) is operating (Latané & Nida, 1981). In experiments, the proof of the effect of each inhibition process in isolation is achieved by varying the number of communication channels available to bystanders. If communication is open, all processes of social inhibition may come into play. If communication channels are restricted, only one or two processes of social inhibition may occur.

With the use of an intercom system it is possible to manipulate the availability of communication channels (Latané & Darley, 1976). Let us consider the example of Mike, who participates in a study on emergency intervention. Diffusion of responsibility can occur if Mike has the knowledge that other witnesses are present, although he is not able to communicate with them. Pluralistic ignorance is added if Mike is able to observe what other witnesses do. Finally, audience effects are operative if other witnesses are able to observe what Mike does.

In an experiment (Latané & Darley, 1976), students were watching on a monitor an experimenter who was working on a shock generator in a room nearby, when a problem apparently occurred: The experimenter cried out in pain, jumped up into the air, and was thrown against the wall. Finally, he fell to the ground, outside the view of the camera, and only his feet were to be seen on the monitor. In addition, participants heard the experimenter moaning. This accident was staged in five different conditions:

(1) The student observed another witness on a second monitor and had the impression that he himself was being observed, because a camera that was directed towards him was on.

(2) The student saw another witness on the second monitor, but he himself was apparently not under observation, because the camera was directed towards the ceiling of the room.

(3) The student could not observe the other witness, but the camera directed towards him was on.

(4) The student neither saw another witness nor was it likely that another witness was able to see him; however, he knew that another witness was present.

(5) The student assumed that he was the only witness (alone condition).

In the first four conditions the experimenter's confederate was a co-witness of the accident to the experimenter. Therefore, in these four conditions the process of diffusion of responsibility was likely to be activated. In contrast, in the alone condition no social inhibition of prosocial tendencies was likely to occur. In condition (1) the additional activation of pluralistic ignorance and audience effects is likely; in condition (2) only the additional activation of pluralistic ignorance is likely; and in condition (3) only additional audience effects are likely. Finally, the comparison of condition (4) with condition (5) focuses exclusively on potential diffusion of responsibility effects.

First of all, the results showed that the conditions were different with respect to intervention rates. As expected, highest intervention was observed in the alone condition, in which no social inhibition effects were plausible. Condition (4), in which only the awareness of

Altruistic personality 16

Although laypersons will generally acknowledge that there is something like an altruistic personality, social psychologists have expressed serious doubts about its existence (e.g., Batson, 1991; Latané & Darley, 1970; Piliavin et al., 1981). Only recently has the notion of an altruistic personality reappeared in the scientific debate as a viable concept. The new evidence is based on two different sources: differences in personality between people who were willing to offer help in real life involving great expense and a control group on the one hand, and evidence on the stability of prosocial responding in longitudinal research on the other hand. The altruistic (or prosocial) personality is defined as "an enduring tendency to think about the welfare and rights of other people, to feel concern and empathy for them, and to act in a way that benefits them" (Penner & Finkelstein, 1998, p. 526).

Rescuers of Jews

A study based on retrospective interviews was conducted on rescuers of Jews, who were identified through an Israeli archive of registered rescuers of Jewish people in Nazi Germany (Oliner & Oliner, 1988). Results indicated that rescuers were similar to nonrescuers in many characteristics. For example, the risks involved in helping were quite similar for both groups. In addition, the opportunities to help were quite comparable. Another point of similarity was that rescuers and nonrescuers were equally critical about the Nazi ideology. Finally, geographic location played only a subordinate role.

However, rescuers were different from their comparison group, which was matched with respect to characteristics such as age and status, in that they showed more benevolence towards Jews, placed more emphasis on adhering to ethical rules, and attached more importance to personal responsibility. Therefore, the conclusion is justified that their help was an expression of the ethical principles that they considered generally valid, as well as further considerations about issues of justice that were violated by the Nazi terror against Jews. In correspondence with this analysis, rescuers scored higher on a Social Responsibility Scale (Berkowitz & Daniels, 1964) compared to nonrescuers. In addition, rescuers scored higher on internal locus of control.

This profile of rescuers is not meant to indicate that rescuers were a homogeneous group. Quite the contrary, several subgroups of helpers may be distinguished: those who had close contact with Jews; those who were characterised by high personal responsibility; and those who emphasised justice and equality. But the systematic differences between rescuers and nonrescuers show that a prosocial personality plays an important role. This is in agreement with experimental studies on emergency intervention (Eisenberg et al., 1989c; Staub, 1974).

Situational factors are not completely irrelevant to being a rescuer of Jews. For example, rescuers were more likely to work together with Jews than nonrescuers (34% vs 17%). In addition, rescuers (59%) were more likely to have Jews as friends than nonrescuers (34%). Although the general living conditions of rescuers and nonrescuers were similar, rescuers had more rooms available than nonrescuers. They also received more social support from their family (60% vs 35%) and were more likely to be members of resistance groups (44% vs 29%). In addition, rescuers reported that their parents talked about Jews more frequently (74%) than nonrescuers (54%).

In general rescuers tended to use stereotypes to a lesser extent than nonrescuers. They placed more emphasis on values of caring and generosity, and believed more in the general applicability of ethical rules (39% vs 15%). In contrast, nonrescuers placed more emphasis on values relating to the self, especially economic competence. Not surprisingly they believed more in the value of obedience to authority than rescuers. The general level of patriotism was similar in both groups.

Rescuers more than nonrescuers felt closer to their mother, expressed more social responsibility, agreed more with items like "I can't feel good if others around me feel bad", and had a stronger belief in their ability to control their environment. Oliner and Oliner (1988, p. 177) comment: "They . . . perceive themselves as actors, capable of making and implementing plans and willing to accept the consequences."

Level of self-esteem did not differ between rescuers and nonrescuers. However, when looking back rescuers derived some self-pride from their prosocial actions which contributed to their personal integrity. They experienced gratitude from others and social approval. In contrast, nonrescuers were defensive and had feelings of collective guilt. Finally, after the war rescuers were more involved in community work than nonrescuers. This demonstrates the continuity of their values of commitment, care, and responsibility which motivated prosocial involvement.

Further results on the altruistic personality

Some of the results on the altruistic personality were replicated in a study of first-aiders who intervened on behalf of injured traffic-accident victims (Bierhoff et al., 1991). Compared with a matched control group of potential nonhelpers, helpers scored higher on a German version of the Berkowitz and Daniels (1964) Social Responsibility Scale, lower on a scale measuring a hostile and selfish intention (M– scale from the EPAQ; Spence et al., 1979), and higher on a German version of the Questionnaire of Emotional Empathy (Mehrabian & Epstein, 1972; see Figure 16.1).

These three scales were correlated with each other and may be considered as measuring an underlying value dimension of "concern for others", which is close to the prosocial value domain described by Schwartz and Bilsky (1990). Social responsibility and empathy indicate high concern for others, whereas hostility taps low concern for others. Two additional results are worth mentioning: Helpers expressed a stronger agreement with items of the internal locus of control scale (Rotter, 1966) than nonhelpers. Finally, helpers scored higher than nonhelpers on the Just World Scale (Rubin & Peplau, 1975), which measures individual differences in the belief that everyone gets what he or she deserves. This result attests to the fact that belief in a just world is a positive factor in helping when it is possible to solve the problem completely (Miller, 1977). Only when helping will not completely alleviate the emergency, is belief in a just world in opposition with prosocial actions (see Chapter 11).

What are the main components of the altruistic personality? One cornerstone seems to be social responsibility. People who disposi-tionally focus on moral obligations tend to act in correspondence with their normative beliefs (Cialdini et al., 1991). Another cornerstone of

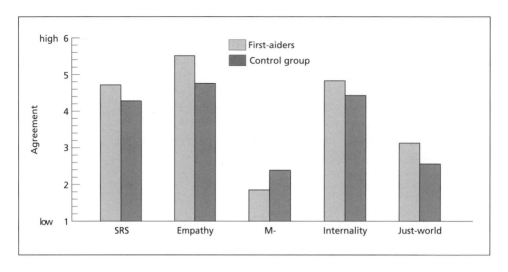

the altruistic personality is dispositional empathy, which is positively correlated with social responsibility in several studies (Omoto & Snyder, 1995; Penner & Finkelstein, 1998). Whereas these field studies show that altruistic dispositions play an important role in planned prosocial behaviour, an experimental approach demonstrates that prosocial orientation predicted helping in a staged emergency (Staub, 1974). Prosocial orientation was a composite of several personality variables including social responsibility, moral reasoning, and Machi-avellianism (Christie & Geis, 1968; reverse scoring). In summary, field and experimental studies show that the altruistic personality pos-sesses a prosocial orientation which is translated into action when another person is in need (see Chapter 21). Dispositional empathy and social responsibility are positive markers of the altruistic per-sonality, whereas Machiavellianism is a negative marker.

The importance of an altruistic personality was acknowledged centuries ago under a different name: Thomas Aquinas described virtues that are compatible with the facets of the altruistic personality (Jeffries, 1998). The virtues are temperance, fortitude, justice, charity, and prudence. It is possible to read the report on the results depicted in this section under these five headings. For example, temperance is linked to impulse control which is inherent in internal locus of control.

Longitudinal research on prosocial dispositions also corresponds with the notion of an altruistic personality (Eisenberg et al., 1999). On the basis of the study on prosocial moral reasoning that was more fully described in Chapter 7 (in the section "Age trends in prosocial orientation: 4–20 years") correlational analyses were performed which showed that spontaneous sharing at age 4–5 (defined as "The child gives away or allows another temporary use of a material object previously in the child's possession") was significantly related to prosocial behaviour at age 15–16 and 17–18 and friends' report of sympathy at age 19–20. These results indicate that prosocial orientation as an individual-difference variable emerged quite early in the preschool years and was quite stable over 15 years. They supplement the findings which show that the altruistic personality explains individual differences in costly helpfulness in real life.

who defines him- or herself as an excellent driver might hesitate to ask about the functions and controls of a new car, because he or she is attempting to project to outsiders the image of a competent driver who does not need to ask any questions before driving off. A further problem is that seeking help might be somewhat embarrassing if the potential helper has similar competencies as the help-seeker. Therefore, level of help seeking is expected to be especially low if the issue touches on a central area of the self-scheme and if only a highly similar helper is available.

Empirical results confirm these ideas. Students frequently ask for help when the potential helper is dissimilar even if a central area of the self-scheme is involved. However, they hesitate to ask for help when the issue is highly relevant and the available helper is highly similar. The suppression of help seeking is even stronger in students who express high self-esteem. For these students the idea of asking a similar person for help in a relevant area is presumably very unpleasant. A similar pattern of results was obtained for students who expressed lower self-esteem but to a lesser extent (Nadler, 1987).

Help seeking is avoided because people who could profit from help frequently have exaggerated anxieties with respect to negative responses of potential helpers. The actual responses of helpers who were asked for help tended to be more accepting than help-seekers expected (Engler & Braun, 1988). Therefore, the anxieties felt by potential help-seekers are at least in part unrealistic.

What are the underlying dimensions of the cognitive representations of help-seeking episodes? To answer this question, help-seeking episodes were collected and similarity judgements between pairs of these episodes were obtained from students (Amato & Saunders, 1985). The multidimensional scaling of these similarity judgements led to four dimensions, three of which were replicated in a second study. These dimensions were characterised as follows:

- The first dimension contrasted serious and embarrassing episodes in which the problem is difficult to solve with non-serious and unembarrassing episodes in which the problem is easy to solve.
- The second dimension referred to type of help source, either friend or stranger.
- The third dimension referred to a second type of help source, either professional or nonprofessional.
- The fourth dimension concerned the issue of reciprocity: Is repayment possible or not?

These dimensions of *help-seeking* episodes have some overlap with the three dimensions of *helping* which were also derived by multi-dimensional scaling (see Chapter 2) because in both analyses a nonserious–serious dimension was found. The three other dimensions that were revealed in the analysis of help-seeking episodes seem to be specific for the role of help-recipient: Help seeking is differentiated according to whether it is characterised by opportunity to repay or not, whether it is linked to the social relationship as friend or stranger with the addressee, and whether help is from a professional source or not.

People who need help sometimes avoid asking for it. Why should this be? A first answer to this question is built on a multidimensional scaling study of reasons for not seeking help (Amato & Bradshaw, 1985). The second answer is based on social impact theory (Williams & Williams, 1983a,b).

People were asked to indicate reasons why they had hesitated to seek help when they needed it because of a distressing problem (Amato & Bradshaw, 1985). In a second study, respondents indicated how much each of the 25 reasons identified in the first study contributed to their not seeking help when they were facing a difficult problem. The reasons for not seeking help that were mentioned most frequently were (Amato & Bradshaw, 1985, p. 25):

- I knew I could solve the problem myself.
- I dislike burdening others with my problems.
- I hoped the problem would right itself.
- I felt the helper would not be of much help.
- I had feelings of not being ready to ask for help.
- I feared loss of face in exposing the problem.

The correlation matrix of the importance ratings was analysed by multidimensional scaling. Several clusters of reasons emerged: fear and stigma associated with help seeking, difficulty in defining or accepting the problem, negative helper evaluation, external barriers, and independence. These results indicate that reluctance to seek help is multidimensionally determined. Simple explanations are obviously not adequate because avoidance of help seeking seems to be determined by situational constraints, definition of the situation, trust in one's own competencies, and anxieties.

From a theoretical point of view, inhibition to seek help may be predicted by social impact theory (Williams & Williams, 1983a,b) which assumes that inhibition is a function of strength, immediacy, and number of sources (Latané, 1981; see Chapter 15). Strength varies, for example, with social status because higher-status people presumably exert a stronger influence than lower-status people. Immediacy varies directly with proximity of others. Taking these variables into account, the hypothesis follows that help seeking becomes more inhibited the greater the number of people hearing the call for help, the closer these people are, and the higher their status.

These assumptions were partly supported by the results of an experiment in which number of potential helpers, their proximity, and their social status were varied. After the computer on which the participants were working broke down, they waited longer before calling for help if three helpers instead of one helper were available. In addition, low-status others were asked for help earlier than high-status others. These results were partly mirrored by data on self-help: Participants attempted to solve the computer problem themselves to a greater degree when three helpers were available. Finally, the participants who waited the longest to ask for help and were more involved in self-help were those in the three-helpers, high-status condition (Williams & Williams, 1983a).

Although the expected results for immediacy of others were not obtained, the results partially support social impact theory. It is a fascinating idea that factors that inhibit helpers (which are predicted by social impact theory, see Chapter 15) also inhibit people who need to ask for help. This parallel pattern is found with respect to number of helpers. Several psychological mechanisms may explain the results for help seeking. For example, it is probably more embarrassing and self-threatening to ask three people for help than to ask one person. In addition, presumably more reactance is elicited in the three-helpers condition than in the one-helper condition because more pressure is felt to return the favour (cf. Brehm & Brehm, 1981).

Which factors influence the reactions of help-recipients?

The reactions of help-recipients are not always characterised by gratitude and joy. Under which conditions do the reactions of help recipients turn out negatively or positively? Table 17.1 gives an overview of research results on conditions that influence reactions to receiving help. In the following, these influencing factors will be

TABLE 17.1

Overview of some conditions that trigger self-support or self-threat after receiving help

Self-support	Self-threat
Dissimilarity between giver and recipient	Similarity between giver and recipient
Service in return possible	Service in return impossible
Help is normatively adequate	Help is normatively inadequate
Low resources of giver	High resources of giver
Without previous request for help	After previous request for help

Source: Based on Fisher, Nadler, & Whitcher-Alagna, 1983.

examined in more detail. Following that, a theoretical approach will be discussed which offers an explanatory tool for the psychology of seeking and receiving help. Finally, I examine how public help programmes should be planned.

Similarity and friendship as potential cues of inferiority and failure

Similarity in personality traits, values, and attitudes is often a facilitating factor for interpersonal relations. Similar people often come together, for instance, because they have the same hobby or because they have the same political opinions. Similarity does not only facilitate communication in general because there is mutual agreement. It also allows a comparison with other people which, for example, influences how one's own life satisfaction is calibrated (Filipp & Ferring, 1998). Older women often judge their own situation by comparing themselves with persons of the same age who seem to be in a worse position. The tendency to carry out downward comparisons using people who seem to be or who really are in a worse position than the comparing person herself/himself is widespread (Wills, 1991).

The possibility of coming out worse than expected in social comparison with similar people bears a certain threat to self-esteem which can render social comparisons problematic. If a person compares him- or herself to others who had the same starting position, and if he or she finds that he or she comes out worse than these comparison persons, weakness and inferiority is indicated by that comparison. To know less than others under the same preconditions means that the others are better than oneself, at least to a certain extent.

In social comparison processes, help-recipients may experience feelings of inferiority. The helpers possess abilities and means that

help on evaluation of the donor were avoided. Therefore, reciprocity was not limited to the donor himself but was generalised to other people (generalised reciprocity).

The interest in reciprocity presumably varies from situation to situation. When it is relatively easy to repay the help received (as in two conditions of the experiment by Castro, 1974) the interest in reciprocity is assumed to be greater than if the repayment is costly. If the costs of repayment are high, many help-recipients would presumably prefer symbolic reciprocity over proportional reciprocity. In addition, if repayment is very expensive and surpasses the help received (e.g., because of interest rates), a defensive response by help-recipients is likely (Gergen, Ellsworth, Maslach, & Seipel, 1975). Under these circumstances defensive responses were obtained in American as well as Swedish and Japanese students.

The importance of reciprocity depends on the social setting (Cook & Pelfrey, 1985). If the relationship is co-operative due to a shared task, the issue of reciprocity is likely to be of minimal importance. Co-operation means that help is given to co-workers who need it in order to achieve a common group goal. Only in a nonco-operative atmosphere is the issue of reciprocity likely to be relevant. Besides situational influences, individual differences in the degree of felt obligation in connection with the norm of reciprocity are important. Results indicate that primarily persons who expressed high self-esteem responded negatively to receiving help (DePaulo et al., 1981). Participants who expressed low self-esteem did not respond differently to help that was given by similar or dissimilar others.

The hypothesis is justified that people who are high in self-esteem place more emphasis on the norm of reciprocity than people who are low in self-esteem. In a questionnaire study with students from Israel a significant correlation of $r = 0.33$ was found between self-esteem and adherence to the norm of reciprocity (Nadler, Mayseless, Peri, & Chemerinski, 1985). The modifying role of type of interpersonal relationship was also evident because the principle of reciprocity towards neighbours and colleagues at work was emphasised more than towards relatives and strangers.

In another study with 12–13-year-old pupils (Nadler, 1987) the similarity of determinants of receiving help and asking for help was demonstrated. The willingness to ask another pupil for help was lower among pupils who expressed high self-esteem than among pupils who expressed lower self-esteem. This effect of self-esteem primarily occurred when no opportunity for repayment was expected. If such an opportunity was expected, help-seeking behaviour did not differ between high- and low-self-esteem pupils. The conclusion is that high self-esteem is compatible with help-seeking behaviour as long as an opportunity to repay is available. Only when such an opportunity was missing did high-self-esteem pupils suppress help-seeking efforts.

High resources of the donor: Discounting an altruistic motive

Donors differ with respect to the resources they have available. A donation of £100 would be trivial for a millionaire, whereas such a donation would be very generous for a student. Large resources of the donor make his or her donation of £100 appear rather small from the perspective of the observer. A bystander may infer that the rich donor did not invest very much and may even insinuate that the donor has negative intentions. For example, the bystander might assume that the wealthy donor wanted to buy off his or her responsibility.

In contrast, low resources of the donor are likely to lead to the assumption that help was only possible because of great effort. From an attributional point of view, low resources of the donor are a reason for not giving help. Low resources are among the inhibiting factors that make generosity unlikely. A donation that is made even when resources are low will probably be attributed to strong altruistic motives because, in the thinking of the attributor, only strong altruism is likely to overpower the inhibiting influence of low resources. In contrast, large resources are not considered an inhibiting factor of prosocial behaviour. Therefore, observers are unlikely to infer a strong altruistic motive. Instead, generosity is explained on the basis of the fact that ample resources are available. As a consequence. an altruistic motive is discounted (Hewstone, 1989).

This attributional analysis leads to the conclusion that a donor who has low resources will be perceived as more altruistic than a donor who has large resources. This hypothesis was confirmed in an experiment conducted in Japan, Sweden, and the United States (Gergen et al., 1975). During a game, students whose game capital was nearly used up received 10 additional chips from a co-player. This help was given either by a player who had small resources or by a player who had large resources. Especially in Japan, but also in Sweden and the United States, the helper who had fewer resources was more liked. The receiver of the chips had the opportunity to support the donor at a later point in time. More chips were reciprocated in the case where the original donor had limited resources than when the original donor had high resources. These differences were visible in all three cultures.

The norm of reciprocity is used in many cultures and may be considered a universal one (Gouldner, 1960; Komter, 1996; Triandis, 1978). The results show that adherence to the norm of reciprocity depends, at least in part, on the prosperity of the donor. In an earlier experiment with male students, similar results were obtained in the context of a social dilemma (Pruitt, 1968). The game consisted of three blocks of three trials each. The student played the game with a partner whose responses were pre-programmed. The two players alternately received a certain number of chips, the value of which was expressed in dollars. If the chips were sent to the partner, the value of the chips was multiplied by 1.5 and the value was transferred to the partner. If the partners co-operated by sending the chips to each other, they were able to earn more money than if they did not co-operate. In this social-dilemma situation in which co-operation only pays if the other party also co-operates, three conditions were established by varying the co-operative behaviour of the partner in the first three trials:

(1)   The partner's resources were $1 per trial and he sent out 80% ($0.80).
(2)   The partner's resources were $1 per trial and he sent out 20% ($0.20).
(3)   The partner's resources were $4 per trial and he sent out 20% ($0.80).

In the second block of trials the students had $3 available in each trial. The dependent variable consisted of the amount of money that they sent to their partner. The comparison between the first and the third condition indicates whether the level of resources of the partner influenced reciprocity. Results showed that more chip money was sent out in the first condition than in the third condition. Even the students who played the game in the second condition sent out more money than those in the third condition. Thus, co-operation varied with condition (1) being highest, condition (2) intermediate, and condition (3) lowest. Additional results indicated that those students co-operated more who expected to receive more chip money from the partner in the third block of trials ($r = .57$).

In the same experiment another variable was manipulated: the future resources of the partner in the last three trials were either high ($2 per trial) or small ($0.50 per trial). The hypothesis was that students who expected a "richer" partner in the third block would send out more money than students who expected a "poorer" partner. This expectation was borne out by the data: More money was provided to the "rich" than to the "poor" partner (Pruitt, 1968).

The adherence to the norm of reciprocity is at least in part dependent on the convictions of the actor, which may be described as reciprocity ideologies (Eisenberger, Cotterell, & Marvel, 1987) or personal norm of reciprocity (Perugini & Gallucci, in press). One ideology is that it is appropriate to take more than to give. People who agree with such a "realistic policy" are not influenced in their reciprocity by the level of co-operation of the partner as much as are people who do not agree with such a policy. Nevertheless, even the students who agree with such a realistic policy show a greater willingness to provide rewards to the more co-operative partner.

Perugini and Gallucci (in press) define reciprocity both as a strategy and as a goal. As a strategy, reciprocity can be instrumental in achieving an egoistic goal (e.g., to maximise outcome in a situation of interdependence). As a goal, reciprocity may be understood as an individual preference which has been internalised as a social value orientation. The prosocial orientation that is characterised by the goal of enhancing joint profits and by an interest in achieving equality in outcomes seems to be positively linked to reciprocity in a co-operative context (van Lange, 1999). But it is not viable to equate reciprocity completely with prosocial orientation, because reciprocal behaviour is also observed in the context of negative interpersonal behaviour (e.g., competition; Perugini & Gallucci, in press).

Offered vs requested help

In the following, the psychological meaning of two types of situations is compared: (1) A social welfare recipient has to ask for help before it is given, and (2) he or she receives a visit by a social worker who offers help before it is asked for. What does it mean to request help as in the first situation? What does it mean if help is offered as in the second situation?

Asking for help is not completely unproblematic for the help-recipient, because the question includes an explicit admission of dependency from a helping measure. The plea for help may be understood as a sign of weakness or inferiority (Nadler & Fisher, 1986). Empirical results show that to ask for help leads to a more negative evaluation of the helper than when the help is offered (Broll, Gross, & Piliavin, 1974).

responsibility exert a much stronger influence on helpfulness than subjective competence. The results of a path-analytic procedure was that although the direct influence of subjective competence was low, an indirect path from subjective competence via responsibility to helpfulness was significant. This path indicates that high subjective competence heightens feelings of responsibility which, in turn, facilitate helpfulness.

The fit of the path model depicted in Figure 18.1 is quite satisfactory if standard criteria of fit are applied (Jöreskog & Sörbom, 1984). The same path model was tested in a scenario that described the fall of a cyclist and in a scenario that described a truck accident. In all scenarios tested, the same pattern of results was found: Responsibility was a strong predictor of helpfulness, and subjective competence had an indirect influence on helpfulness via increasing feelings of responsibility. Training in first-aid and age were predictors of subjective competence with better trained and older participants feeling more competent.

The fit of the path models is very good. A large amount of variance of helpfulness is explained by the variables that were included in the model. Note that the age range investigated was between 20 and 60 years, and 92% of respondents were younger than 50 years. Therefore, the possibility exists that subjective competence will decrease among older respondents over 65 years. As the results in Figure 18.1 show, age also positively influenced responsibility, although the effect of age on responsibility was quite low. Other factors that are not represented in the model presumably exert a stronger influence on responsibility.

Therefore, an extended model that includes decision confidence was developed with the goal of explaining more variance in responsibility. In the study just described, participants were asked "How confident would you be that you would be able to help?" Decision confidence includes dispositional aspects (in the sense of resolution) as well as situational aspects, because confidence is expected to be higher in situations that are unequivocal. The extended model is based on several additional assumptions:

- The influence of subjective competence on responsibility is mediated by decision confidence.
- A path from training in first-aid via subjective competence, decision confidence, and responsibility to helpfulness is significant. Such a chain would connect objective knowledge with likelihood of intervention.

- Decision confidence also has a direct positive influence on helpfulness.
- Decision confidence is influenced by instrumental traits which are measured by the Extended Personal Attribute Questionnaire (Spence et al., 1979). An instrumental, agentic personality (characterised by independence, resolution, and self-confidence) is assumed to facilitate decision confidence. As a measure of this basic personality dimension, which was originally labelled masculinity in the context of the measurement of sex-role attributes, the German Extended Personal Attribute Questionnaire (Runge, Frey, Gollwitzer, Helmreich, & Spence, 1981) was used.
- Dispositional empathy explains additional variance in responsibility (cf. Zahn-Waxler & Robinson, 1995). Empathy was measured on the basis of the Mehrabian and Epstein (1972) questionnaire using the translation by Schmitt (1982).

This extended path model, which is depicted in Figure 18.2, fitted the data quite well when the conventional path-analytic criteria were applied as standard of judgement. This is true for the scenario of the car collision as well as for the other two accident scenarios. The results in Figure 18.2 indicate that the goal of explaining more variance of responsibility was achieved because decision confidence explained some variance in responsibility. In contrast, the influence of empathy on responsibility was very low. It was not possible to explain further variance in responsibility by the empathy questionnaire. Whether this result is due to the problems with measuring

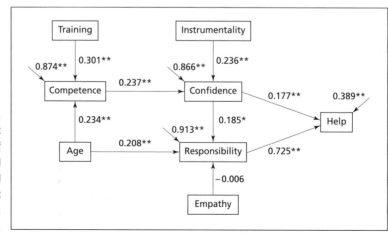

FIG. 18.2.
Help at a car accident as a function of responsibility and competence: Extended model (from Bierhoff et al., 1990, p. 57). Key: *p<.05; **p<.01.

empathy (see Chapter 9) or to the fact that responsibility is situation-specific, whereas empathy is a dispositional measure, is unclear.

All assumptions that refer to decision confidence were confirmed. Instrumental traits as well as subjective competence were significant predictors of decision confidence. In addition, the path from training in first-aid to helpfulness was significant, confirming the assumption that a chain extends from objective knowledge to helpfulness. This chain also reveals that the effects of training in first-aid on helpfulness were mainly indirect. The training heightened subjective competence which, in turn, was a positive factor for facilitating decision confidence. Decision confidence was positively related to helpfulness indirectly via responsibility as well as directly.

Feelings of responsibility were the most important predictor of helpfulness in these scenario studies. This result underlines that responsibility is a key variable in prosocial behaviour. In the introduction to this section, subjective competence was also considered a key variable. The path model gives some credence to this viewpoint if it is assumed that subjective competence is not a direct influence on helpfulness but is mediated via decision confidence.

Determinants of subjective competence

Intervention in an emergency depends on motivation and competence. Whereas much research has referred to motivational factors, little is known about subjective competence. From the path model that was described in the last section we know that age of participant and training in first-aid were significant determinants of subjective competence. In this section the determinants of subjective competence are considered more closely.

With respect to emergency intervention, subjective competence depends in part on training in first-aid. In addition, bystanders may have task-related competence which facilitates their intervention in a specific situation. In an empirical study of emergency intervention (Clark & Word, 1974) an accident to a mechanic in a laboratory was simulated—it looked as if the mechanic had received an electric shock (see Chapter 12). On the basis of their responses to a questionnaire on subject knowledge, observers of this emergency situation were divided into two groups. One group had knowledge in the use of electrical equipment, whereas the other group had no such knowledge. Competent students intervened more frequently (90%) than less competent students (58%). Therefore, (subjective) competence height-ened the likelihood of intervention. Task-related competence was also a predictor of helping behaviour when the prosocial behaviour was connected with costs (receiving electric shocks for prosocial beha-viour; Midlarsky, 1971; Midlarsky & Midlarksy, 1973, 1976).

In the experiment by Clark and Word (1974) the influence of competence was not limited to the likelihood of intervention. Com-petent students helped in ways that ensured their personal safety. In contrast, only 57% of the less competent students were able to provide help in a safe way. High competence, therefore, influenced the likelihood of intervention and improved the quality of help.

The analysis of the determinants of competence is based on a distinction between objective and subjective competence. One assumption is that objective competence, which is closely linked to training level in first-aid, influences willingness to intervene only via subjective competence (see earlier). Subjective competence is meas-ured by self-assessment. Such assessments may refer to a general competence or to specific competences that are necessary to intervene under specific circumstances (e.g., heart attack of the victim, traffic accident, etc.).

What are the determinants of subjective competence? A first determinant is objective competence (see earlier). On the one hand, the amount of training in first-aid will contribute to subjective com-petence. On the other hand, the time point of training is important, because a training course that took place just a few weeks ago is likely to lead to high feelings of subjective competence in the present, whereas a training course several years ago will contribute much less to current subjective competence.

Additional factors that are likely to influence subjective competence are demographic variables. Among these factors, age and gender are of special importance. Because age is correlated with more experience and maturity one can expect a positive correlation between age and prosocial behaviour, at least until the beginning of old age, when age-related impairments may lead to less helpfulness. Gender differences in prosocial behaviour are a topic of interesting speculations. For example, because women tend to be more other-oriented and more empathic, it is tempting to conclude that they are more helpful than men on the average. But a meta-analysis of prosocial behaviour depending on gender came to a contra-intuitive result (Eagly & Crowley, 1986, see Chapter 4): Men help more than women. Gener-alising from this result, the conclusion is justified that males are more likely than females to actively intervene in emergencies (Eagly, 1987).

What is the reason for this gender difference? One factor is subjective competence. Gender roles support stereotypes which indicate that men are more competent in achievement situations than women. When these stereotypical beliefs are repeated during socialisation over and over again, they may contribute to differences in self-schemes of men and women, with women attributing less competence in achievement situations to themselves than do men.

Bierhoff et al. (1990) report the results of a study on the determinants of subjective competence. Subjective competence was systematically influenced by four variables:

- Level of objective competence, as indicated by the number of first-aid courses that the person had participated in. The larger the number of courses, the higher the subjective competence ($r = .36$).
- The timing of training was also a significant factor which explained the variance in subjective competence. When the training had taken place a longer while ago, subjective competence was assessed as lower ($r = -.28$).
- Males reported higher subjective competence than females. The means of scores on a scale ranging from 1 (low competence) to 9 (high competence) are quite different for males (M = 5.59) and females (M = 3.74). This difference is reflected in a correlation of $r = .43$ between gender and subjective competence. The same difference in subjective competence depending on gender was found in a nationally representative opinion poll on first-aid conducted in Germany in 1984 by the opinion research institute EMNID.
- Finally, an age effect emerged, because older respondents indicated higher subjective competence than younger respondents. Note that the participants of the study were between 20 and 40 years of age. It is possible that subjective competence decreases in elderly respondents.

The results of this study are summarised in Figure 18.3. A multiple regression analysis indicated that each of the four factors had an

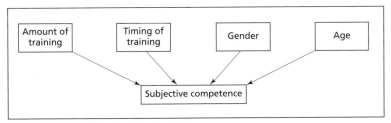

FIG. 18.3.
Factors that determine subjective competence (from Bierhoff et al., 1990, p. 20).

independent influence on subjective competence. Altogether, the four variables explained 38% of variance of subjective competence.

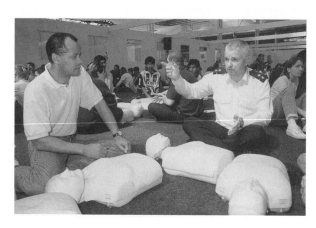

Is there any evidence that training in first-aid increases likelihood of intervention in emergencies? In a study on people who intervened on behalf of the victim during a crime (Huston, Ruggiero, Conner, & Geis, 1981), it was shown that people who intervened were better trained in first-aid than people who did not intervene. In addition, a strong gender difference was observed. From the 42 persons who intervened, 31 were male.

Credit: Art Directors and TRIP.

The results of the path-analytic study of Bierhoff et al. (1990) also confirm the relationship between subjective competence and helpfulness. The same positive association is also evident in the representative sample of Germans obtained by EMNID in 1984. In that sample a reliable association between objective and subjective competence was found as well as a reliable association between subjective competence and reported helpfulness. In contrast, the direct influence of objective competence on reported helpfulness was low and not significant.

These results show that subjective competence is a key factor in emergency intervention. Programmes that are designed to increase the likelihood of emergency intervention in everyday situations are well advised to consider measures that increase subjective competence. In this context the gender gap with respect to emergency intervention is also relevant. Training in first-aid that is targeted towards women should emphasise the subjective competence they have acquired during the course. Finally, the role of regular repetition of first-aid courses is of obvious significance.

supportive, cooperative to other individuals or collectivities and based on or associated with a sense of obligation or value-based commitment." In the following, two types of solidarity are distinguished: Joint action on the basis of common interests, and joint action on the basis of the interests of others. The two types of joint action may be illustrated by examples: The union movement, the women's movement, or the protests by cyclists taking part in the *Tour de France* illustrate joint action on the basis of common interests of the participants. The attempt to reduce discrimination against people in the Third World is an example of solidarity on the basis of different interests. Another example is when people provide meals for the homeless or serve as consultants in crisis centres without payment. The movement of "volunteerism" clearly shows that people are willing to work for the welfare of the needy without expecting any repayment (see Chapter 21).

The distinction between solidarity based on common interests and on the interests of others is justified given the empirically validated difference between values that refer to self-enhancement and values that refer to self-transcendence (Schwartz, 1992, 1994): *Self-enhancement* includes values such as wealth, social power, authority, social recognition, freedom, ambition, success, family security, and pleasure. *Self-transcendence* includes values such as helpfulness, responsibility, honesty, loyalty, social justice, a world at peace, inner harmony, equality, and unity with nature

Self-enhancement and self-transcendence tend to be mutually exclusive, as demonstrated by 97 samples in 44 countries (Schwartz, 1992, 1994). The preference for values that refer to self-enhancement and the preference for values related to self-transcendence are negatively correlated—people who emphasise self-enhancement tend to de-emphasise self-transcendence and vice versa (Feather, 1995). Self-enhancement and self-transcendence describe a basic dimension of social values. Solidarity on the basis of common interests is related to self-enhancement. The goal is to improve one's own situation. If the interests are the same, joint action is described as fight solidarity because the community of interests is frequently directed against the interests of other groups (Bayertz, 1998). In contrast, solidarity on the basis of interests of others is related to self-transcendence. Personal interests are de-emphasised and the fulfilment of moral obligations is emphasised. Is this type of solidarity nothing other than charity? This question is answerable if one considers that this second type of solidarity is concerned with the elimination of discrimination (Bayertz, 1998). Solidarity with underprivileged people is based on a value-orientation to which the person is obligated. Such actions of unconditional co-operation are frequently based on decisions of conscience which are motivated by social responsibility, guilt over affluence, and fairness considerations (Montada, 2001b).

Different uses of the term solidarity

One hundred years ago, Durkheim (1902) distinguished between mechanic and organic solidarity. He contrasted solidarity that is based on similarity and community with solidarity that is based on the division of labour. In his book, Durkheim analysed the effects of the division of labour in modern societies compared to primitive societies and contrasted mechanic solidarity in primitive societies with organic solidarity in modern societies. He used the term "solidarity" to describe forces that contribute to the cohesion of society in cases where society threatens to fall apart because of individualistic tendencies. The question is which factors contribute to the integration of society given that individualism prevails?

Bergson (1933) distinguished between instinctive and open solidarity. He contrasted a limited solidarity with a solidarity that is intended to serve all people in the world. Bayertz (1998) distinguished between fight solidarity and community solidarity. Whereas fight solidarity serves the realisation of common interests, community solidarity is based on partisanship for certain groups (e.g., the family). Finally, the distinction between altruistic solidarity (with underprivileged people) and co-operative solidarity based on common interests was introduced by Voland (1999) who suggested a sociobiological perspective on solidary action.

Cialdini and his co-workers (1997) found that people help close relatives more than distant relatives or strangers (see Chapter 13). This pattern of results may be predicted on the basis of the principle of inclusive fitness (Hamilton, 1964). Voland (1999) assumed that parents influence the conscience of their children in such a way as to ensure that they are willing to support their parents. This socialisation is the basis for altruistic behaviour in other contexts. In general, parents expect more altruism from their children than the children are willing to show on the basis of their own decisions. Conscience may be understood as an agency which serves the interests of the parents and is located in the children. The children are willing to follow the standards of their parents because they learn to adapt to the complex environment by imitation. At the same time, the price of facilitation of successful adaptation is that their parents ask for trust and obedience. After the conscience has developed, other individuals can profit from the moral obligations that are seated in the conscience (Voland, 1999).

Co-operative solidarity is based on the norm of reciprocity. Reciprocal co-operation may be the result of evolution, as the costs of co-operation are usually lower than the rewards that are produced. Generalised reciprocity is advantageous if success is highly uncertain and if it depends on circumstances beyond the control of the individual person (Hinde, 2001). Under aversive circumstances reciprocal co-operation maximises personal advantages in the long run.

It is hard to say whether the frequency of joint action has increased or decreased during the last decade. Although some evidence is available which points to the decline of solidarity, citizen initiatives and self-help groups show that a new type of solidarity has developed, which can be summarised under the term "new social movements". They are characterised by voluntary participation, setting time limits for involvement, and specifying goals (Bayertz, 1998).

Frequently, joint action is described in the context of common interests. As mentioned earlier, I use a more comprehensive notion of solidarity which includes reciprocal and unconditional co-operation (cf. Gintis, 2000; Thome, 1999). Solidary action that serves own interests seems to be determined by factors that are quite different from the determinants that shape solidarity with underprivileged people (Bierhoff & Küpper, 1999). Such differences are to be expected from a sociobiological point of view: Whereas solidarity in the first sense corresponds with in-group favouritism and may be understood as part of human nature, solidarity of the second type is more the result of cultural norms and political leadership (Hinde, 2001). Another viewpoint on solidarity is inherent in the empathy–altruism hypothesis (see Chapter 13): Whereas solidarity that serves own interests is related to egoistically motivated helping, solidarity that serves the interests of under-privileged people (excluding oneself) is related to altruistically motivated helping which is based on perspective taking (cf. Batson et al., 1999). In the following, this difference between the two forms of solidarity, which is illustrated in Figure 19.1, will be described in more detail.

FIG. 19.1.
Two types of solidarity.

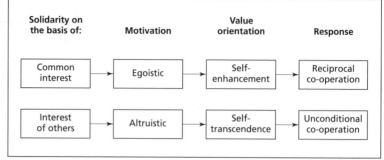

Solidarity on the basis of:	Motivation	Value orientation	Response
Common interest	Egoistic	Self-enhancement	Reciprocal co-operation
Interest of others	Altruistic	Self-transcendence	Unconditional co-operation

Common interests

Solidarity as a social dilemma

The Prisoners' Dilemma

This game holds a particular fascination for psychologists, because it tests co-operation between people: The outcome of the game always depends on the choices both people make and the degree of co-operation between them. In its typical format, the players are given the hypothetical situation of being arrested for working together to commit a crime. The two "prisoners" are kept apart, and each is questioned by the "police". The same suggestion is made to each one: If he or she (A) will agree to confess and give evidence against the other prisoner (B), then A will be released and B will be severely punished. Each player has two choices: to keep silent in co-operation with their partner, or to defect and confess all.

Both players gain when they co-operate with each other, as each will receive the same small punishment (there being little or no evidence against either). If both players confess, they both lose, because there is now evidence against them both and the penalties will be more severe. However, if one remains silent and the other confesses, the confessor gets away without a penalty while the other player receives the severe punishment. The dilemma is, of course, that one person can never be sure of the other person's decision.

The well-known "prisoners' dilemma" offers two choices: co-operation and competition. It is representative of many social situations in which rational egoists tend to choose the competitive alternative, although co-operation would be feasible. Two features are characteristic for prisoners' dilemmas (Messick & Brewer, 1983): (1) Each person has an individual rational choice which he or she prefers over all other choices; (2) If all participants insist upon their individual preference, the outcome for each individual is less positive than if every person selects the "irrational" choice.

These features imply that a conflict arises between an individual's short-term interest and collective interest. An example is the "tragedy of the commons". The tendency to overuse common grazing ground by farmers who have free access to the land is the result of an individual cost–reward calculation: Each individual farmer is better off if the number of sheep that he or she keeps on the common ground is high rather than low. The problem is that other farmers follow the same egoistic plan, leading to an overuse and finally destruction of the common grazing ground. In the long run all farmers would be better off if they restricted their use of the commons, although the immediate incentive to do so is quite weak because they are only interested in maximising their own benefits.

Two-person prisoners' dilemmas are less representative of real-world collective dilemmas than N-person prisoners' dilemmas. Only in N-person dilemmas does anonymity occur with respect to who co-operates and who competes. Because anonymity is a certain protection against being identified as an unco-operative person by others, the temptation to free-ride is stronger in N-person prisoners' dilemmas (Messick & Brewer, 1983).

One motive behind free riding is egoistic maximisation of individual benefits. Yamagishi and Sato (1986) have pointed to another motive (besides self-interest) which gives rise to competitive behaviour: mistrust in the solidarity of other group members and a feeling of helplessness that results from this mistrust. The tragedy of the commons may be either the result of egoistic pursuit of self-interest or the result of the insight that unilateral co-operation is useless, because a single farmer cannot save the common ground by restraining his/her consumption of the public good. As a result, a completely different motivation for disinterest in the collective benefit emerges: fear of uselessness of self-control in a social world in which each other participant seems to be greedy. This motivation not to co-operate is closely linked to mistrust. Lack of trust in the co-operative orientation of others is the cause of feelings of helplessness which motivate fearful nonco-operation.

Both types of motivation—greed and fear—may contribute to the free-riding problem. A questionnaire has been developed to measure these motives. Sample items are (Yamagishi & Sato, 1986, pp. 69–70): "During the oil shock, people rushed to stores to buy a stock of toilet paper because people are concerned only with their own interest and not with the benefit of society" (Fear). "In order to be a successful person in this society, it is important to make use of every opportunity" (Greed).

Empirical results confirmed that fear in addition to greed may contribute to low co-operation. Greed was more relevant when the highest contribution determined the provision of the public good. Fear was a stronger determinant of competition when the lack of co-operation of a single person would be able to destroy the public good (i.e., the lowest contribution determined the provision of the public good; Yamagishi & Sato, 1986). Public goods problems differ with respect to whether they activate either fear or greed. Fear is more likely a hindrance for co-operation if group success depends on the contribution of the least co-operative member, whereas greed is more likely a hindrance if group success depends on the contribution of the most co-operative member.

The distinction between fear and greed is important because it makes clear that besides egoistic pursuit of self-interest, problems of trust and co-ordination among group members are potential causes of lack of co-operation in a prisoners' dilemma situation. One result of the experiment by Yamagishi and Sato (1986) was that friends contributed more to the public good than strangers but only when fear was a relevant hindrance to co-operation. The fear vs greed distinction is related to two basic motivations: fear to lose and hope to win. Fear to lose is grounded in a social scheme of distrust which suggests a negative impression formation towards other group members. Empirical results indicate that in intergroup situations fear is even more pronounced than in interpersonal situations (Insko, Schopler, Hoyle, Dardis, & Graetz, 1990; Schopler et al., 1993). Greed also seems to be more pronounced in intergroup situations, than in interpersonal situations because social support among group members tends to intensify their uncompromising attitude.

Fear as a hindrance to solidarity is especially relevant in the context of pro-environmental behaviour. As mentioned earlier, the structure of problems like air pollution and water contamination is well represented by the paradigm of the tragedy of the commons. In public, communications about pro-environmental behaviour call attention to the insufficient willingness of citizens to contribute to the public good. Much of the debate focuses on irresponsible citizens and governments. Therefore, one may easily get the impression that individual efforts to preserve the environment are useless because others will damage the environment anyway. As a consequence, people are tempted to give up pro-environmental behaviour in order to protect themselves. They mistrust others and the public discussion makes them worry about the possibility that their good intentions could be exploited.

One problem for social systems built on solidarity is the danger that people prefer free riding over contributing (cf. Hinde, 2001). The phenomenon of free riding is most closely linked to public goods that are equally available to all members of society, such as air and water. Free riding is a real threat to solidarity. Voland (1999) assumes that social intelligence has developed so that instances of betrayal and exploitation can be detected. Solidarity is more likely: if people are familiar with each other and trust each other; if they interact with each other for a long period of time; if they stay at the same place and in the same community for a long time; and if sanctions are directed against betrayal and exploitation.

Experimental simulations of prisoners' dilemmas that are played repeatedly have shown that the tit-for-tat strategy is the best choice, in the sense that it maximises individual gains (Axelrod, 1984). Tit-for-tat means that the first choice is co-operation and the following choices are an imitation of the choice of the other player in the previous round. The advantages of tit-for-tat are the following:

- Tit-for-tat does not provoke competitive interactions because it prefers co-operation as long as the other party co-operates. In this sense, tit-for-tat is a fair strategy.
- Tit-for-tat leads to competitive behaviour only if the other party competes.
- Tit-for-tat is built on the principle of reciprocity. The application of the principle is straightforward: It is enough to remember the last action of the opponent when deciding about the next choice.
- Tit-for-tat is generous in the sense that it quickly forgives competitive choices of the other party. Therefore, negative echo effects and the escalation of conflicts are avoided.

Tit-for-tat is especially successful if it is combined with successful partner strategies. In contrast, partner strategies that prefer com-petition and tend to lead to negative outcomes are also a problem for tit-for-tat. Egoistic behaviour of other persons provokes retaliation by tit-for-tat which leads to negative consequences in the long run.

In social relationships that extend over a larger time frame and in which one must expect retaliation to occur, even rational egoists learn that co-operation is the better choice (Pruitt & Kimmel, 1977) and that co-operation is rewarded by high gains. From the experience that mutual co-operation leads to success, the individual develops a preference for the employment of reciprocity in the future. Reciprocal behaviour is acquired as a strategy that may serve several goals simultaneously (e.g., to serve self-interest and to achieve equity in the relationship; Perugini & Gallucci, in press). However, one prerequisite is that the number of co-operative persons exceeds the number of competitive persons in a given population (Orbell & Dawes, 1993). If the proportion of competitive people is high, there is a high likelihood that they will frequently meet each other, and so they will not be able to regularly experience the success resulting from co-operative behaviour.

In the case of repeated interactions, co-operation is profitable for all players in a prisoners' dilemma. Co-operation is expected if the members of the group trust each other. Trust is transmitted by communication. If the partners communicate about the interaction problem, the willingness to co-operate increases (Dawes, McTavish, & Shaklee, 1977; Liebrand, 1984; Sally, 1995). A critical factor is a binding promise to behave in a co-operative way, because that helps the partners in such a situation to trust each other (Chen & Komorita, 1994).

The goal/expectancy theory (Pruitt & Kimmel, 1977) refers to two conditions of joint action: own willingness to co-operate, and the expectancy that the other person will co-operate (i.e., trust). Because of the structure of the prisoners' dilemma, one's own preference for co-operation is not a necessary and sufficient condition of co-operation, because the danger of exploitation exists if the other party is not trustworthy. Goal/expectancy theory predicts that co-operation will be chosen only if the individual expects the other party to co-operate. Social exchange has a time problem because contributions are exchanged with a time lag. In addition, there is an information problem, because it is not certain if the interaction partners will keep their promises. In conclusion, the prisoners' dilemma may be under-stood as a trust dilemma. Constructive approaches include a solution to this trust dilemma, for example on the basis of encouraging com-munication, reduction of risk of being exploited, or positive examples of others.

Reciprocity

"Tit-for-tat" is characterised by mutual exchange. Therefore, it is closely linked to the norm of reciprocity (see Chapter 17). In solidarity movements members are willing to contribute something because they expect to receive something in return. Therefore, joint action on the basis of common interest is egoistically motivated. This egoism is based on the insight that interdependence forces the individuals to work together. The expectation of reciprocity leads to a diffuse obli-gation of repayment. "What one party receives from the other does require some return, so that giving and receiving are mutually contingent" (Gouldner, 1960, p. 169). In correspondence with this proposition, prosocial reciprocity occurs because people help in return for having been helped (Stapleton, Nacci, & Tedeschi, 1973). The theory of reciprocal altruism (Trivers, 1971) goes beyond the description of reciprocity in social life by assuming that altruism which follows the principle of reciprocity is the result of natural evolution (see Chapter 5).

Group deprivation and social identity

The key insight of group deprivation theory is that "the crucial factor in promoting collective action is a shift in causal attribution on the part of the disadvantaged group members from internal attribution for lack of success, for example, insufficient ability, to external attributions, such as discriminatory actions of the dominant group" (Kelly & Breinlinger, 1996, pp. 43–44). Joint action on the basis of group deprivation was investigated in the context of gender relations (Kelly & Breinlinger, 1996). What are the factors that lead to an active involvement in women's groups and campaigns? To answer this question participation was measured with respect to: collective protest (e.g., attending demonstrations); participation in women's groups (e.g., attending meetings); informal participation (e.g., discussing women's issues); and individual protest (e.g., contacting your MP). Several dimensions of social beliefs were measured:

- Collective relative deprivation (e.g., "Women as a group deserve a better deal in society").
- Gender identity (e.g., "I feel strong ties with other women").
- Political efficacy vs powerlessness (e.g., "Every individual can have an impact on the political process").
- Collectivist orientation with respect to gender (e.g., "Women must act as a group rather than as individuals").
- Collectivist orientation in general (e.g., "Working with others is usually more trouble than it's worth" [reverse scoring]).

Relationships between these social beliefs and participation were analysed using multiple regression: Gender identity was the most powerful predictor across the four dependent variables. In addition, feelings of relative deprivation were significantly related to participation in a gender context (except for participation in women's groups). Finally, political efficacy (vs feelings of powerlessness) was positively related to action (except in the domain of informal participation). Collectivist orientations did not contribute much to the explanation of activity. Further analyses underlined the pivotal importance of gender identity as a determinant of reported activism. Gender identity is an indicator of collective identification with other women. In addition, the importance attached to doing something positive for women and self-perception of an activist were relevant predictors of participation in the gender context.

The powerful influence of gender identity on social movement participation is congruent with predictions of social identity theory (Tajfel & Turner, 1986). Specifically, participation is expected to depend on the relative dominance of collective identity and individual identity or "we" and "me", respectively (Simon, 1997). The importance of collective identity for solidarity was also demonstrated in the context of volunteerism (Simon, Stürmer, & Steffens, 2000). Members of an AIDS volunteer service organisation who were either homosexuals or heterosexuals participated in the study. Willingness to volunteer (e.g., fundraising for World AIDS Day, AIDS education in schools) was the dependent variable. A new feature of the study was that collective identification was contrasted with individual identification. Measures of collective identification were obtained with respect to homosexuals and heterosexuals (e.g., "I am aware of my being homosexual/heterosexual)". Individual identification was measured with items that stressed the importance of individuality (e.g., "My individuality is important to me").

The hypothesis was that collective identification with the category of homosexuals would contribute to willingness to volunteer, whereas collective identification with the category of heterosexuals would predict less engagement. In contrast, individual identification was assumed to reduce level of engagement in homosexuals and to increase it in heterosexuals. This complex hypothesis was borne out by the data. For homosexuals, collective identification increased and individual identification decreased willingness to volunteer, whereas for heterosexuals collective identification decreased and individual identification increased it. The results pinpoint collective and individual identification. In combination with other results (Simon et al., 1998) they confirm the role of collective identification as a determinant of participation in social movements. In addition, the results show that individual identification does not always mean indifference but may actually increase willingness to volunteer.

Solidarity on the basis of interests of others

Altruistic motives are relevant in the context of the second type of solidarity, which is characterised by improving the situation of people who exist outside the horizon of personal interests. This unconditional co-operation depends in part on the perception of discrimination against other people which violates value ideals and/or activates feelings of moral obligation. This form of solidarity has gained importance in the last decade. The involvement of people in this form of solidarity is high, as shown by the generous donations in response to catastrophes, such as earthquakes in Turkey and famine in Ethiopia and southern Sudan. A recent example is the "walk for reconciliation" in Sydney, in which 300,000 Australians supporting for the rights of Aborigines participated.

It is likely that willingness to help underprivileged people is based on socialisation in the family (Voland, 1999). Moral socialisation and development of conscience contribute to the willingness to sacrifice time and money for the well-being of strangers who live in remote parts of the world. Such personal sacrifices are in agreement with values that are related to self-transcendence (Feather, 1995).

Social responsibility and human rights

The concept of social responsibility was treated in Chapter 11. Here the link between social responsibility and involvement in human rights will be considered. The Universal Declaration of Human Rights was proclaimed in 1948 by the United Nations. The understanding of the importance and involvement in human rights has changed during the last 50 years (Spini & Doise, 1998). For a long time the protection of human rights was considered to be an exclusive task of governments; however, in recent years the efforts of non-governmental organisations (e.g., Amnesty International) and of democratic people in general have become increasingly important. In correspondence with this trend, the inhabitants of a democratic country are considered to be more responsible for the political situation than the government, a conviction that is not shared in dictatorships, where the belief is exactly the opposite (Staerklé, Clémence, & Doise, 1998).

In general, people associate human rights most strongly with public and political freedom (e.g., that everyone has the right to freedom of opinion and expression; Doise, Spini, Jesuino, Ng, & Emler, 1994). Involvement in human rights may be interpreted as solidarity behaviour. Recent political debates have made it clear that human rights may be pursued on the basis of two quite different strategies: nonviolent and violent.

In a study with university students the relationship between social responsibility and human rights was analysed (Bierhoff, 2000b). Responsibility was measured by four scales: The German version of the Berkowitz and Daniels (1964) questionnaire allows the distinction of two components of responsibility: moral fulfilment of justified expectations of others, and adherence to social rules (see Chapter 11). In addition, responsibility was measured on the Inventory of Motive Structure of Volunteers (see Chapter 21). In this context two dimensions were distinguished: social responsibility (e.g., need to help needy people) and political responsibility (e.g., effort to call attention to societal problems). Attitudes towards human rights were measured with two scales: involvement in human rights (e.g., "I actively participate in human rights demonstrations"), and military enforcement of human rights (e.g., "I support the enforcement of human rights through military interventions").

The association between involvement in human rights and military enforcement of human rights was very low ($r = -.12$). Therefore, two independent dimensions of attitudes towards human rights were empirically identified. The results, which are depicted in Table 19.1, indicate that the correlation between social responsibility and involvement in human rights was significant. The only exception to this result was obtained for adherence to social rules. In contrast, social responsibility and military enforcement of human rights were essentially uncorrelated. In addition, the correlations with involvement in human rights were significantly higher than the correlations with military enforcement of human rights.

TABLE 19.1
Social responsibility and human rights

	Involvement in human rights	Correlations significantly different?	Military enforcement of human rights
SRS Fulfilment	.33**	Yes	.04
SRS Social rules	−.12	No	.12
V Social responsibility	.26*	Yes	.03
V Political responsibility	.25*	Yes	−.10

Source: from Bierhoff, 2000b.

$p < .05$; ** $p < .01$.

SRS = Social Responsibility Scale; V = Inventory of Motive Structure of Volunteers.

The positive relationship between social responsibility and involvement in human rights is corroborated by the result that personal involvement in human rights is positively linked to the endorsement of prosocial value types which can be subsumed under values of self-transcendence (e.g., universalism and benevolence; Spini & Doise, 1998). The correlates of military enforcement of human rights were not found in this prosocial domain. They are likely to be located in beliefs that relate to aggressive sanctioning and Machiavellianism (Fetchenhauer & Bierhoff, 2002).

Guilt over affluence

Guilt over affluence was more fully discussed in Chapter 10. It is highly correlated with felt responsibility to support the needy and prosocial commitment (Montada & Schneider, 1991). Further results highlight the cognitive structure that connects guilt over affluence with prosocial commitments: Perceived interconnection of own advantages and the disadvantages of others is associated with perceived injustice, which in turn is related to readiness for prosocial commitment (Montada & Schneider, 1991). This chain of dependencies supports the assumption that guilt over affluence is a result of perceived injustice on a global level.

Guilt over affluence is not dependent on direct confrontation with the suffering of other people. It is sufficient that the discrimination and unjust treatment of other people is evident (Montada, 2001b). The bad fate of underprivileged groups, which is either directly experienced or reported on in the media, is understood in the context of one's own prosperity. This interconnection is interpreted as an unfair advantage which threatens social norms based on the equality or the need principle. A possible solution is reparation in the sense of doing something good for those who are underprivileged or politically contributing to affirmative action, which promises to reduce future injustice (or use of psychological justifications by denial of discrimination or distorted attributions for the cause of the discrimination).

Empathy

Empathy was more fully discussed in Chapter 9. Much of the research on prosocial behaviour is dominated by Batson's empathy–altruism hypothesis. Batson (1991) assumed that altruistic motivation is based on the ultimate goal of increasing another person's welfare. He equated this type of altruistic motivation with empathic emotion.

If another person is perceived to be in need, feelings of sympathy, compassion, and tenderness are elicited. In correspondence with this assumption it was shown that high-empathy conditions (e.g., high similarity) heighten the readiness to value another person's welfare (e.g., on items like "How important is it to you that this person is happy"; Batson et al., 1995, p. 302).

The likelihood of arousing empathy depends on the characteristics of the other person. Friends and similar others elicit more empathy and co-operation than strangers (Batson, 1995; Van Lange & Kuhlman, 1994). The empathy–altruism hypothesis leads to the conclusion that the scope of prosocial behaviour will be quite limited, as empathy is focused on people who elicit compassion (not on global problems like exploitation of the Third World, population control, or environmental preservation; Batson, Shaw, & Slingsby, 1991). Empirical results confirmed that empathy is not an important determinant of solidarity with people in the Third World, whereas guilt over affluence and moral outrage predicted prosocial commitment in this context (Montada, 2001b). People presumably do not experience strong feelings of empathy with human beings in general, not even with the group of owners of small coffee plantations in Central America.

Principlism and just-world-belief

"Principlism is motivation with the ultimate goal of upholding some moral principle, such as justice or the greatest good for the greatest number" (Batson, 1995, p. 370). Moral principles might motivate solidarity towards members of minorities who are considered underprivileged or victims of misfortune. Principlism is a moral orientation that takes into account moral values and cultural norms which are related to justice as a basis of action. Religion tends to support joint action on behalf of victims and the underprivileged in general. The message of the biblical parable of the Good Samaritan is that we should help those who need our help, as did the Samaritan who saved the man who fell among thieves (cf. Gunnoe, Hetherington, & Reiss, 1999).

The Christian tradition includes cultural virtues that exert an influence on social, political, and economic developments (Jeffries, 1998). Cultural traditions not only define the ultimate goal of living up to moral virtues, they also inspire people to develop social strategies that serve their moral matter of concern. Virtues inspire institutions and organisations that reinforce and disseminate Christian values (Misra & Hicks, 1994).

The solidarity-enhancing message of principlism is frequently limited by moral hypocrisy (Batson et al., 1999). In addition, belief in a just world, which assumes that people get what they deserve (Lerner, 1980; see Chapter 9), is relevant: Because the just world belief does not correspond to what is going on in the world, it is an illusion (cf. Taylor & Brown, 1988, 1994) and serves as a psychological protection against the threat that fate is uncontrollable and arbitrary. If the world is basically a just place, solidary action is not necessary. Religion disseminates ideas that include just world beliefs. Strong believers in a just world admire successful people and derogate the victims of misfortune and underprivileged people in general (Dalbert, 1996). Therefore, it is likely that just world belief reduces the impact of principlism on prosocial inclinations.

Conclusions

Modern themes of solidarity include pollution of the environment, right of political asylum, and the exploitation of the Third World. A classic example of joint action is the success of the Polish trade unions in the early 1980s. Whereas trade unions exemplify joint action in one's own interest, solidarity with the Third World supports people from a different culture who are only loosely linked to the benefactors. The distinction between solidarity on the basis of common interests and on the basis of interests of others centres on a motivational difference. Both forms of solidarity appear superficially similar; however, their motive structure is quite different, indicated by the differences in value orientations that are presumably linked to both forms of solidarity. Whereas self-enhancement provides the value platform of solidarity on the basis of common interests, self-transcendence is the value platform of solidarity on the basis of different interests.

The divergence between both uses of solidarity does not preclude the possibility that gradual transitions between both forms may be observed. The gradual transition from self-transcendence to self-enhancement corresponds to our daily experience. In most cases the separation line between altruistic and egoistic motivation is clear; however, borderline cases may emerge.

Voluntary work engagement in organisations 20

If you are paid for work, it is natural to assume that what you do is done because of the contract between your employer and yourself. However, some jobs, for example working on an assembly line, clearly involve no prosocial behaviour. But when the work is done by teams of co-operating members, prosocial behaviour may contribute to the efficiency of the team. For example, if a customer shows up and the employee who is usually his consultant is absent, a colleague may help out. In general, co-operation of this kind may increase the success of the firm. This episode is an example of self-responsible organisational behaviour (Organ & Ryan, 1995; Podsakoff, Mac-Kenzie, Paine, & Bachrach, 2000).

Self-responsible organisational behaviour

Which factors contribute to the activation of the norm of social responsibility? Organisational citizenship behaviour may be understood as responsible behaviour at the workplace. The parallel goes even further: The basic paradigm in which the activation of the norm of social responsibility was studied is the co-worker–supervisor relationship (Berkowitz & Daniels, 1963). It is assumed that dependency is the crucial factor that elicits prosocial behaviour in such an organisational setting. The hypothesis is that the greater the dependency of the supervisor, the more effort the co-worker will invest on behalf of his/her supervisor.

Dependency was varied by the amount of support that the supervisor needed from his/her co-worker to do his/her job successfully. His/her success was made to directly depend on the contribution of the co-worker. Dependency was manipulated by instructing the co-worker that his/her supervisor's success was, for example, 20% or 80% dependent on the performance of the co-worker. The norm of social responsibility prescribes giving help to people who are dependent on help. The greater the dependency, the stronger the altruistic motivation.

The dependency–responsibility hypothesis was tested in a situation in which a measure of leadership effectiveness was supposedly obtained. Participants in the experiment arrived in pairs at the laboratory. They were informed that the purpose of the experiment was the development of a test of supervisory ability in the context of work samples. One student would play the role of the supervisor who writes down the instructions for the worker (how to make paper boxes), whereas the other student would play the role of the worker who constructs the paper boxes. The students assumed that one of them was the supervisor and the other the worker. In reality, both were informed that they would be the worker, and they were assigned to different rooms. The instructions, which were supposedly prepared by the supervisor, were presented in written form.

After receiving these instructions, the students-as-workers practised producing the paper boxes for 15 minutes (Berkowitz & Daniels, 1963, Exp. 2). After that the students were informed that the assessment of the supervisor was a function of how well he had written the instructions and that the best supervisor would win a five-dollar prize. In the high-dependency condition it was added that the evaluation also heavily depended on the worker's productivity. In the low-dependency condition it was explicitly stated that the supervisor's evaluation was completely independent of the worker's output. Then the 30-minute work period began.

Although the students-as-workers believed that the supervisor would not receive immediate feedback about their performance, a significant effect of dependency emerged. The increase in productivity from the practice period to the work period was much higher in the high-dependency condition than in the low-dependency condition. If the dependency in the worker–supervisor paradigm was gradually increased from 20% to 50% and then 80%, a parallel increase in productivity was observed (Berkowitz & Connor, 1966). A meta-analytic review of 23 studies on the dependency–helping relationship confirmed that high-dependent people receive more help than low-dependent people (Bornstein, 1994).

Prosocial behaviour may play an important role in an organisational context. Patterns of individual behaviour required for organisational functioning include joining and staying in the organisation, role performance in the organisation, and innovative and spontaneous behaviour (Katz & Kahn, 1978). The latter are described as "performance beyond role requirements for accomplishment of organisational functions" (p. 403). These behaviours include five subcategories:

- Informal help-giving among co-workers on the job.
- Protection of the organisation against damage.
- Suggestions for improving methods of production or maintenance.
- Developing oneself by self-initiated learning.
- Spreading of a favourable climate for the organisation in public.

Current theories of organisational leadership have incorporated the prosocial behaviour concept in the analysis of the supervisor–co-worker relationship. For example the vertical dyad linkage approach implies that supervisor and co-worker may form an exchange relationship characterised by mutual support, influence, and trust (Dansereau, Graen, & Haga, 1975; Graen & Uhl-Bien, 1995). In contrast, the exchange may be restricted with respect to trust and commitment, leading to low relationship quality between supervisor and co-worker. The basic idea is that organisational leadership is rooted in dyadic relationships that have either a low or a high quality and which lead either to low or to high levels of co-operation (Graen & Scandura, 1987). Results indicate that the development of an in-group as an expression of high relationship quality is associated with high organisational commitment, work satisfaction, and willingness to invest effort on behalf of the organisation (see also Lee, Carswell, & Allen, 2000).

Three interrelated concepts refer to prosocial behaviour in the organisational setting: organisational citizenship behaviour (OCB), prosocial organisational behaviour (POB), and organisational spontaneity (OS). Among these three concepts OCB is clearly the most popular although each of the three concepts makes its own contribution to organisational psychology.

Organisational citizenship behaviour

Organisational citizenship behaviour is defined as discretionary behaviour of employees that contributes to the effectiveness of the organisation (Organ, 1988). It is based on a multidimensional approach which is grounded on a questionnaire for the assessment of two components of organisational behaviour: altruism and generalised compliance (Smith et al., 1983; see also Organ & Ryan, 1995). Altruism is measured by the following items:

- Helps others who have been absent.
- Volunteers for things that are not required.
- Orients new people even though it is not required.
- Helps others who have heavy work load.

Generalised compliance is represented by the following items:

- Punctuality.
- Takes undeserved breaks (reverse scoring).
- Attendance at work is above the norm.
- Coasts towards the end of the day (reverse scoring).

Results of factor analyses indicate that altruism and generalised compliance refer to independent dimensions (Schnake, 1991). Here the emphasis is on altruism which may be subdivided into several facets that are positively correlated with each other (Podsakoff, Ahearne, & MacKenzie, 1997):

- Helping ("Help each other out if someone falls behind in his/her work").
- Civic virtue ("Provide constructive suggestions about how the crew can improve its effectiveness").
- Sportsmanship ("Always focus on what is wrong with our situation, rather than the positive side" [reverse scoring]).

Regression analyses showed that helping and sportsmanship have a positive relationship with quantity of output, whereas helping alone is a significant predictor of product quality among machine crews in a paper mill (Podsakoff et al., 1997).

With respect to the determinants of altruism, organisational justice is important (Organ, 1988). Higher justice is associated with more prosocial behaviour. Specifically, high procedural fairness, which refers to the treatment of employees by the management (e.g., whether promises are kept, rules of consistency and impartiality are followed, and participation in decisions is possible), fosters OCB at the workplace (Farth, Podsakoff, & Organ, 1990; Podsakoff et al., 2000). In addition, high distributional fairness, which refers to income, privileges, and prospects of promotion, contributes to OCB (Scholl, Cooper, & McKenna, 1987).

Increasing organisational fairness by a training programme contributes to the development of OCB (Skarlicki & Latham, 1996). In a training programme for union officers, principles of procedural fairness and methods of implementation of these principles in the union were discussed. Three months later a higher level of OCB was reported among union members whose officers had participated in the training than among other union members.

Other results that were obtained with employees of a retail store indicate that prosocial personality contributes to OCB (Penner, Midili, & Kegelmeyer, 1997). Prosocial personality was measured by the Prosocial Personality Battery which is based on two prosocial factors: other-oriented empathy (empathy combined with responsibility) and helpfulness (self-reported tendency to act prosocially). In a regression analysis both dimensions of the Prosocial Personality Battery explained significant portions of the variance of the altruism scale of OCB after mood and job satisfaction were controlled for. In addition, other-oriented empathy was a significant predictor of generalised compliance.

In summary, OCB is a multidimensional construct that includes prosocial behaviour in organisations. Specifically, the altruism scale taps the tendency to help other employees during work. Results indicate that it is determined by situational influences (organisational justice) as well as dispositional factors (prosocial personality). These are only two of the many determinants that mould OCB (e.g., mood, job satisfaction, prosocial models, prosocial communication, and work ethics; Bierhoff & Herner, 1999; Schnake, 1991).

Penner et al. (1997) suggest a conceptual model that includes a dynamic element because it is assumed that active involvement in OCB leads to the formation of a citizen role identity which, in turn, is a predictor of long-lasting OCB. In earlier work the concept of role identity was applied as an explanation of repeated blood donations (cf. Piliavin & Callero, 1991; see Chapter 8). The concept of role identity expresses the idea that individuals who behave prosocially in many situations acquire a corresponding self-scheme which functions as a guideline that promotes the further development of the prosocial habit once it has been acquired. As a consequence, if OCB occurs in the present, there is a high likelihood that OCB will occur in the future.

Prosocial organisational behaviour

Prosocial organisational behaviour is defined as "behaviour which is (a) performed by a member of an organisation, (b) directed toward an individual, group, or organisation with whom he or she interacts while carrying out his or her organisational role, and (c) performed with the intention of promoting the welfare of the individual, group, or organisation toward which it is directed" (Brief & Motowidlo, 1986, p. 711).

Examples are: assisting co-workers with job-related and personal matters; showing leniency in personnel decisions (e.g., in perform-ance appraisals); providing services or products to consumers in organisationally consistent ways on the basis of the conviction that the consumer will benefit from the product; helping consumers with personal matters (e.g., giving directions); compliance with organ-isational values, policies, and regulations; and suggesting procedural, administrative, or organisational improvements. These examples illustrate that POB: is either functional or dysfunctional for the organisation involved; refers to prescribed or extra-role behaviours; and is directed towards individuals or the organisation as a whole.

The concept of POB is very broad in order to offer a descriptive framework that encompasses all possible forms of prosocial beha-viour that may occur in organisations. Theorists and researchers have generally focused on the functional forms of prosocial behaviour. They are the most interesting from the perspective of organisational psychology because the promotion of these (e.g., suggesting pro-cedural, administrative, or organisational improvements) is in the best interest of the organisation.

Organisational spontaneity: Mood and group atmosphere as predictors of prosocial behaviour

A third approach that focuses on prosocial behaviour in organisations is organisational spontaneity (George, 1996; George & Brief, 1992). The "performances beyond role requirement", as described by Katz and Kahn (1978), were termed OS, emphasising that they are voluntary, creative in nature, and not predictable on the basis of officially assigned roles. OS is defined as voluntary acts that facilitate the accomplishment of organisational goals (George & Brief, 1992).

It was assumed that the primary work group is of central importance for the development of OS and that positive mood at work is the decisive mediator of the influence of these antecedent variables on prosocial behaviour: individual factors (e.g., extroversion, neuroticism); primary work group characteristics (especially the affective tone of primary work group); contextual characteristics (e.g., the physical environment of work setting); and motivational patterns (i.e., external rewards, internalised motivation).

In accordance with studies on mood states (Watson et al., 1988), it was assumed that mood is a two-dimensional construct with positive and negative mood constituting independent dimensions. Measures of mood are obtained by adjective lists. An example is the Positive and Negative Affect Schedule (PANAS; Watson et al., 1988) which is based on two 10-item subscales. Adjectives that describe feelings and emotions are assessed on a scale from 1 (very slightly or not at all) to 5 (extremely). Time instructions refer either to the moment of answering, the day of answering, or the past few days, etc. Adjectives on the positive affect scale include enthusiastic, interested, determined, excited, and inspired, whereas examples of adjectives on the negative affect scale are scared, afraid, upset, distressed, and jittery. Not surprisingly, respondents report more positive affect than negative affect. Independent of the time frame, the correlation of the positive scale with the negative scale is very low, ranging from −.12 to −.23. Additional data indicate that the PANAS scales show a substantial level of stability over time. This is interpreted as a strong dispositional component of affect because even momentary moods reflect to a certain degree dispositional affectivity. In agreement with such an interpretation, the negative affect scale correlated highly positively with depression, whereas the positive affect scale was negatively correlated with depression.

In a field study (George & Bettenhausen, 1990) prosocial behaviour was aggregated on the group level. Such an aggregation is justified by the fact that individual members of work groups tend to be similar (George, 1996). It is assumed that similar people are attracted to the group, are motivated to stay in the group, and—as a result of group socialisation—become more similar over time (Schneider, 1987). As a result, homogeneity in attitudes and dispositions among group members is expected. Salespeople in 33 shops of a retail chain took part in a questionnaire study which assessed group cohesiveness, socialisation emphasis on prosocial orientation of newcomers to a team, prosocial activities with respect to customers, and voluntary turnover during the last 6 months. In addition, the manager assessed his/her mood, and sales in dollars were obtained at the shop level.

Prosocial behaviour was positively correlated with group cohesiveness, socialisation emphasis, and manager's positive mood. Prosocial behaviour was higher when initial socialisation emphasised a prosocial orientation and when cohesiveness was experienced as high. In addition, the manager's positive mood contributed to the occurrence of prosocial activities. Sales performance correlated with prosocial behaviour ($r = .33$). Therefore, emphasis on prosocial activities led to better business success. In addition, manager's positive mood also contributed positively to sales ($r = .35$). These results show that, at least in the context of retail shops, prosocial behaviour may heighten productivity (cf., Podsakoff et al., 1997).

In another study (George, 1991) in a retail chain, measures of positive mood of salespersons and of their prosocial behaviour (on a modified version of the altruism scale of the OCB questionnaire) were obtained. In addition, customer-service behaviour was taken into account, which was understood as prosocial behaviour directed at customers. A sample item is "informs a customer of the important features of an item". Data were analysed on an individual basis. Altruism scale score and customer-service behaviour, which were both rated by the supervisor, correlated quite highly ($r = .53$). Only one predictor influenced both indicators of OS in the same way, namely positive mood ($r = .24$ and $r = .26$, respectively). Finally, customer-service behaviour correlated positively with sales ($r = .20$). Together these studies show that mood is a consistent predictor of OS both at the individual and at the group level. This generalisation corresponds with many other studies which show that positive mood is a reliable predictor of prosocial behaviour (Carlson et al., 1988). Positive mood is also a determinant of volunteer work (see Chapter 21).

The conceptual framework of OS is the basis of the model of voluntary work motivation (Bierhoff & Müller, 1999) which distinguishes between input variables, mediator variables, and output variables (see Figure 20.1). Compared with OS, the model simplifies the side of the antecedent variables by distinguishing only between dispositional and situational variables. On a more theoretical level, the model considers the finding that perceived group atmosphere correlates higher with co-operative support than mood at work. Therefore, a chain of influence is postulated which includes two mediator variables: mood at work, which influences group atmosphere, which in turn is the proximal variable influencing co-operative support.

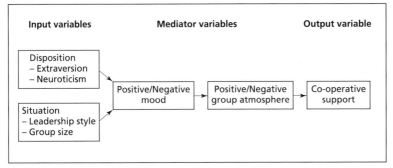

FIG. 20.1.
Model of voluntary
work motivation (from
Bierhoff & Müller, 1999,
p. 181). Reproduced
with the kind
permission of Hans
Huber AG (publishers).

Bierhoff and Müller (1999) replicated the finding that mood was correlated with prosocial behaviour as measured by the altruism scale of the OCB. Results that were computed on the group level indicated that positive mood correlated positively ($r = .60$) and negative mood negatively ($r = -.45$) with prosocial behaviour in the group. In addition, a measure of group atmosphere was included which was a modification of the Team Climate Inventory (Anderson & West, 1994). This questionnaire contains two subscales that measure positive and negative group atmosphere. Ten attributes constitute each subscale. Positive group atmosphere is based on attributes like active, open, and friendly. Negative group atmosphere refers to attributes like tense, chilly, and irritated. Results indicate that both positive and negative group atmosphere are highly correlated with prosocial behaviour in the group ($r = .81$ and $r = -.55$, respectively). These correlations with prosocial behaviour tend to be higher than those with positive and negative mood.

The voluntary work motivation model attempts to account for the fact that group atmosphere is a stronger correlate of prosocial behaviour than mood. We assume that the transient feelings constitute a meaningful sequence that goes from individual affect to group affect which is the proximal cause of altruism in the work setting. The justification for this sequence is straightforward: People have feelings while they attend the work setting. These feelings are represented by the two-dimensional structure described by the PANAS and other related scales. These feelings of individual team members are transformed into the group affective tone by averaging across the group members (cf. George, 1996).

Our results, as those of other researchers, indicate that individual moods of group members are quite similar, justifying aggregation into a global team measure (Bierhoff & Müller, 1999). By the very fact that people work in teams they experience the group atmosphere, which itself is two-dimensional with a positive and a negative dimension involved. While group atmosphere is directly related to the experience in groups, it is at the same time an expression of individual moods of group members.

Path-analytic results that refer to the results reported earlier support the voluntary work motivation model (Müller & Bierhoff, 2001). It was assumed that mood influences group atmosphere, which in turn influences prosocial behaviour. The analysis was carried out at the group level. Three data sets were obtained across 3 months in a longitudinal design. At the first measurement point data on mood and group atmosphere were obtained. The second and third measurement points included measures of prosocial behaviour. Prosocial behaviour was represented by a latent variable which was predicted by mood via group atmosphere. The model explained a substantial proportion of variance in prosocial behaviour. The fit of the LISREL model was satisfactory, indicating that the correlation structure corresponds quite well with the proposed model. Specifically, mood and group atmosphere constitute a chain of influence on prosocial behaviour. Whereas positive feelings exert a positive influence on prosocial behaviour, negative feelings turn out to be negative determinants of prosocial behaviour.

From an applied perspective, feeling states in work groups are relevant for the activation of self-organisation among group members (Rohmann, Bierhoff, & Müller, 2000). Specifically, group atmosphere seems to be a key variable for the development and maintenance of self-initiative and organisational responsibility.

Comparison between OCB, POB, and OS

The comparison between OCB, POB, and OS reveals similarities and differences (George & Brief, 1992). Whereas POB includes both functional and dysfunctional behaviours, the other two constructs are limited to functional behaviour patterns only. Whereas POB and OCB include role-prescribed as well as extra-role behaviours, OS is limited to extra-role behaviours. If we consider only the altruism factor in OCB, it corresponds with OS in this respect. OS and the subcategories of the altruism dimension of OCB refer to active behaviours that demand the self-initiative of the employees. In contrast, POB is broader and also includes passive adherence to rules, which also applies to the generalised compliance factor of OCB. Note that the subcategory of sportsmanship in OCB also describes a passive response, namely to do nothing if some conditions at work are not optimal or temporarily worse than what is expected.

moment. Responses were given on 9-point scales with 1 meaning "completely unimportant" and 9 meaning "very important" as a reason.

The Inventory of Motive Structure of Volunteers was developed to measure nine motives (e.g., social attachment, social responsibility). The 9-factor structure of the inventory on which item construction was based was confirmed by the results of factor analyses. The following motive scales were formed:

- Social attachment (e.g., "want to find people with whom I am connected by a shared activity").
- Self experience (e.g., "want to learn something about my own strengths").
- Social responsibility (e.g., "feel obligated to help people who are worse off than I am").
- Self-esteem/recognition (e.g., "want to do something significant").
- Identification with the organisation (e.g., "influence of members of my family").
- Compensation for stress at work (e.g., "want a satisfying task as a change from what I do on the job").
- Career advancement (e.g., "interested in getting a foot in the door of the organisation because I would like to work in it").
- Political responsibility (e.g., "want to contribute to societal change").
- Personal experience (e.g., "relied on the organisation in the past for help").

Each scale comprised 5 to 10 items. The internal consistency of the scales was satisfactory with the lowest reliability occurring for identification with the organisation. Of all subscales, social and political responsibility were rated as most important (as current motives $M = 6.0$ and $M = 5.6$, respectively), whereas the means of the importance ratings on the other scales were lower (current motives ranging between $M = 3.1$ for career development and $M = 5.0$ for self-experience). The correlations between scales were positive and varied between .20 and .60. (The factor structures on the item level revealed many double loadings.) The scale correlations were similar in both instruction conditions.

Omoto and Snyder (1995, p. 675) distinguished five motivation scales in their study of volunteers who were members of AIDS support organisations. Specifically the scales refer to values (e.g., "because I enjoy helping other people"); understanding (e.g., "to understand AIDS and what it does to people"); personal development (e.g., "to meet new people and make new friends"); community concern (e.g., "to help members of the gay community"); and esteem enhancement (e.g., "to feel needed"). Each scale, which consisted of five items, was internally consistent. In addition, positive correlations were found across the different scales.

Clary et al. (1998) developed the Volunteer Functions Inventory which partially follows the earlier motivation questionnaire, although the items were newly formulated and did not specifically address AIDS service organisations. The values and understanding scales correspond with the earlier scales with identical names. Enhancement refers to promotion of self-esteem and making new friends, whereas social refers to encouragement by members of the social network of the volunteer. Finally, career refers to career development, and protective refers to defence against negative feelings (e.g., "Volunteering is a good escape from my own troubles"; Clary et al., 1998, p. 1520).

Internal consistency of the 5-item scales was good. The factor structure of the scales confirmed the distinction between six scales and was similar in samples of volunteers and students. Nearly all items loaded unequivocally on their factor. Additional results showed that the functions assessed by the Volunteer Functions Inventory were quite stable over a 4-week interval with test–retest correlations in the range of .64 to .78. Finally, volunteers who experienced their work as confirming their primary functions as measured by the Volunteer Function Inventory were more satisfied with their service and more committed.

Frisch and Gerrard (1981) investigated the motives of volunteers of the Red Cross. A factor analysis of the items of their questionnaire revealed two underlying dimensions which were labelled altruistic and egoistic motives. Similar results were obtained on the basis of the nine motive scales (Tietz & Bierhoff, 1996). A factor analysis revealed two factors, which were labelled altruistic and egoistic orientation, both for current and for prior motives. The altruistic factor was characterised by high loadings of political and social responsibility. The egoistic factor comprised high loadings of all other scales. Social attachment, self-experience, self-esteem/recognition, compensation for stress at work, and career development were unequivocally located on this factor. Two scales exhibited double loadings: identification with the organisation, and personal experience. In summary, the basic structure of the Inventory of Motive Structure of Volunteers is two-dimensional with one factor corresponding to altruism and the other factor corresponding to egoism. This pattern of results is an indirect confirmation of Batson's (1991) distinction between ego-istically and altruistically motivated prosocial behaviour.

Reports of volunteer motives are only minimally influenced by social desirability (Allen & Rushton, 1983). This result was confirmed in a study by Bierhoff, Burkart, & Wörsdörfer (1995) which showed that motives of volunteers correlated at a low level with social desirability (see also Benson et al., 1980).

Role-identity model

Volunteers assessed their current motives and their prior motives when they first began working for their organisation. Although the factor structure of both data sets was similar, an important difference also emerged: The importance of current motives was rated higher than the importance of prior motives (Tietz & Bierhoff, 1996).

This result may be interpreted as a socialisation effect. Long-term activity in the organisation may contribute to an increase in the importance of motives that are fulfilled by volunteer work. Such a socialisation effect is compatible with the role-identity model (Grube & Piliavin, 2000; Penner & Finkelstein, 1998). The habit of volunteering, which is acquired over months of participation, influences personal inferences about what kind of person the volunteer is; the result is a colouring of the self-scheme in correspondence with the habit that has emerged. Such personal inferences on the basis of the regular experi-ence of a volunteer may evoke processes of self-perception which lead to attitudes that are more congruent with the activity.

This speculation needs corroboration by empirical data. In one study of volunteers, involvement in volunteering was predicted by organisational commitment. In a multiple regression analysis, volun-teer role identity accounted for the relationship between commitment and involvement (Grube & Piliavin, 2000). Although this result does not prove that processes of self-perception modify the role identity of the volunteers, it demonstrates that role identity is an important determinant of volunteering which mediates the influence of organ-isational commitment.

Indirect evidence that supports the role-identity model was derived from the fact that prior amount of volunteer activity was a better predictor of later amount of volunteer activity than prior organisational commitment (Penner & Finkelstein, 1998). Organisational commitment was measured by items that referred to feelings of acceptance by the organisation, desire for additional involvement in the organisation, and importance that was attributed to attending activities within the organisation. Amount of volunteer activities was measured by two items that referred to time spent volunteering and number of organisational meetings attended. Data were collected in a three-wave panel study of volunteers in an AIDS service organisation. The time span between each of the three waves was 4 to 5 months. It was assumed that processes of role identity would be visible if the influence of organisational commitment at time 1 on activity level at time 3 was be mediated by activity level at time 2. In support of the role-identity formation hypothesis, organisational commitment at time 1 was a significant predictor of activity level at time 3. However, inclusion of activity level at time 2 in the regression equation rendered organisational commitment nonsignificant. Therefore, the common variance of amount of volunteer activity at time 3 and organisational commitment at time 1 was mediated by volunteer activity at time 2.

These results taken together yield impressive support for the role-identity model of volunteering. Because the role-identity model is compatible with the result that collective identity contributes to solidarity (see Chapter 19), the importance of identity-promoting processes in the explanation of volunteering is underscored.

Altruistic personality, motives of volunteers, and religious orientation

Altruistic personality, which was measured by the Prosocial Personality Battery (see Chapter 20), correlated positively with length of service in an AIDS service organisation (Penner & Finkelstein, 1998). Both dimensions of prosocial personality that are tapped by the questionnaire—other-oriented empathy and helpfulness—were significant correlates of length of service. In another study, communal orientation measured by items like "I believe people should go out of their way to be helpful" (cf. Clark & Mills, 1993) was a correlate of intentions to support the homeless (Bryan, Hammer, & Fisher, 2000). A summary of the results of 19 studies on community mental health workers, which compared motives and personality variables of volunteers and nonvolunteers, showed that volunteers scored higher on empathy, social responsibility, intimacy of self-disclosure, competence, internal control, self-esteem, and emotional stability compared with nonvolunteers (Allen & Rushton, 1983).

How do the motive scales relate to the amount of commitment and evaluation of the activity? In the study by Tietz and Bierhoff (1996) level of commitment was measured by the average number of hours per week that were devoted to the volunteer activity as reported by respondents. Evaluation was measured by satisfaction with the activity. All nine motive scales were entered into a stepwise multiple regression analysis with commitment as the dependent variable. Results indicated that social responsibility was the only significant predictor that explained 4.4% of the variance in commitment. For evaluation of the activity the same pattern of results emerged: Only social responsibility was a significant predictor, explaining 6.8% of the variance. In another study, social responsibility predicted number of volunteer commitments (Moschner, 1998). Volunteers who worked for several organisations scored higher on social responsibility than volunteers who worked for only one organisation. Furthermore, in the three-wave study of AIDS volunteers (Penner & Finkelstein, 1998) humanitarian values were a positive predictor of the extent to which their volunteer work had brought them into direct contact with someone who had AIDS at time 3.

As mentioned earlier, egoistic attitudes may also contribute to involvement in volunteering. In a study of volunteers who worked in different organisations (e.g., Amnesty International, prevention of child abuse), social attachment was the strongest predictor of number of hours worked per week and explained 14.4% of the variance (Küpper & Bierhoff, 1999). In the study of AIDS volunteers, which was described more fully earlier, the functions of knowledge and understanding, and to a lesser extent humanitarian values, were significant predictors of willingness to volunteer (Simon et al., 2000). Identification with the organisation also contributed to explaining willingness.

In addition, importance of religion was an independent predictor of number of hours worked as a volunteer (Küpper & Bierhoff, 1999). Volunteers who considered religion to be more important tended to be more involved than volunteers who were not so much interested in religion. Research on rescuers of Jews in Nazi Europe also indicates that religious commitment was associated with rescuing Jews (Oliner & Oliner, 1988). Social attachment and importance of religion explained 27% of the variance in involvement as volunteers (Küpper & Bierhoff, 1999). In the study of AIDS volunteers, social integration, humanitarian values, skill development, and knowledge and understanding explained 15% of the willingness to volunteer (Simon et al., 2000).

In summary, involvement in volunteering is influenced by a cluster of attitudes that includes altruistic and egoistic dimensions. Taking this evidence into account, welfare organisations are well advised if they base their organisation of volunteering on the knowledge that altruistic and egoistic motives (as well as religious orientation and identification with the organisation) are relevant. It is likely that social responsibility is an important factor for volunteering in general, whereas egoistic motives such as social attachment facilitate the maintenance of involvement in volunteerism.

Research on voluntary work engagement (see earlier) provides further advice: As predicted by the attraction–selection–attrition hypothesis, groups will be more successful if group leaders and group members express similar attitudes and values (Schneider, 1987). It is likely that volunteers who express similar values tend to co-operate well with one another. For example, if group members agree that social responsibility is an important concern, it is likely that harmony and co-operation will be higher than if they disagree.

Conclusions

Involvement in volunteer work has been measured differently in different studies. Whereas some researchers focused on willingness to volunteer, others concentrated on length of service, amount of hours spent working for the volunteer organisation, or number of welfare organisations in which respondents were active. It is likely that the results differ somewhat depending on the type of measure used. Specifically, intentions might be predicted better by verbal measures than by measures that reflect time spent working (Küpper & Bierhoff, 1999). On the one hand, verbal measures of attitudes and intentions tend to correlate highly, whereas correlations of attitudes with reports of behaviour tend to be lower (Ajzen, 1988). On the other hand, the time people spend on a given activity is determined by a multitude of factors. Therefore, it is unlikely that high proportions of explained variance of time spent on an activity will be found on the basis of a single factor.

Among the factors that were identified as predictors of amount of volunteer work and willingness to volunteer several clusters are of relevance:

- Social identity as reflected in volunteer role identity and collective identity (e.g., as homosexuals).
- Identification with the organisation.
- Altruistic personality.
- Religious orientation as reflected in the personal importance assigned to religion.
- Volunteer motives which encompass egoistic and altruistic motives.

Beyond the determinants of volunteer work that have been discussed in this chapter, there is one other relevant determinant which was also important as an explanation of organisational citizenship behaviour (see Chapter 20): positive feelings about being a volunteer were positively correlated with length of service (Penner & Finkelstein, 1998).

Postscript

In the introduction, the five major parts of this book were outlined: the social phenomenon of prosocial behaviour; learning and development; processes of prosocial behaviour; theories; and applications. Each part contributes to the existing body of knowledge about prosocial behaviour. This knowledge base includes, for example, information about expected levels of prosocial behaviour in specific situations, which was summarised in Chapter 3 as a hypothetical profile of helpfulness. In addition, it contains information on the development of prosocial behaviour, which was presented in Chapter 7 and Chapter 8, as well as information on determinants of prosocial behaviour (summarised in Chapters 12–17). Finally, the knowledge base also informs about issues of application: How have theoretical insights been used to set up guidelines for the solution of social problems? How can theories contribute to structuring specific real-life situations in such a way that desirable goals are attained?

In the following, a number of conclusions and prospects for the future are discussed. With respect to conclusions, the role of theories is emphasised at the level of community as the unit of analysis, and at the level of the individual as the unit of analysis, respectively. With respect to theories, sociobiology, the altruism question, and issues of individual differences are considered. With respect to prospects for the future, expectations concerning the direction of future research on prosocial behaviour are outlined.

The community as the unit of analysis

Whereas most of the research on prosocial behaviour uses the individual as the unit of analysis, research on cultural differences indicates that substantial variation in the amount of prosocial behaviour emerges on the level of the community. Some communities have a social climate that is more favourable to prosocial behaviour than others. For example, a systematic relationship was reported between population density and level of prosocial behaviour, with higher levels of density being associated with lower levels of helping.

What are the reasons for this intriguing association between demographic variables and prosocial behaviour which was found on the level of the community? As was mentioned in Chapter 3, one explanation for the correlation with level of population density is offered by the information overload hypothesis. Higher population density is likely to elicit frequent information overload in the individual, who—as a consequence of population density—is confronted with a multitude of social and nonsocial (e.g., noise) stimuli. This is a good example for an important lesson that is revealed by this kind of research: Prosocial behaviour is embedded in spatial environments and influenced by cultural factors that predict its likelihood on a community level. Therefore, a more comprehensive understanding is achieved if we broaden our perspective and consider evidence from environmental psychology, which indicates that environmental factors influence cognitive processing, which in turn shapes behaviour in the environment. Urbanism and population growth are also important topics of social change in the modern world, which will undoubtedly influence the occurrence of prosocial behaviour in real life. Another explanation of the inhibiting effect of high social density is based on the notion of diffusion of responsibility. Both of these explanations imply that population growth may have negative side-effects, in that it reduces the likelihood that humans will act with compassion and empathy.

Another important result that points to the influence of social status as a moderator of prosocial behaviour is that higher cost of living in a community is negatively correlated with willingness to act prosocially. As cost of living is highly correlated with per capita income, the conclusion is justified that certain facets of social status are systematically linked with prosocial behaviour. This result also has important implications for the prediction of the level of prosocial behaviour in societies in which the income level is rising. It points to the possibility of the emergence of a society in which a combination of high income and low compassion will lead to wealth but cold-heartedness.

It would be interesting to develop a more comprehensive socio-logical understanding of prosocial behaviour, which is currently only beginning to emerge. Social status, which is related to economic differences between social classes, constitutes one of the most important systems of inequality in society. Whereas the independence of the upper and middle classes rests upon possessions and high-level skills, the solidary working-class communities are charac-terised by a social tradition of reciprocal support systems. It would be interesting to find out more about these social roots of prosocial behaviour. Some of this is reflected in the discussion of solidarity in Chapter 19. Theoretical concepts like social dilemma, group deprivation, and reciprocity ideology are of pivotal theoretical importance in this debate.

These brief notes on the explanation of community-dependent helping point to the important role of theory in our understanding of prosocial behaviour. Although theoretical lines have been visible in many places in this book, and one part has dealt with them exclusively, the emphasis was placed more on what is known about prosocial behaviour. This final chapter is a welcome opportunity to say more about the theoretical integration of research on prosocial behaviour.

Sociobiological perspective and socialisation processes

One important theoretical viewpoint is based on the biological perspective, which was described more fully in Chapter 5. Sociobiology offers new insights into the dynamics of prosocial behaviour. For example, the assumed effect of felt oneness on willingness to help (see Chapter 13) may be understood on the basis of the hypothesis that kin selection leads to prosocial behaviour among relatives because one indicator of relatedness is closeness, which presumably fosters felt oneness. The principle of inclusive fitness leads to the prediction that prosocial behaviour, which is exemplified by the parent who cares for his or her child, is extended to relatives and—in general—to persons who might fall into the category of relatives. The sociobiological unit is reproductive success, which presumably is not only pursued by egoistic goal setting but also by prosocial behaviour that is directed by possible indicators of relatedness (e.g., similarity, closeness, and attachment).

These considerations invite us to look for connections between human and animal behaviour. Although such a connection may be possible, it is not very likely. Information processing in humans occurs on a much higher level than in lower animals. Furthermore, humans live in highly developed cultural settings, which are increasingly creating a technological reality, detached from evolutionary processes. The principles of inclusive fitness are applicable to humans as well as to lower animals. They imply that situational factors that indicate relatedness are important in directing prosocial behaviour, favouring those persons as help-recipients who are similar or close. However, the situational dynamics in which humans act are more complex than those in which lower animals behave. One reason why human action is not easily understood on the basis of animal behaviour is that the social-cognitive dimension has to be considered in humans. For example, the step-by-step development of empathy, guilt feelings, and responsibility is unique in human beings, not matched by comparable processes in lower animals.

Nevertheless, some viable sociobiological hypotheses on human prosocial behaviour remain which are supported by empirical evidence. For example, the predisposition to develop empathy and guilt feelings may well be innate. As described in Chapters 7, 9, and 10, twin studies show that a significant heritability component is present in empathy, guilt feelings, and prosocial behaviour. This heritability component is especially evident in 1-year-olds but tends to diminish as the cumulative influences of socialisation increase in older children.

The interplay of innate factors and socialisation processes leads to the conclusion that a one-sided perspective focusing exclusively on innate factors or social-learning factors is too simple. Rather, these factors represent two sides of the same coin. The empirical issue is to determine which share of prosocial development is due to innate factors and which is due to social factors that impinge on the child during socialisation and contribute to the internalisation of conscience, guilt feelings, and responsible action as a citizen in a democratic society. Evidence for a genetic basis was found in adolescents' adherence to the norm of social responsibility (see Chapter 11), but environmental factors played a decisive role in the change of responsibility across different age groups.

In addition, strong cultural variation was found in the meaning of responsible action, with Far Eastern cultures putting more emphasis on the fulfilment of social roles and connected obligations than Western cultures (Shaver & Schutte, 2001). As a consequence, in Far Eastern cultures the assignment of responsibility takes social roles and the social network into account, whereas in Western cultures responsibility is assigned to a single person, ignoring the social embeddedness of his or her deeds. This cultural difference is explained by the stronger emphasis on the connectedness of the individual in the group in Far Eastern cultures, whereas in Western cultures the dominant ideology is characterised by the independence of the (isolated) self.

Cultural collectivism, which is found in Far Eastern cultures, is based on the viewpoint that the self is anchored in a social system represented by family, school, and profession. The social value system includes cultural proclivities that either encourage solidary action or the pursuit of individual advantages. The Far Eastern viewpoint seems to correspond more with what research on the development of the self-scheme has found than the Western viewpoint (cf. Baumeister, 1998b). There is some reason to consider the Far Eastern approach to social responsibility as more in line with the scientific data base than the American and European approach. In fact, the Western perspective has been described as an example of the fundamental attribution error—that is, action that is under the control of situational constraints is erroneously interpreted as an outcome of individual decisions, which rests upon dispositions and personal preferences (Shaver & Schutte, 2001).

Additional research that points to systematic differences in prosocial moral reasoning between Spanish-speaking and English-speaking cultures may also be mentioned as evidence on cultural determination of prosocial orientation (see Chapter 7). In summary, genetic factors as determinants of prosocial behaviour co-exist with socialisation influences. It may well be argued that the genetic propensities include the child's openness to social influence. Appropriate comparisons (e.g., between cultures) show that substantial differences in social value orientation and prosocial moral reasoning are found, which are relevant for prosocial behaviour in general and for social responsibility in particular. It is likely that the importance of genetic factors is considered to be higher in a homogeneous culture, whereas the importance of socialisation is assessed as higher when comparing culturally heterogeneous societies.

Situational vs dispositional explanations

The interplay of situational and dispositional factors in prosocial behaviour is another important theoretical issue. Whereas many studies demonstrated situational influence on prosocial behaviour, leading to the conviction that prosocial behaviour is primarily under situational control—a conviction that emerged in the context of the studies on bystander apathy and diffusion of responsibility in the late 1960s and early 1970s—much research evidence has accumulated in the meantime which shows that dispositional factors related to the concept of altruistic personality are equally relevant. This new insight is strengthened by the results of a longitudinal study which spans nearly 20 years and reveals substantial individual stability in the level of prosocial behaviour (Eisenberg et al., 1999). According to these researchers, the results show that this individual stability can be taken as an indication that the altruistic personality disposition is formed in early childhood.

Additional evidence summarised in Chapters 18–21 indicates that prosocial behaviour in applied settings is influenced by dispositional variables. Because the study of situational determinants of prosocial behaviour is usually performed in the laboratory, which tends to bring out situational influences in a very strong way, the study of prosocial behaviour in everyday situations is an important methodological advancement. In general, results of studies conducted outside the laboratory indicate that situational factors are important determinants of prosocial behaviour, as demonstrated by the number effect of bystanders, which has been confirmed in the laboratory as well as in field studies and which may also contribute to differences on the community level with higher population density leading to less inclination of the inhabitants to act prosocially. But field studies also show that situational factors are not all-important, because systematic individual differences in prosocial behaviour are observed. For example, volunteers who work several hours a week on behalf of the needy differ in their personality structure from nonvolunteers (see Chapter 21).

These individual differences, which influence willingness to act prosocially, may be summarised under the heading of the virtues of temperance, fortitude, justice, charity, and prudence (Jeffries, 1998). These five virtues illustrate that the altruistic personality is a multidimensional construct. It is not based on a single personality dimension, but instead several facets of personality contribute to prosocial behaviour, including impulse control, initiative, fairness-related convictions, compassion, and far-sightedness. It is possible that traits influence the prosocial behaviour of some persons more consistently than that of others (for a similar argument see Harter & Jackson, 1992). If this is so, the prosocial behaviour of some people might be more under the control of traits than that of others, whose prosocial behaviour is more under the control of situation-specific influences. These are speculations that might be investigated in future studies on the altruistic personality.

Theorising on these individual differences is in an early stage, but a promising new approach is the theoretical model of Eisenberg and her colleagues (e.g., Eisenberg & Fabes, 1992) in which emotional regulation (vs impulsivity) and emotionality (i.e., emotional intensity) are taken into account as predictors of empathic concern or sympathy. The balancing role of emotional regulation in interaction with emotionality is an indication of the foundation of empathic feelings in temperamental factors. Temperament, which is in part innately determined, seems to regulate emotional experiences in general and empathy in particular. Other results which were reported in Chapter 14 confirm the importance of emotionality as a factor in prosocial behaviour because children who exhibited underarousal responded with less empathy in an experimental situation than children who showed high reactivity in the temperament assessment.

Altruism vs egoism

No topic has contributed more to the interest in prosocial behaviour since the 1980s than the distinction between egoistically and altruistically motivated helping. In Chapter 1 a distinction was drawn between prosocial behaviour and altruism as a subset of prosocial behaviour. It was pointed out that the definition of altruism implies that the helper is motivated by the goal of reducing the suffering of the victim, which is related to empathic concern elicited in the situation. Conceptually, prosocial behaviour is based on either egoistically motivated goals or altruistically motivated goals.

Although it is theoretically easy to draw a distinction between prosocial behaviour in general and altruism specifically, it is much harder to obtain experimental evidence that unequivocally confirms the relevance of the assumed altruistic motive system (see Chapter 13). Dozens of experiments have been conducted in the attempt to prove the existence of an altruistic motive system that is independent of the egoistic motive system. Batson (1991) has been quite ingenious in devising experimental designs that allow conclusions about the issue of true altruism. The sum of his research points to a high likelihood that a unitary altruistic motive system directs human behaviour in a number of situations. This altruistic motive system is effective either in isolation or—what seems to be more common—in combination with the egoistic motive system. As a result, in many real-life examples a mixture of altruistic and egoistic goals seems to motivate prosocial behaviour.

The question of whether a second motive system beyond the egoistic one exists is obviously of great theoretical importance, because the default assumption in social psychology is that human behaviour is understandable if one assumes that people are motivated to act selfishly. The same assumption is implicit in sociobiology, although here selfishness is attributed to the genes instead of the person. As we have seen, sociobiology is able to account for prosocial behaviour as a dominant strategy under specific circumstances, some of which are equivalent to the conditions that are assumed to facilitate empathic concern (e.g., similarity and closeness between helper and help-recipient). In the future, theoretical discussions may clarify whether the altruistic motive system proposed by Batson (1991) is compatible with the principle of inclusive fitness.

The dual-process model of prosocial behaviour coincides with dual-process notions in other psychological theories which are based on the distinction of two separate processes (Chaiken & Trope, 1999). An example is the elaboration likelihood theory of Petty and Wegener (1999) which contrasts a central route of persuasion with a peripheral route. Other dual-process theories contrast spontaneous and intentional inferences (Uleman, 1999) and deliberative and implemental mindsets in the control of action (Gollwitzer & Bayer, 1999). Dual-process theories are based on the assumption that the explanation of complex responses, which include inconsistent responses in different settings, rests on the activation of two independent processes. In most of these theories, a fast, associative, and unconscious process is supplemented by a slow, controlled, and conscious process. Sigmund Freud was one of the first dual-process theorists because he drew a distinction between irrational processes that take place in the Id, and Ego processes that are described as much more rational and cognitive than the Id processes.

Dual-process notions imply basic questions in terms of systems theory (Gilbert, 1999): Batson's model assumes that either one process (e.g., the altruistic one) is activated while the other process is not activated, or that both are activated simultaneously. In addition, his model is based on the assumption that both processes control prosocial behaviour independently of each other. It would be interesting to formulate and test a model of prosocial behaviour in which one process (e.g., the egoistic one) modifies the other process (e.g., the altruistic one). Such corrective models have the advantage that they can keep a system's stability high (Gilbert, 1999). Another parallel between Batson's dual-process models and dual-process models in social cognition is that one of the processes (i.e., the egoistic process) is more under intentional control than the other process (i.e., the altruistic process), which seems to occur spontaneously and

References

Ainsworth, M.D.S., Blehar, M.C., Waters, S., & Wall, S. (1978). *Patterns of attachment: A psychological study of the strange situation*. Hillsdale, NJ: Lawrence Erlbaum Associates Inc.

Ajzen, I. (1988). *Attitudes, personality, and behaviour*. Milton Keynes, UK: Open University Press.

Ajzen, I. (1991). The theory of planned behavior. *Organizational Behavior and Human Decision Processes, 50*, 179–211.

Alexander, R.D. (1987). *The biology of moral systems*. Chicago: Aldine.

Allen, H. (1972). Bystander intervention and helping on the subway. In L. Bickman & T. Henchy (Eds.), *Beyond the laboratory: Field research in social psychology* (pp. 22–33). New York: McGraw-Hill.

Allen, N., & Rushton, J.P. (1983). Personality characteristics of community mental health volunteers: A review. *Journal of Voluntary Action Research, 12*, 36–49.

Alloy, L.B., & Abramson, L.Y. (1979). Judgments of contingency in depressed and nondepressed students: Sadder but wiser? *Journal of Experimental Psychology: General, 108*, 441–485.

Allport, F.H. (1933). *Institutional behavior*. Chapel Hill, NC: University of North Carolina Press.

Altmann, J. (1974). Observational study of behavior: Sampling methods. *Behaviour, 49*, 227–263.

Amato, P.R. (1983). Helping behavior in urban and rural environments: Field studies based on a taxonomic organization of helping episodes. *Journal of Personality and Social Psychology, 45*, 571–586.

Amato, P.R. (1985). An investigation of planned helping behavior. *Journal of Research in Personality, 19*, 232–252.

Amato, P.R., & Bradshaw, R. (1985). An exploratory study of people's reasons for delaying or avoiding helpseeking. *Australian Psychologist, 20*, 21–31.

Amato, P.R., & Saunders, J. (1985). The perceived dimensions of help-seeking episodes. *Social Psychology Quarterly, 48*, 130–138.

Anderson, N.R., & West, M.A. (1994). *The team climate inventory: Manual and user's guide*. Windsor, UK: Nelson Press.

Archer, J. (2001). Evolutionary social psychology. In M. Hewstone & W. Stroebe (Eds.), *Introduction to social psychology* (pp. 23–46). Oxford: Blackwell.

Archer, R.L., Diaz-Loving, R., Gollwitzer, P.M., Davis, M.H., & Foushee, H.C. (1981). The role of dispositional empathy and social evaluation in the empathic mediation of helping. *Journal of Personality and Social Psychology, 40*, 786–796.

Aron, A., Aron, E.N., & Smollan, D. (1992). Inclusion of Other in the Self Scale and the structure of interpersonal closeness. *Journal of Personality and Social Psychology, 63*, 596–612.

Aronfreed, J. (1976). Moral development from the standpoint of a general psychological theory. In T. Lickona (Ed.), *Moral development and behavior* (pp. 54–69). New York: Holt.

Auhagen, A.E. (2000). On the psychology of meaning of life. *Swiss Journal of Psychology, 59*, 34–48.

Auhagen, A.E. (2001). Responsibility in everyday life. In A.E. Auhagen & H.W. Bierhoff (Eds.), *Responsibility—the many faces of a phenomenon* (pp. 61–77). London: Routledge.

Auhagen, A.E., & Bierhoff, H.W. (Eds.). (2001). *Responsibility—the many faces of a social phenomenon.* London: Routledge.

Axelrod, L.J., & Lehman, D.R. (1993). Responding to environmental concern: What factors guide individual action? *Journal of Environmental Psychology, 13*(2), 149–159.

Axelrod, R. (1984). *The evolution of cooperation.* New York: Basic Books.

Bagozzi, R.P. (1986). Attitude formation under the theory of reasoned action and a purposeful behaviour reformulation. *British Journal of Social Psychology, 25*, 95–107.

Bakan, D. (1966). *The duality of human existence.* Boston: Beacon.

Bamberg, S. (2000). The promotion of new behavior by forming an implementation intention—results of a field experiment. *Journal of Applied Social Psychology, 30*, 1903–1922.

Bandura, A. (1971). Analysis of modeling processes. In A. Bandura (Ed.), *Psychological modeling* (pp. 1–62). Chicago: Aldine.

Bandura, A. (1978). The self system in reciprocal determinism. *American Psychologist, 33*, 344–358.

Bandura, A. (1986). *Social foundation of thought and action: A social cognitive theory.* Englewood Cliffs, NJ: Prentice-Hall.

Bandura, A. (1997). *Self-efficacy: The exercise of control.* New York: Freeman.

Bandura, A., Grusec, J.E., & Menlove, F.L. (1967). Some social determinants of self-monitoring reinforcement systems. *Journal of Personality and Social Psychology, 5*, 449–455.

Bandura, A., & Huston, A.C. (1961). Identification as a process of incidental learning. *Journal of Abnormal and Social Psychology, 63*, 311–318.

Bandura, A., Ross, D., & Ross, S.A. (1963). Imitation of film-mediated aggressive models. *Journal of Abnormal and Social Psychology, 66*, 3–11.

Bandura, A., & Walters, R.H. (1963). *Social learning and personality development.* New York: Holt.

Barnett, M.A., Howard, J.A., King, L.M., & Dino, G.A. (1980). Antecedents of empathy: Retrospective accounts of early socialization. *Personality and Social Psychology Bulletin, 6*, 361–365.

Barnett, M.A., Howard, J.A., King, L.M., & Dino, G.A. (1981). Helping behavior and the transfer of empathy. *Journal of Social Psychology, 115*, 125–132.

Baron, R.A. (1987). Interviewer's moods and reactions to job applicants: The influence of affective states on applied social judgments. *Journal of Applied Social Psychology, 17*, 911–926.

Baron, R.S. (1986). Distraction-conflict theory: Progress and problems. In L. Berkowitz (Ed.), *Advances in experimental social psychology* (Vol. 19, pp. 1–40). New York: Academic Press.

Barrett, K.C. (1998). The origins of guilt in early childhood. In J. Bybee (Ed.), *Guilt and children* (pp. 75–90). San Diego, CA: Academic Press.

Batson, C.D. (1983). Sociobiology and the role of religion in promoting social behaviour: An alternative view. *Journal of Personality and Psychology, 45*, 1380–1385.

Batson, C.D. (1987). Prosocial motivation: Is it ever truly altruistic? In L. Berkowitz (Ed.), *Advances in experimental social psychology* (Vol. 20, pp. 65–122). San Diego, CA: Academic Press.

Batson, C.D. (1991). *The altruism question: Toward a social-psychological answer.* Hillsdale, NJ: Lawrence Erlbaum Associates Inc.

Batson, C.D. (1995). Prosocial motivation: Why do we help others? In A. Tesser (Ed.), *Advanced social psychology* (pp. 333–381). New York: McGraw-Hill.

Batson, C.D. (2000). Unto others: A service . . . and a disservice. *Journal of Consciousness Studies, 7,* 207–210.

Batson, C.D., Batson, J.G., Griffitt, C.A., Barrientos, S., Brandt, J.R., Sprengelmeyer, P., & Bayly, M.J. (1989). Negative-state relief and the empathy–altruism hypothesis. *Journal of Personality and Social Psychology, 56,* 922–933.

Batson, C.D., Bolen, M.H., Cross, J.A., & Neuringer-Benefiel, H.E. (1986). Where is the altruism in the prosocial personality? *Journal of Personality and Social Psychology, 50,* 212–20.

Batson, C.D., Duncan, B.D., Ackerman, P., Buckley, T., & Birch, K. (1981). Is empathic emotion a source of altruistic motivation? *Journal of Personality and Social Psychology, 40,* 290–302.

Batson, C.D., Dyck, J., Brandt, J.R., Batson, J.G., Powell, A.L., McMaster, M.R., & Griffitt, C. (1988). Five studies testing two new egoistic alternatives to the empathy–altruism hypothesis. *Journal of Personality and Social Psychology, 55,* 52–77.

Batson, C.D., Fultz, J., & Schoenrade, P.A. (1987). Distress and empathy: Two qualitatively distinct vicarious emotions with different motivational consequences. *Journal of Personality, 55,* 21–39.

Batson, C.D., Harris, A.C., McCaul, K.D., Davis, M., & Schmidt, T. (1979). Compassion or compliance: Alternative dispositional attributions for one's helping behavior. *Social Psychology Quarterly, 42,* 405–409.

Batson, C.D., O'Quinn, K., Fultz, J., Vanderplas, M., & Isen, A. (1983). Self-reported distress and empathy and egoistic versus altruistic motivation for helping. *Journal of Personality and Social Psychology, 45,* 706–718.

Batson, C.D., Sager, K., Garst, E., Kang, M., Rubchinsky, K., & Dawson, K. (1997). Is empathy-induced helping due to self–other merging? *Journal of Personality and Social Psychology, 73,* 495—509.

Batson, C.D., Shaw, L.L., & Slingsby, J.K. (1991). Practical implications of the empathy–altruism hypothesis: Some reflections. In L. Montada & H.W. Bierhoff (Eds.), *Altruism in social systems* (pp. 27–40). Lewiston, NY: Hogrefe.

Batson, C.D., Thompson, E.R., Seuferling, G., Whitney, H., & Strongman, J.A. (1999). Moral hypocrisy: Appearing moral to oneself without being so. *Journal of Personality and Social Psychology, 77,* 525–537.

Batson, C.D., Turk, C.L., Shaw, L.L., & Klein, T.R. (1995). Information function of empathic emotion: Learning that we value the other's welfare. *Journal of Personality and Social Psychology, 68,* 300–313.

Baumann, D.J., Cialdini, R.B., & Kenrick, D.L. (1981). Altruism as hedonism: Helping and self-gratification as equivalent responses. *Journal of Personality and Social Psychology, 40,* 1039–1046.

Baumeister, R.F. (1998a). Inducing guilt. In J. Bybee (Ed.), *Guilt and children* (pp. 127–138). San Diego, CA: Academic Press.

Baumeister, R.F. (1998b). The self. In D.T. Gilbert, S.T. Fiske, & G. Lindzey (Eds.), *The handbook of social psychology* (Vol. 1, pp. 680–740). Boston: McGraw-Hill.

Baumeister, R.F., & Leary, M.R. (1995). The need to belong: Desire for interpersonal attachments as a fundamental human motivation. *Psychological Bulletin, 117,* 497–529.

Baumeister, R.F., Reis, H.T., & Delespaul, P.A.E.G. (1995a). Subjective and experiential correlates of guilt in everyday life. *Personality and Social Psychology Bulletin, 21,* 1256–1268.

Baumeister, R.F., Stillwell, A.M., & Heatherton, T.F. (1994). Guilt: An interpersonal approach. *Psychological Bulletin, 115,* 243–267.

Baumeister, R.F., Stillwell, A.M., & Heatherton, T.F. (1995b). Interpersonal aspects of guilt: Evidence from narrative studies. In J.P. Tangney & K.W. Fischer (Eds.), *Self-conscious emotions* (pp. 255–273). New York: Guilford Press.

Bayertz, K. (1998). Begriff und Problem der Solidarität [Concept and problem of solidarity]. In K. Byertz (Ed.), *Solidarität [Solidarity]* (pp. 11–53). Frankfurt: Suhrkamp.

Bem, D. (1972). Self-perception theory. In L. Berkowitz (Ed.), *Advances in experimental social psychology* (Vol. 6, pp. 1–62). New York: Academic Press.

Benson, P.L., Dehority, J., Garman, L., Hanson, E., Hochschwender, U., Lebold, C., Rohr, R., & Sullivan, J. (1980). Intrapersonal correlates of nonspontaneous helping behavior. *Journal of Social Psychology, 110,* 87–95.

Bentler, P.M., & Speckart, G. (1979). Models of attitude–behavior relations. *Psychological Review, 86,* 452–464.

Bergson, H. (1933). *The two sources of morality and religion* [A. Audra & C. Brereton, Trans.]. New York: Holt.

Berkowitz, L., & Connor, W.H. (1966). Success, failure, and social responsibility. *Journal of Personality and Social Psychology, 4,* 664–669.

Berkowitz, L., & Daniels, L.R. (1963). Responsibility and dependency. *Journal of Abnormal and Social Psychology, 66,* 429–437.

Berkowitz, L., & Daniels, L.R. (1964). Affecting the salience of the social responsibility norm: Effects of past help on the response to dependency relationships. *Journal of Abnormal and Social Psychology, 68,* 275–281.

Berkowitz, L., & Heimer, K. (1989). On the construction of the anger experience: Aversive events and negative priming in the formation of feelings. In L. Berkowitz (Ed.), *Advances in experimental social psychology* (Vol. 22, pp. 1–37). San Diego, CA: Academic Press.

Berkowitz, L., & Lutterman, K.G. (1968). The traditional socially responsible personality. *Public Opinion Quarterly, 32,* 169–187.

Berscheid, E., & Walster, E. (1967). When does a harm-doer compensate a victim? *Journal of Personality and Social Psychology, 6,* 435–441.

Bickman, L., & Kamzan, M. (1973). The effect of race and need on helping behavior. *Journal of Social Psychology, 89,* 73–77.

Bierhoff, H.W. (1983). Wie hilfreich ist der Mensch? [How helpful is the human being?] *Bild der Wissenschaft, 20*(12), 118–126.

Bierhoff, H.W. (1988). Affect, cognition, and prosocial behavior. In H. Fiedler & J. Forgas (Eds.), *Affect, cognition and social behavior* (pp. 167–182). Toronto: Hogrefe.

Bierhoff, H.W. (2000a). Skala der sozialen Verantwortung nach Berkowitz und Daniels: Entwicklung und Validierung [Berkowitz and Daniels' Social Responsibility Scale: Development and validation]. *Diagnostica, 46,* 18–28.

Bierhoff, H.W. (2000b). *Zwei Dimensionen von Einstellungen zu den Menschenrechten [Two dimensions of attitudes toward human rights].* 42. Kongress der Deutschen Gesellschaft für Psychologie in Jena (Paper presented at the 42nd convention of the German Psychological Association in Jena).

Bierhoff, H.W. (2001a). Prosocial behaviour. In M. Hewstone & W. Stroebe (Eds.), *Introduction to social psychology* (3rd ed.). Oxford: Blackwell.

Bierhoff, H.W. (2001b). Responsibility and altruism: The role of volunteerism. In A.E. Auhagen & H.W. Bierhoff (Eds.), *Responsibility—the many faces of a phenomenon* (pp. 149–166). London: Routledge.

Bierhoff, H.W. (2002). Just world, social responsibility and helping behaviour. In M. Ross & D.T. Miller (Eds.), *The justice motive in everyday life* (pp. 189–203). New York: Cambridge University Press.

Bierhoff, H.W., Burkart, T., & Wörsdörfer, C. (1995). Einstellungen und Motive ehrenamtlicher Helfer [Attitudes and motives of volunteers]. *Gruppendynamik, 26*, 373–386.

Bierhoff, H.W., & Herner, M.J. (1999). Arbeitsengagement aus freien Stücken: Zur Rolle der Führung [Voluntary work engagement: The role of leadership]. In G. Schreyögg & J. Sydow (Eds.), *Managementforschung* [Management research] (Vol. 9, pp. 55–87). Berlin: deGruyter.

Bierhoff, H.W., Klein, R., & Kramp, P. (1986). Social context and perceived justice. In H.W. Bierhoff, R.L. Cohen, & J. Greenberg (Eds.), *Justice in social relations* (pp. 165–185). New York: Plenum.

Bierhoff, H.W., Klein, R., & Kramp, P. (1990). Hemmschwellen zur Hilfeleistung. Untersuchung der Ursachen und Empfehlung von Maßnahmen zum Abbau [Factors inhibiting the giving of help: Studies on the causes and recommendations on how to reduce them]. *Forschungsberichte des Bundesanstalt für Straßenwesen* [*Research reports of the Federal Agency of Road Traffic*]. Aachen: Mainz.

Bierhoff, H.W., Klein, R., & Kramp, P. (1991). Evidence for the altruistic personality from data on accident research. *Journal of Personality, 59*, 263–280.

Bierhoff, H.W., & Küpper, B. (1999). Social psychology of solidarity. In K. Bayertz (Ed.), *Solidarity* (pp. 133–156). Dordrecht: Kluwer.

Bierhoff, H.W., & Müller, G.F. (1999). Positive feelings, cooperative support, and performance: Organizational spontaneity in project groups. *Swiss Journal of Social Psychology, 58*, 180–190.

Bischof-Köhler, D. (1991). The development of empathy in infants. In M.E. Lamb & H. Keller (Eds.), *Infant development: Perspectives from German-speaking countries* (pp. 1–33). Hillsdale, NJ: Lawrence Erlbaum Associates Inc.

Black, J.S., Stern, P.C., & Elsworth, J.T. (1985). Personal and contextual influences on household energy adaptations. *Journal of Applied Psychology, 70*, 3–21.

Boggiano, A.K., & Ruble, D.N. (1979). Competence and the overjustification effect: A developmental study. *Journal of Personality and Social Psychology, 37*, 1462–1468.

Bornstein, R.F. (1994). Dependency as a social cue: A meta-analytic review of research on the dependency-helping relationship. *Journal of Research in Personality, 28*, 182–213.

Bowlby, J. (1969). *Attachment*. New York: Basic Books.

Brehm, J.W., & Cole, A.H. (1966). Effect of a favor which reduces freedom. *Journal of Personality and Social Psychology, 3*, 420–426.

Brehm, S.S., & Brehm, J.W. (1981). *Psychological reactance: A theory of freedom and control*. New York: Academic Press.

Brickman, P., Kidder, L.H., Coates, D., Rabinowitz, V., Cohn, E., & Karuza, J. (1983). The dilemmas of helping:

Making aid fair and effective. In J.D. Fisher, A. Nadler, & B.M. DePaulo (Eds.), *New directions in helping* (Vol. 1, pp. 17–49). New York: Academic Press.

Brief, A.P., & Motowidlo, S.J. (1986). Prosocial organizational behavior. *Academy of Management Review, 11,* 710–725.

Broll, L., Gross, A.E., & Piliavin, I. (1974). Effects of offered and requested help on help seeking and reactions to being helped. *Journal of Applied Social Psychology, 4,* 244–258.

Brown, P., & Elliot, R. (1965). Control of aggression in nursery school class. *Journal of Experimental Child Psychology, 2,* 103–107.

Brown, R., & Herrnstein, R.J. (1975). *Psychology.* London: Methuen.

Bryan, A.D., Hammer, J.C., & Fisher, J.D. (2000). Whose hands reach out to the homeless? Patterns of helping among high and low communally oriented individuals. *Journal of Applied Social Psychology, 30,* 887–905.

Bryan, J.H. (1972). Why children help: A review. *Journal of Social Issues, 28*(3), 87–104.

Bryan, J.H., & Schwartz, T. (1971). Effects of film material upon children's behavior. *Psychological Bulletin, 75,* 50–59.

Bryan, J.H., & Test, M. (1967). Models and helping. Naturalistic studies in aiding behaviour. *Journal of Personality and Social Psychology, 6,* 400–407.

Bryan, J.H., & Walbek, N.H. (1970). Preaching and practising generosity: Children's action and reactions. *Child Development, 41,* 329–353.

Bryant, B.K. (1982). An index of empathy for children and adolescents. *Child Development, 53,* 413–425.

Burleson, B.R., Albrecht, T.L., Goldsmith, D.J., & Sarason, I.G. (1994). Introduction: The communication of social support. In B.R. Burleson, T.L. Albrecht, & I.G. Sarason (Eds.), *Communication of social support* (pp. xi–xxx). Thousand Oaks, CA: Sage.

Buss, A.H., & Plomin, R.A. (1975). *A temperament theory of personality development.* New York: Wiley.

Butler, R., & Neuman, O. (1995). Effects of task and ego achievement goals on help-seeking behaviors and attitudes. *Journal of Educational Psychology, 87,* 261–271.

Buunk, B.P. Collins, R.L., Taylor, S.E., VanYperen, N.W., & Dakof, G.A. (1990). The affective consequences of social comparison: Either direction has its ups and downs. *Journal of Personality and Social Psychology, 59,* 1238–1249.

Buunk, B.P., VanYperen, N.W., Taylor, S.E., & Collins, R.L. (1991). Social comparison and the drive upward revisited: Affiliation as a response to marital stress. *European Journal of Social Psychology, 21,* 529–546.

Bybee, J. (1998). The emergence of gender. Differences in guilt during adolescence. In J. Bybee (Ed.), *Guilt and children* (pp. 113–125). San Diego, CA: Academic Press.

Bybee, J., Merisca, R., & Velasco, R. (1998). The development of reactions to guilt-producing events. In J. Bybee (Ed.), *Guilt and children* (pp. 185–213). San Diego, CA: Academic Press.

Bybee, J., & Quiles, Z.N. (1998). Guilt and mental health. In J. Bybee (Ed.), *Guilt and children* (pp. 269–291). San Diego, CA: Academic Press.

Bybee, J.A., Zigler, E., Berliner, D., & Merisca, R. (1996). Guilt, guilt-evoking events, depression and eating disorders. *Current Psychology: Developmental, Learning, Personality, Social, 15,* 113–127.

Byrne, D. (1971). *The attraction paradigm.* New York: Academic Press.

Cairns, R.B., & Green, J.A. (1979). How to assess personality and social patterns: Observations or ratings? In R.B. Cairns

(Ed.), *The analysis of social interactions* (pp. 209–226). Hillsdale, NJ: Lawrence Erlbaum Associates Inc.

Campbell, D.T. (1965). Ethnocentric and other altruistic motives. In D. Levine (Ed.), *Nebraska Symposium on Motivation* (Vol. 13, pp. 283–311). Lincoln, NE: University of Nebraska Press.

Campbell, D.T. (1975). On the conflicts between biological and social evolution and between psychology and moral tradition. *American Psychologist, 30,* 1103–1126.

Carlo, G., Eisenberg, N., & Knight, G.P. (1992). An objective measure of prosocial moral reasoning. *Journal of Research in Adolescence, 2,* 331–349.

Carlo, G., Eisenberg, N., Troyer, D., Switzer, G., & Speer, A.L. (1991a). The altruistic personality: In what contexts is it apparent? *Journal of Personality and Social Psychology, 61,* 450–458.

Carlo, G., Fabes, R.A., Laible, D., & Kupanoff, K. (1999). Early adolescence and prosocial/moral behavior II: The role of social and contextual influences. *Journal of Early Adolescence, 19,* 133–147.

Carlo, G., Knight, G.P., Eisenberg, N., & Rotenberg, C. (1991b). Cognitive processes and prosocial behaviour among children: The role of affective attributions and reconciliations. *Developmental Psychology, 27,* 456–461.

Carlo, G., Koller, S.H., & Eisenberg, N. (1998). Prosocial moral reasoning in institutionalized delinquent, orphaned, and noninstitutionalized Brazilian adolescents. *Journal of Adolescent Research, 13,* 363–376.

Carlo, G., Koller, S.H., Eisenberg, N., Da Silva, M.S., & Frohlich, C.B. (1996). A cross-national study on the relations among prosocial moral reasoning, gender role orientation, and prosocial behaviors. *Developmental Psychology, 32,* 231–240.

Carlsmith, J.M., & Gross, A.E. (1969). Some effects of guilt on compliance. *Journal of Personality and Social Psychology, 11,* 232–239.

Carlson, M., Charlin, V., & Miller, N. (1988). Positive mood and helping behavior: A test of six hypotheses. *Journal of Personality and Social Psychology, 55,* 211–29.

Carlson, M., & Miller, N. (1987). Explanation of the relation between negative mood and helping. *Psychological Bulletin, 102,* 91–108.

Carver, C.S., & Scheier, M.F. (1990). Origins and functions of positive and negative affect: A control-process view. *Psychological Review, 97,* 19–35.

Castro, M.A. (1974). Reactions to receiving aid as a function of cost to donor and opportunity to aid. *Journal of Applied Social Psychology, 4,* 194–209.

Chen, X.P., & Komorita, S.S. (1994). The effects of communication and commitment in a public goods social dilemma. *Organizational Behavior and Human Decision Processes, 60,* 367–386.

Chaiken, S., & Trope, Y. (Eds.). (1999). *Dual-process theories in social psychology.* New York: Guilford Press.

Christie, R., & Geis, F. (1968). *Studies in Machiavellianism.* New York: Academic Press.

Cialdini, R.B., Borden, R.J., Thorne, A., Walker, M.R., Freeman, S., & Sloan, L.R. (1976). Basking in reflected glory: Three (football) field studies. *Journal of Personality and Social Psychology, 34,* 366–375.

Cialdini, R.B., Brown, S.L., Lewis, B.P., Luce, C., & Neuberg, S.L. (1997). Reinterpreting the empathy–altruism relationship: When one into one equals oneness. *Journal of Personality and Social Psychology, 73,* 481–494.

Cialdini, R.B., Darby, B.L., & Vincent, J.E. (1973). Transgression and altruism: A case for hedonism. *Journal of Experimental Social Psychology, 9,* 502–516.

Cialdini, R.B., Kallgren, C.A., & Reno, R.R. (1991). A focus theory of normative conduct: A theoretical refinement and reevaluation of the role of norms in human behavior. In M.P. Zanna (Ed.), *Advances in experimental social psychology* (Vol. 24, pp. 202–234). San Diego, CA: Academic Press.

Cialdini, R.B., & Kenrick, D.T. (1976). Altruism as hedonism: A social development perspective on the relationship of negative mood state and helping. *Journal of Personality and Social Psychology, 34,* 907–914.

Cialdini, R.B., Kenrick, D.T., & Baumann, D.J. (1982). Effects of mood on prosocial behavior in children and adults. In N. Eisenberg (Ed.), *The development of prosocial behavior* (pp. 339–359). New York: Academic Press.

Cialdini, R.B., Schaller, M., Houlihan, D., Arps, K., Fultz, J., & Beaman, A.L. (1987). Empathy-based helping: It is selflessly or selfishly motivated? *Journal of Personality and Social Psychology, 52,* 749–758.

Citrin, J., & Muste, C. (1999). Trust in government. In J.P. Robinson, P.R. Shaver, & L.S. Wrightsman (Eds.), *Measurement of political attitudes* (pp. 465–532). San Diego, CA: Academic Press.

Clark, M.S., & Mills, J. (1993). The difference between communal and exchange relationships: What it is and is not. *Personality and Social Psychology Bulletin, 19,* 684–691.

Clark, R.D. (1976). On the Piliavin and Piliavin model of helping behavior: Costs are in the eye of the beholder. *Journal of Applied Social Psychology, 6,* 322–328.

Clark, R.D., & Word, L.E. (1972). Why don't bystanders help? Because of ambiguity? *Journal of Personality and Social Psychology, 24,* 392–400.

Clark, R.D., & Word, L.E. (1974). Where is the apathetic bystander? Situational characteristics of the emergency. *Journal of Personality and Social Psychology, 29,* 279–287.

Clary, E.G., & Miller, J. (1986). Socialization and situational influences on sustained altruism. *Child Development, 57,* 1358–1369.

Clary, E.G., & Snyder, M. (1991). A functional analysis of altruism and prosocial behavior: The case of volunteerism. In M.S. Clark (Ed.), *Prosocial behavior* (pp. 119–148). Newbury Park, CA: Sage.

Clary, E.G., Snyder, M., Ridge, R.D., Copeland, J., Stukas, A.A., Haugen, J., & Miene, P. (1998). Understanding and assessing the motivations of volunteers: A functional approach. *Journal of Personality and Social Psychology, 74,* 1516–1530.

Coates, B., Pusser, H.E., & Goodman, I. (1976). The influence of "Sesame Street" and "Mister Roger's Neighborhood" on children's social behaviour in the preschool. *Child Development, 47,* 138–144.

Coke, J.S., Batson, C.D., & McDavis, K. (1978). Empathic mediation of helping: A two-stage model. *Journal of Personality and Social Psychology, 36,* 752–766.

Cole, E.R., & Stewart, A.J. (1996). Meanings of political participation among black and white women: Political identity and social responsibility. *Journal of Personality and Social Psychology, 71,* 130–140.

Coleman, J.S. (1990). *Foundations of social theory.* Cambridge, MA: Harvard University Press.

Cook, S.W., & Pelfrey, M. (1985). Reactions to being helped in cooperating interracial groups: A context effect. *Journal of Personality and Social Psychology, 49,* 1231–1245.

Cottrell, N.B. (1972). Social facilitation. In C.G. McClintock (Ed.), *Experimental social psychology* (pp. 185–236). New York: Holt.

Crick, N.R., & Dodge, K.A. (1994). A review and reformulation of social information-processing mechanisms in children's social adjustment. *Psychological Bulletin, 115,* 74–101.

Crittenden, K.S., & Bae, H. (1994). Self-effacement and social responsibility. *American Behavioral Scientist, 37,* 653–671.

Cronbach, L.J. (1990). *Essentials of psychological testing* (5th ed.). New York: Harper.

Crowne, D.P., & Marlowe, D. (1960). A new scale of social desirability independent of psychopathology. *Journal of Consulting Psychology, 24,* 349–354.

Dalbert, C. (1996). *Über den Umgang mit Ungerechtigkeit [On dealing with injustice].* Bern: Huber.

Dalbert, C. (1999). The world is more just for me than generally: About the personal belief in a just world scale's validity. *Social Justice Research, 12,* 79–98.

D'Amato, M.R. (1969). Instrumental conditioning. In M.H. Marx (Ed.), *Learning processes* (pp. 33–75). New York: Macmillan.

Dansereau, F., Graen, G., & Haga, W.J. (1975). A vertical dyad linkage approach to leadership within formal organizations: A longitudinal investigation of the role making process. *Organizational Behavior and Human Performance, 13,* 46–78.

Darley, J., & Cooper, J. (1972). The "clean for Gene" phenomenon: The effects of students' appearance on political campaigning. *Journal of Applied Social Psychology, 2,* 24–33.

Darley, J.M., & Batson, C.D. (1973). From Jerusalem to Jericho: A study of situational and dispositional variables in helping behaviour. *Journal of Personality and Social Psychology, 27,* 100–108.

Darley, J.M., & Latané, B. (1968). Bystander intervention in emergencies: Diffusion of responsibility. *Journal of Personality and Social Psychology, 8,* 377–383.

Darley, J.M., Teger, A.I., & Lewis, L.D. (1973). Do groups always inhibit individuals' responses to potential emergencies? *Journal of Personality and Social Psychology, 26,* 395–399.

Darlington, R.B., & Macker, C.E. (1966). Displacement of guilt-produced altruistic behavior. *Journal of Personality and Social Psychology, 4,* 442–443.

Davis, M.H. (1983a). Empathic concern and the muscular dystrophy telethon: Empathy as a multidimensional construct. *Personality and Social Psychology Bulletin, 9,* 223–229.

Davis, M.H. (1983b). Measuring individual differences in empathy: Evidence for a multidimensional approach. *Journal of Personality and Social Psychology, 44,* 113–126.

Davis, M.H. (1994). *Empathy: A social psychological approach.* Madison, WI: Brown & Benchmark.

Davis, M.H., & Franzoi, S.L. (1991). Stability and change in adolescent self-consciousness and empathy. *Journal of Research in Personality, 25,* 70–87.

Dawes, R.M., McTavish, J., & Shaklee, H. (1977). Behavior, communication and assumptions about other people's behavior in a common dilemma situation. *Journal of Personality and Social Psychology, 35,* 1–11.

Deaux, K. (1974). Anonymous altruism: Extending the lost letter technique. *Journal of Social Psychology, 92,* 61–66.

Deci, E.L., & Ryan, R.M. (1985). *Intrinsic motivation and self-determination of human behavior.* New York: Plenum.

DeJong, W. (1979). An examination of self-perception mediation of the foot-in-the-door effect. *Journal of Personality and Social Psychology, 37,* 2221–2239.

DePaulo, D.M., Brown, P.L., Ishii, S., & Fisher, J.D. (1981). Help that works: The effects of aid on subsequent task performance. *Journal of Personality and Social Psychology, 41,* 478–487.

DePaulo, B.M., & Fisher, J.D. (1980). The costs of asking for help. *Basic and Applied Social Psychology, 1,* 23–35.

Derryberry, D., & Rothbart, M.K. (1988). Arousal, affect, and attention as components of temperament. *Journal of Personality and Social Psychology, 55,* 958–966.

Deutsch, M. (1986). Cooperation, conflict and justice. In H.W. Bierhoff, R.L. Cohen, & J. Greenberg (Eds.), *Justice and social relations* (pp. 3–18). New York: Plenum.

Dietz, T., Stern, P.C., & Guagnano, G.A. (1998). Social structural and social psychological bases of environmental concern. *Environment and Behavior, 30,* 450–471.

Dillard, J.P., & Hunter, J.E. (1989). On the use and interpretation of the Emotional Empathy Scale, the Self-Consciousness Scales, and the Self-Monitoring Scale. *Communication Research, 16,* 104–129.

Dlugokinski, E.L., & Firestone, I.J. (1974). Other centeredness and susceptibility to charitable appeals: Effects of perceived discipline. *Developmental Psychology, 10,* 21–28.

Doise, W., Spini, D., Jesuino, J.C., Ng, S., & Emler, N. (1994). Values and perceived conflicts in the social representations of human rights: Feasibility of a cross-national study. *Swiss Journal of Psychology, 53,* 240–251.

Dovidio, J.F., Allen, J., & Schroeder, D.A. (1990). The specificity of empathy-induced helping: Evidence for altruism. *Journal of Personality and Social Psychology, 59,* 249–260.

Dovidio, J.F., & Morris, W.N. (1975). Effects of stress and commonality of fate on helping behavior. *Journal of Personality and Social Psychology, 31,* 145–149.

Durkheim, E. (1997). *On the division of labor in society* [W.D. Halls, Trans.]. New York: Free Press. (Original work published 1902.)

Durkin, K. (1995). *Developmental social psychology.* Oxford: Blackwell.

Eagly, A.H. (1987). *Sex differences in social behavior: A social-role interpretation.* Hillsdale, NJ: Lawrence Erlbaum Associates Inc.

Eagly, A.H., & Crowley, M. (1986). Gender and helping behavior: A meta-analytic review of the social psychological literature. *Psychological Bulletin, 100,* 283–308.

Earley, P.C. (1994). Self or group? Cultural effects of training on self-efficacy and performance. *Administrative Science Quarterly, 39,* 89–117.

Eisenberg, N. (1982). The development of reasoning regarding prosocial behavior. In N. Eisenberg (Ed.), *The development of prosocial behavior* (pp. 219–249). New York: Academic Press.

Eisenberg, N. (1986). *Altruistic emotion, cognition, and behavior.* Hillsdale, NJ: Lawrence Erlbaum Associates Inc.

Eisenberg, N. (2000). Emotion, regulation, and moral development. *Annual Review of Psychology, 51,* 665–697.

Eisenberg, N., Cameron, E., Tryon, K., & Dodez, R. (1981). Socialization of prosocial behavior in the preschool classroom. *Developmental Psychology, 17,* 773–782.

Eisenberg, N., Carlo, G., Murphy, B., & van Court, P. (1995). Prosocial development in late adolescence: A longitudinal study. *Child Development, 66,* 1179–1197.

Eisenberg, N., Cialdini, R.B., McCreath, H., & Shell, R. (1987a). Consistency-based compliance: When and why do children become vulnerable? *Journal of Personality and Social Psychology, 52,* 1174–1181.

Eisenberg, N., Cialdini, R.B., McCreath, H., & Shell, R. (1989a). Consistency-based compliance in children: When and why do consistency procedures have immediate effects? *International Journal of Behavioural Development, 12,* 351–367.

Eisenberg, N., & Fabes, R.A. (1990). Empathy: Conceptualization, assessment, and relation to prosocial behavior. *Motivation and Emotion, 14,* 131–149.

Eisenberg, N., & Fabes, R.A. (1992). Emotion, regulation, and the development of social competence. In M.S. Clark (Ed.), *Emotion and social behavior* (pp. 119–150). Newbury Park, CA: Sage.

Eisenberg, N., & Fabes, R.A. (1998). Prosocial development. In N. Eisenberg (Ed.), *Handbook of child development* (5th ed., Vol. 3, pp. 701–778). New York: Wiley.

Eisenberg, N., Fabes, R.A., Carlo, G., Speer, A.L., Switzer, G., Karbon, M., & Troyer, D. (1993). The relations of empathy-related emotions and maternal practices to children's comforting behavior. *Journal of Experimental Child Psychology, 55,* 131–150.

Eisenberg, N., Fabes, R.A., Guthrie, I.K., & Reiser, M. (2000). Dispositional emotionality and regulation: Their role in predicting quality of social functioning. *Journal of Personality and Social Psychology, 78,* 136–157.

Eisenberg, N., Fabes, R.A., Murphy, B., Karbon, M., Maszk, P., Smith, M., O'Boyle, C., & Suh, K. (1994). The relations of emotionality and regulation to dispositional and situational empathy-related responding. *Journal of Personality and Social Psychology, 66,* 776–797.

Eisenberg, N., Fabes, R.A., Shepard, S.A., Murphy, B.C., Jones, S., & Guthrie, I.K. (1998). Contemporaneous and longitudinal prediction of children's sympathy from dispositional regulation and emotionality. *Developmental Psychology, 34,* 910–924.

Eisenberg, N., Guthrie, I.K., Murphy, B.C., Shepard, S.A., Cumberland, A., &

Carlo, G. (1999). Consistency and development of prosocial dispositions: A longitudinal study. *Child Development, 70,* 1360–1372.

Eisenberg, N., & Lennon, R. (1983). Sex differences in empathy and related capacities. *Psychological Bulletin, 94,* 100–131.

Eisenberg, N., McCreath, H., & Ahn, R. (1988). Vicarious emotional responsiveness and prosocial behavior. Their interrelations in young children. *Personality and Social Psychology Bulletin, 14,* 298–311.

Eisenberg, N., & Miller, P.A. (1987). The relation of empathy to prosocial and related behaviors. *Psychological Bulletin, 101,* 91–119.

Eisenberg, N., Miller, P.A., Schaller, M., Fabes, R.A., Fultz, J., Shell, R., & Shea, C.L. (1989b). The role of sympathy and altruistic personality traits in helping: A reexamination. *Journal of Personality, 57,* 41–67.

Eisenberg, N., Miller, P.A., Shell, R., McNally, S., & Shea, C. (1991). Prosocial development in adolescence: A longitudinal study. *Developmental Psychology, 27,* 849–857.

Eisenberg, N., & Murphy, B. (1995). Parenting and children's moral development. In M.H. Bornstein (Ed.), *Handbook of parenting* (Vol. 4, pp. 227–257). Mahwah, NJ: Lawrence Erlbaum Associates Inc.

Eisenberg, N., Pasternack, J.F., Cameron, E., & Tryon, K. (1984). The relation of quantity and mode of prosocial behavior to moral cognitions and social style. *Child Development, 55,* 1479–1485.

Eisenberg, N., & Strayer, J. (1987b). Critical issues in the study of empathy. In N. Eisenberg & J. Strayer (Eds.), *Empathy and its development* (pp. 3–13). Cambridge: Cambridge University Press.

Eisenberger, R., Cotterell, N., & Marvel, J. (1987c). Reciprocation ideology. *Journal* of *Personality and Social Psychology, 53,* 743–750.

Ekman, P., & Friesen, W.V. (1975). Unmasking the face. *A guide to recognizing emotions from facial clues.* Englewood Cliffs, NJ: Prentice Hall

Emler, N.P., & Rushton, J.P. (1974). Cognitive-developmental factors in children's generosity. *British Journal of Social and Clinical Psychology, 13,* 277–281.

Emswiller, T., Deaux, K., & Willits, J.E. (1971). Similarity, sex and request for small favors. *Journal of Applied Social Psychology, 1,* 284–291.

Engler, V. & Braun, O. (1988). Hilfesuchen und helferbezogene Gedanken [Help-seeking and thoughts about the helper]. In H.W. Bierhoff & L. Montada (Eds.), *Altruismus [Altruism]* (pp. 253–263). Göttingen: Hogrefe.

Epley, N., & Dunning, D. (2000). Feeling "holier than thou": Are self-serving assessments produced by errors in self- or social prediction? *Journal of Personality and Social Psychology, 79,* 861–875.

Erber, R., Wegner, D.M., & Therriault, N. (1996). On being cool and collected: Mood regulation in anticipation of social interactions. *Journal of Personality and Social Psychology, 70,* 757–766.

Erikson, E.H. (1963). *Insight and responsibility.* New York: Norton.

Erikson, E.H. (1968). *Identity: Youth and crisis.* New York: Norton.

Erlanger, D.M. (1998). Identity status and empathic response patterns: A multidimensional investigation. *Journal of Adolescence, 21,* 323–335.

Estrada-Hollenbeck, M., & Heatherton, T.F. (1998). Avoiding and alleviating guilt through prosocial behavior. In J. Bybee (Ed.), *Guilt and children* (pp. 215–231). San Diego, CA: Academic Press.

Eysenck, M. (2000). *Psychology: A student's handbook.* Hove, UK: Psychology Press.

Fabes, R.A., Carlo, G., Kupanoff, K., & Laible, D. (1999). Early adolescence and prosocial/moral behavior I: The role of individual processes. *Journal of Early Adolescence, 19,* 5–16.

Fabes, R.A., Eisenberg, N., Karbon, M., Bernzweig, J., Speer, A.L., & Carlo, G. (1994a). Socialization of children's vicarious emotional responding and prosocial behavior: Relations with mothers' perceptions of children's emotional reactivity. *Developmental Psychology, 30,* 44–55.

Fabes, R.A., Eisenberg, N., Karbon, M., Troyer, D., & Switzer, G. (1994b). The relations of children's emotion regulation to their vicarious emotional responses and comforting behaviors. *Child Development, 65,* 1678–1693.

Fabes, R.A., Eisenberg, N., McCormick, S.E., & Wilson, M.S. (1988). Preschoolers' attributions of the situational determinants of others' naturally occurring emotions. *Developmental Psychology, 24,* 376–385.

Fabes, R.A., Eisenberg, N., Nyman, M., & Michealieu, Q. (1991). Young children's appraisals of others' spontaneous emotional reactions. *Developmental Psychology, 27,* 858–866.

Fabes, R.A., Fultz, J., Eisenberg, N., May-Plumlee, T., & Christopher, F.S. (1989). Effects of rewards on children's prosocial motivation: A socialization study. *Developmental Psychology, 25,* 509–515.

Farth, J.L., Podsakoff, P.M., & Organ, D.W. (1990). Accounting for organizational citizenship behavior: Leader fairness and task scope versus satisfaction. *Journal of Management, 16,* 705–721.

Feather, N.T. (1995). Values, valences, and choice: The influence of values on the perceived attractiveness and choice of alternatives. *Journal of Personality and Social Psychology, 68,* 1135–1151.

Fehr, E., & Gachter, S. (2000). Cooperation and punishment in public goods experiments. *American Economic Review*, 90, 980–994.

Feldman, R.E. (1968). Response to compatriot and foreigner who seek assistance. *Journal of Personality and Social Psychology, 10,* 202–214.

Ferguson, T.J., & Stegge, H. (1998). Measuring guilt in children: A rose of any other name still has thorns. In J. Bybee (Ed.), *Guilt and children* (pp. 19–74). San Diego, CA: Academic Press.

Festinger, L. (1954). A theory of social comparison processes. *Human Relations, 7,* 117–140.

Fetchenhauer, D., & Bierhoff, H.W. (2002). *Attitudes toward a military enforcement of human rights.* Manuscript in preparation.

Filipp, S.H., & Ferring, D. (1998). Befindlichkeitsregulation durch temporale und soziale Vergleichsprozesse im Alter? [State regulation by temporal and social comparisons in old age?] *Zeitschrift für Klinische Psychologie, 27,* 93–97.

Fincham, F.D., & Jaspars, J.M. (1980). Attribution of responsibility: From man the scientist to man as lawyer. In L. Berkowitz (Ed.), *Advances in experimental social psychology* (Vol. 13, pp. 81–138). New York: Academic Press.

Fincham, F.D., & Jaspars, J.M. (1983). A subjective probability approach in responsibility attribution. *British Journal of Social Psychology, 22,* 145–162.

Fincham, F.D., & Roberts, C. (1985). Intervening causation and the mitigation of responsibility for harm doing: II. The role of limited mental capacities. *Journal of Experimental Social Psychology, 21,* 178–194.

Fishbein, M., & Ajzen, I. (1975). *Belief, attitude, intention and behavior.* Reading, MA: Addison-Wesley.

Fisher, J.D., Harrison, C.L., & Nadler, A. (1978). Exploring the generalizability of donor-recipient similarity effects. *Personality and Social Psychology Bulletin, 4,* 627–630.

Fisher, J.D., & Nadler, A. (1974). The effect of similarity between donor and recipient on recipient's reaction to help. *Journal of Applied Social Psychology, 4,* 230–243.

Fisher, J.D., Nadler, A., & Whitcher-Alagna, S. (1983). Four conceptualizations of reactions to aid. In J.D. Fischer, A. Nadler, & B.M. DePaulo (Eds.), *New directions in helping* (pp. 51–84). New York: Academic Press.

Freedman, J.L. (1970). Transgression, compliance and guilt. In J. Macaulay & L. Berkowitz (Eds.), *Altruism and helping behavior* (pp. 155–161). New York: Academic Press.

Freedman, J.L., & Fraser, S.C. (1966). Compliance without pressure: The foot-in-the-door technique. *Journal of Personality and Social Psychology, 4,* 195–202.

Freedman, J.L., Wallington, S.A., & Bless, E. (1967). Compliance without pressure: The effect of guilt. *Journal of Personality and Social Psychology, 7,* 117–124.

Freeman, S., Walker, M.R., Borden, R., & Latané, B. (1975). Diffusion of responsibility and restaurant tipping: Cheaper by the bunch. *Personality and Social Psychology Bulletin, 1,* 584–587.

Friedrich, L.K., & Stein, A.H. (1973). Aggressive and prosocial television programs and the natural behavior of preschool children. *Monographs of the Society for Research in Child Development, 38* (4, Serial No. 151).

Friedrich, L.K., & Stein, A.H. (1975). Prosocial television and young children: The effects of verbal labeling and role playing on learning and behavior. *Child Development, 46,* 27–38.

Frisch, M.B., & Gerrard, M. (1981). Natural helping systems: A survey of Red Cross Volunteers. *American Journal of Community Psychology, 9,* 567–579.

Froming, W.J., Walker, G.R., & Lopyan, K.J. (1982). Public and private self-awareness: When personal attitudes conflict with societal expectations. *Journal of Experimental Social Psychology, 18,* 476–487.

Fukuyama, F. (1999). *The great disruption: Human nature and the reconstitution of social order.* New York: Free Press.

Fultz, J., Batson, C.D., Fortenbach, V.A., McCarthy, P.M., & Varney, L.L. (1986). Social evaluation and the empathy–altruism hypothesis. *Journal of Personality and Social Psychology, 50,* 761–769.

Gaertner, S.L., & Dovidio, J.E. (1977). The subtlety of white racism, arousal, and helping behaviour. *Journal of Personality and Social Psychology, 35,* 691–707.

Gangestad, S.W., & Snyder, M. (2000). Self-monitoring: Appraisal and reappraisal. *Psychological Bulletin, 126,* 530–555.

Gaskin, K., Smith, J.D., & Paulwitz, I. (1996). *Ein neues bürgerliches Europa [A new civic Europe].* Freiburg: Lambertus.

Gelfand, D.M., & Hartmann, D.P. (1982). Response consequences and attributions: Two contributors to prosocial behavior. In N. Eisenberg (Ed.), *The development of prosocial behavior* (pp. 167–196). New York: Academic Press.

George, J.M. (1991). State or trait: Effects of positive mood on prosocial behaviors at work. *Journal of Applied Psychology, 76,* 299–307.

George, J.M. (1996). Group affective tone. In M.A. West (Ed.), *Handbook of work group psychology* (pp. 77–93). Chicester, UK: Wiley.

George, J.M., & Bettenhausen, K. (1990). Understanding prosocial behavior, sales performance, and turnover. *Journal of Applied Psychology, 75,* 698–709.

George, J.M., & Brief, A.P. (1992). Feeling good–doing good: A conceptual analysis of the mood at work–organizational spontaneity relationship. *Psychological Bulletin, 112,* 310–329.

Gergen, K.J. (1974). Toward a psychology of receiving help. *Journal of Applied Social Psychology, 4,* 187–193.

Gergen, K.J., Ellsworth, P., Maslach, C., & Seipel, M. (1975). Obligation, donor resources, and reactions to aid in three countries. *Journal of Personality and Social Psychology, 31,* 390–400.

Gergen, K.J., & Gergen, M.M. (1983). The social construction of helping relationships. In J.D. Fisher, A. Nadler, & B.M. DePaulo (Eds.), *New directions in helping* (Vol. 1, pp. 143–163). New York: Academic Press.

Gilbert, D.T. (1998). Ordinary personology. In D.T. Gilbert, S.T. Fiske, & G. Lindzey (Eds.), *The handbook of social psychology* (Vol. 2, pp. 89–150). Boston: McGraw-Hill.

Gilbert, D.T. (1999). What the mind's not. In S. Chaiken & Y. Trope (Eds.), *Dual-process theories in social psychology* (pp. 3–11). New York: Guilford Press.

Gilbert, D.T., & Silvera, D.H. (1996). Overhelping. *Journal of Personality and Social Psychology, 70,* 678–690.

Gintis, H. (2000). Strong reciprocity and human sociality. *Journal of Theoretical Biology, 206,* 169–179.

Glick, P., & Fiske, S.T. (1996). The ambivalent sexism inventory: Differentiating hostile and benevolent sexism. *Journal of Personality and Social Psychology, 70,* 491–512.

Goethals, G.R., & Darley, J.M. (1977). Social comparison theory. An attributional approach. In J.M. Suls & R.L. Miller (Eds.), *Social comparison processes* (pp. 259–278). Washington, DC: Hemisphere.

Gollwitzer, P.M., & Bayer, U. (1999). Deliberative versus implemental mindsets in the control of action. In S. Chaiken & Y. Trope (Eds.), *Dual-process theories in social psychology* (pp. 403–422). New York: Guilford Press.

Gorenflo, D.W., & Crano, W.D. (1989). Judgmental subjectivity/objectivity and locus of choice in social comparison. *Journal of Personality and Social Psychology, 57,* 605–614.

Gough, H.G. (1975). *Manual for the California Psychological Inventory* (Rev. ed.). Palo Alto, CA: Consulting Psychologists Press.

Gouldner, A.W. (1960). The norm of reciprocity: A preliminary statement. *American Sociological Review, 25,* 161–178.

Graen, G.B., & Scandura, T.A. (1987). Toward a psychology of dyadic organizing. In L.L. Cummings & B.M. Staw (Eds.), *Research in organizational behavior* (Vol. 9, pp. 175–208). Greenwich, CT: JAI Press.

Graen, G.B., & Uhl-Bien, M. (1995). Führungstheorien: von Dyaden zu Teams [Leadership theories: From dyads to teams]. In A. Kieser, G. Reber, & R. Wunderer (Eds.), *Handwörterbuch der Führung* [*Pocket dictionary of leadership*] (2nd ed., pp. 1045–1058). Stuttgart: Schäffer-Poeschel.

Gross, A.E., Wallston, B.S., & Piliavin, I.M. (1975). Beneficiary attractiveness and cost as determinants of responses to routine requests for help. *Sociometry, 38,* 131–140.

Gross, A.E., Wallston, B.S., & Piliavin, I.M. (1979). Reactance, attribution, equity and the help recipient. *Journal of Applied Social Psychology, 9,* 297–313.

Grube, J.A., & Piliavin, J.A. (2000). Role identity, organizational experiences and volunteer performance. *Personality and Social Psychology Bulletin, 26,* 1108–1119.

Grusec, J.E. (1971). Power and the internalization of self-denial. *Child Development, 42,* 93–105.

Grusec, J.E. (1972). Demand characteristics of the modeling element: Altruism as a function of age and aggression. *Journal*

of Personality and Social Psychology, 22, 139–148.

Grusec, J.E. (1982). The socialization of altruism. In N. Eisenberg (Ed.), *The development of prosocial behavior* (pp. 139–166). New York: Academic Press.

Grusec, J.E. (1991). Socializing concern for others in the home. *Developmental Psychology, 27,* 338–342.

Grusec, J.E., Kuczynski, L., Rushton, J.P., & Simutis, Z. (1978). Modeling, direct instruction, and attribution: Effects on altruism. *Developmental Psychology, 14,* 51–57.

Grusec, J.E., & Redler, E. (1980). Attribution, reinforcement and altruism: A developmental analysis. *Developmental Psychology, 16,* 525–534.

Grusec, J.E., & Skubiski, L. (1970). Model nurturance, demand characteristics, and altruism. *Journal of Personality and Social Psychology, 14,* 352–359.

Guerin, B. (1986). Mere presence effects in humans: A review. *Journal of Experimental Social Psychology, 22,* 38–77.

Gunnoe, M.L., Hetherington, E.M., & Reiss, D. (1999). Parental religiosity, parenting style, and adolescent social responsibility. *Journal of Early Adolescence, 19,* 199–225.

Hamilton, V.L., & Sanders, J. (1992). *Everyday justice: Responsibility and the individual in Japan and the United States.* New Haven, CT: Yale University Press.

Hamilton, W.D. (1964). The genetical evolution of social behavior: Part I and II. *Journal of Theoretical Biology, 7,* 1–52.

Harris, M.B., Benson, S.M., & Hall, C.L. (1975). The effects of confession on altruism. *Journal of Social Psychology, 98,* 187–192.

Harris, M.B., & Huang, L.C. (1973). Helping and the attribution process. *Journal of Social Psychology, 90,* 291–297.

Harris, M.B., & Samerotte, G.C. (1976). The effects of actual and attempted theft, need and a previous favor on altruism. *Journal of Social Psychology, 99*, 193–202.

Harter, S., & Jackson, B.K. (1992). Trait vs. nontrait conceptualizations of intrinsic/extrinsic motivational orientation. *Motivation and Emotion, 16*, 209–230.

Hastings, P.D., Zahn-Waxler, C., Robinson, J., Usher, B., & Bridges, D. (2000). The development of concern for others in children with behavior problems. *Developmental Psychology, 36*, 531–546.

Hathaway, S., & McKinley, J. (1951). *The Minnesota Multiphasic Personality Inventory manual*. New York: Psychological Corporation.

Havighurst, R.J. (1953). *Human development and education*. London: Longman.

Hechter, M. (1987). *Theories of group solidarity*. Berkeley, CA: University of California Press.

Heider, F. (1958). *The psychology of interpersonal relations*. New York: Wiley.

Hewstone, M. (1989). *Causal attribution: From cognitive processes to collective beliefs*. Oxford: Blackwell.

Hinde, R.A. (2001). Responsibility: A biological perspective. In A.E. Auhagen & H.W. Bierhoff (Eds.), *Responsibility—the many faces of a social phenomenon* (pp. 23–33). London: Routledge.

Hirschi, T. (1969). *Causes of delinquency*. Berkeley, CA: University of California Press.

Hofer, M. (1999). Community service and social cognitive development in German adolescents. In M. Yates & J. Youniss (Eds.), *Roots of civic identity: International perspectives on community service and activism in youth* (pp. 114–134), Cambridge: Cambridge University Press.

Hoffman, M.L. (1975). Altruistic behavior and the parent–child relationship. *Journal of Personality and Social Psychology, 31*, 937–943.

Hoffman, M.L. (1977). Moral internalization: Current theory and research. In L. Berkowitz (Ed.), *Advances in experimental social psychology* (Vol. 10, pp. 86–135). New York: Academic Press.

Hoffman, M.L. (1978). Empathy, its development and prosocial implications. In C.B. Keasey (Ed.), *Nebraska Symposium on Motivation* (Vol. 25, pp. 169–218). Lincoln, NE: University of Nebraska Press.

Hoffman, M.L. (1982). Development of prosocial motivation: Empathy and guilt. In N. Eisenberg (Ed.), *The development of prosocial behavior* (pp. 281–313). New York: Academic Press.

Hoffman, M.L. (1984). Interaction of affect and cognition in empathy. In C.E. Izard, J. Kagan, & R.B. Zajonc (Eds.), *Emotions, cognition, and behaviour* (pp. 103–131). Cambridge: Cambridge University Press.

Hoffman, M.L. (1987). The contribution of empathy to justice and moral judgment. In N. Eisenberg & J. Strayer (Eds.), *Empathy and its development* (pp. 47–80). New York: Cambridge University Press.

Hoffman, M.L. (1990). Empathy and justice motivation. *Motivation and Emotion, 14*, 151–172.

Hoffman, M.L. (1998). Varieties of empathy-based guilt. In J. Bybee (Ed.), *Guilt and children* (pp. 91–112). San Diego, CA: Academic Press.

Hoffman, M.L. (2000). *Empathy and moral development: Implications for caring and justice*. Cambridge: Cambridge University Press.

Hoffman, M.L., & Saltzstein, H.D. (1967). Parent discipline and the child's moral development. *Journal of Personality and Social Psychology, 5*, 45–57.

Hofstede, G. (1991). *Cultures and organizations*. London: HarperCollins.

Hogan, R. (1969). Development of an empathy scale. *Journal of Consulting and Clinical Psychology, 33*, 307–316.

Holmes, W.G., & Sherman, P.W. (1983).

Kin recognition in animals. *American Scientist, 71,* 46–55.

Holmgren, R.A., Eisenberg, N., & Fabes, R.A. (1998). The relations of children's situational empathy-related emotions to dispositional prosocial behavior. *International Journal of Behavioral Development, 22,* 169–193.

Holz-Ebeling, F., & Steinmetz, M. (1994). Entwicklung eines situationsbezogenen Empathiefragebogens mittels experimenteller Konstruktionsprinzipien [Development of a situation-oriented empathy questionnaire based on experimental construction principles]. *Zeitschrift für Sozialpsychologie, 25,* 155–169.

Holz-Ebeling, F., & Steinmetz, M. (1995). Wie brauchbar sind die vorliegenden Fragebogen zur Messung von Empathie? [How useful are the available empathy questionnaires?] *Zeitschrift für Differentielle und Diagnostische Psychologie, 16,* 11–32.

Hopper, J.R., & Nielsen, J.M. (1991). Recycling as altruistic behavior: Normative and behavioral strategies to expand participation in a community recycling program. *Environment and Behavior, 23,* 195–220.

House, J.S., & Wolf, S. (1978). Effects of urban residence on interpersonal trust and helping behavior. *Journal of Personality and Social Psychology, 36,* 1029–1043.

Hunecke, M., Blöbaum, A., Matthies, E., & Höger, R. (2001). Responsibility and environment—Ecological norm orientation and external factors in the domain of travel mode choice behavior. *Environment and Behavior, 33,* 830–862.

Huston, A.C., & Wright, J.C. (1998). Mass media and children's development. In I.E. Siegel & K.A. Renninger (Eds.), *Handbook of child psychology* (5th ed., Vol. 4, pp. 999–1058). New York: Wiley.

Huston, T.L., Ruggiero, M., Conner, R., & Geis, G. (1981). Bystander intervention into crime: A study based on naturally-occurring episodes. *Social Psychology Quarterly, 44,* 14–23.

Hutz, C.S., De Conti, L., & Vargas, S. (1993). Rules used by Brazilian students in systematic and nonsystematic reward allocation. *Journal of Social Psychology, 134,* 331–338.

Iannotti, R.J. (1978). Effect of role-taking experiences on role taking, empathy, altruism and aggression. *Developmental Psychology, 14,* 119–124.

Ickes, W. (Ed.). (1997). *Empathic accuracy.* New York: Guilford Press.

Ickes, W., Stinson, L., Bissonnette, V., & Garcia, S. (1990). Naturalistic social cognition: Empathic accuracy in mixed-sex dyads. *Journal of Personality and Social Psychology, 59,* 730–742.

Ickes, W.J., & Kidd, R.F. (1976). An attributional analysis of helping behavior. In J.H. Harvey, W.J. Ickes, & R.F. Kidd (Eds.), *New directions in attribution research* (Vol. 1, pp. 311–334). Hillsdale, NJ: Lawrence Erlbaum Associates Inc.

Insko, C.A., & Schopler, J. (1972). *Experimental social psychology.* New York: Academic Press.

Insko, C.A., Schopler, J., Hoyle, R.H., Dardis, G.J., & Graetz, K.A. (1990). Individual–group discontinuity as a function of fear and greed. *Journal of Personality and Social Psychology, 58,* 68–79.

Isen, A.M. (1987). Positive affect, cognitive processes and social behavior. In L. Berkowitz (Ed.), *Advances in experimental social psychology* (Vol. 20, pp. 203–253). San Diego, CA: Academic Press.

Isen, A.M., Shalker, T.E., Clark, M., & Karp, L. (1978). Affect, accessibility of material in memory, and behavior: A cognitive loop? *Journal of Personality and Social Psychology, 36,* 1–12.

Izard, C.E. (1977). *Human emotions.* New York: Plenum.

James, W. (1908/1950). *The principles of psychology*. New York: Dover.

Jeffries, V. (1998). Virtue and the altruistic personality. *Sociological Perspectives, 41,* 151–166.

Johns, G., & Xie, J.L. (1998). Perceptions of absence from work: People's Republic of China versus Canada. *Journal of Applied Psychology, 83,* 515–530.

Johnson, B.T., & Eagly, A.H. (1989). The effects of involvement on persuasion: A meta-analysis. *Psychological Bulletin, 106,* 290–314.

Johnson, J.A., Cheek, J.M., & Smither, R. (1983). The structure of empathy. *Journal of Personality and Social Psychology, 45,* 1299–1312.

Jonas, H. (1985). *The imperative of responsibility*. Chicago, IL: University of Chicago Press. (Original work published 1979.)

Jones, W.H., & Kugler, K. (1990). *Preliminary manual for the Guilt Inventory (GI) [Unpublished instrument]*. University of Tennessee, Knoxville, TN.

Jöreskog, K.G., & Sörbom, D. (1984). *LISREL VI: Analysis of linear structural relationships by the method of maximum likelihood*. Mooresville, IN: Scientific Software.

Jose, P.E. (1990). Just-world reasoning in children's immanent justice judgments. *Child Development, 61,* 1024–1037.

Kaiser, F.G., Fuhrer, U., Weber, O., Ofner, T., & Bühler-Ilieva, E. (2001). Responsibility and ecological behaviour—a meta-analysis of the strength and the extent of a causal link. In A.E. Auhagen & H.W. Bierhoff (Eds.), *Responsibility—the many faces of a social phenomenon* (pp. 109–126). London: Routledge.

Kals, E. (2001). Responsibility appraisals of health protection. In A.E. Auhagen & H.W. Bierhoff (Eds.), *Responsibility—the many faces of a social phenomenon* (pp. 127–138). London: Routledge.

Karau, S.J., & Williams, K.D. (1993). Social loafing: A meta-analytic review and theoretical integration. *Journal of Personality and Social Psychology, 65,* 681–706.

Katz, D. (1960). The functional approach to the study of attitude. *Public Opinion Quarterly, 24,* 163–204.

Katz, D., & Kahn, R.L. (1978). *The social psychology of organizations* (2nd ed.). New York: Wiley.

Kelly, C., & Breinlinger, S. (1996). *The social psychology of collective action*. London: Taylor & Francis Ltd.

Kochanska, G. (1993). Toward a synthesis of parental socialization and child temperament in early development of conscience. *Child Development, 64,* 325–347.

Kochanska, G., DeVet, K., Goldman, M., Murray, K., & Putnam, S.P. (1994). Maternal reports of conscience development and temperament in young children. *Child Development, 65,* 852–868.

Kohlberg, L. (1984). *The psychology of moral development*. San Francisco: Harper.

Komter, A.E. (Ed.). (1996). *The gift: An interdisciplinary perspective*. Amsterdam: Amsterdam University Press.

Konecni, V.J. (1972). Some effects of guilt on compliance: A field replication. *Journal of Personality and Social Psychology, 23,* 30–32.

Korte, C. (1981). Constraints on helping behavior in an urban environment. In J.P. Rushton & R.M. Sorrentino (Eds.), *Altruism and helping behavior* (pp. 315–329). Hillsdale, NJ: Lawrence Erlbaum Associates Inc.

Korte, C., & Ayvalioglu, N. (1981). Helpfulness in Turkey: Cities, towns and urban villages. *Journal of Cross-Cultural Psychology, 12,* 123–131.

Korte, C., & Kerr, N. (1975). Response to altruistic opportunities in urban and nonurban settings. *Journal of Social Psychology, 95,* 183–184.

Korte, C., Ypma, I., & Toppen, A. (1975).

Helpfulness in Dutch society as a function of organization and environmental input level. *Journal of Personality and Social Psychology, 32,* 996–1003.

Krebs, D. (1975). Empathy and altruism. *Journal of Personality and Social Psychology, 32,* 1134–1146.

Krevans, J., & Gibbs, J.C. (1996). Parents' use of inductive discipline: Relations to children's empathy and prosocial behavior. *Child Development, 67,* 3263–3277.

Kuczysnki, L. (1982). Intensity and orientation of reasoning: Motivational determinants of children's compliance to verbal rationales. *Journal of Experimental Child Psychology, 34,* 357–370.

Kuczysnki, L. (1983). Reasoning, prohibitions, and motivations for compliance. *Developmental Psychology, 19,* 126–134.

Kugler, K., & Jones, W.H. (1992). On conceptualizing and assessing guilt. *Journal of Personality and Social Psychology, 62,* 318–327.

Küpper, B., & Bierhoff, H.W. (1999). Liebe Deinen Nächsten, sei hilfreich . . .: Hilfeleistung ehrenamtlicher Helfer in Zusammenhang mit Motiven und Religiosität [Love your neighbour, do good to him . . .: The helping behaviour of volunteers in relation to motives and religiosity]. *Zeitschrift für Differentielle und Diagnostische Psychologie, 20,* 217–230.

Larsen, R.J., & Diener, E. (1987). Affect intensity as an individual difference characteristic: A review. *Journal of Research in Personality, 21,* 1–39.

Latané, B. (1981). The psychology of social impact. *American Psychologist, 36,* 343–356.

Latané, B., & Dabbs, J.M. (1975). Sex, group size and helping in three cities. *Sociometry, 38,* 180–194.

Latané, B., & Darley, J.M. (1968). Group inhibition of bystander intervention in emergencies. *Journal of Personality and Social Psychology, 10,* 215–221.

Latané, B., & Darley, J.M. (1969). Bystander "apathy". *American Scientist, 57,* 244–268.

Latané, B., & Darley, J.M. (1970). *The unresponsive bystander: Why doesn't he help?* New York: Appleton.

Latané, B., & Darley, J.M. (1976). *Help in a crisis: Bystander response to emergency.* Morristown, NJ: General Learning Press.

Latané, B., & Nida, S. (1981). Ten years of research on group size and helping. *Psychological Bulletin, 89,* 308–324.

Latané, B., & Rodin, J. (1969). A lady in distress: Inhibiting effects of friends and strangers on bystander intervention. *Journal of Experimental Social Psychology, 5,* 189–202.

Latané, B., & Wolf, S. (1981). The social impact of majorities and minorities. *Psychological Review, 88,* 438–453.

Lazarus, R.S., & Folkman, S. (1984). *Stress, appraisal, and coping.* New York: Springer.

Lee, K., Carswell, J.J., & Allen, N.J. (2000). A meta-analytic review of occupational commitment: Relations with person- and work-related variables. *Journal of Applied Psychology, 85,* 799–811.

Lefkowitz, M.M., Blake, R.R., & Mouton, J.S. (1955). Status factors in pedestrian violation of traffic signals. *Journal of Abnormal and Social Psychology, 51,* 704–706.

Lenk, H., & Maring, M. (2001). Responsibility and technology. In A.E. Auhagen & H.W. Bierhoff (Eds.), *Responsibility—the many faces of a social phenomenon* (pp. 93–107). London: Routledge.

Lennon, R., & Eisenberg, N. (1987). Gender and age differences in empathy and sympathy. In N. Eisenberg & J. Strayer (Eds.), *Empathy and its development* (pp.

195–217). Cambridge: Cambridge University Press.

Lerner, M.J. (1980). *The belief in a just world: A fundamental delusion*. New York: Plenum.

Leventhal, H. (1974). Emotions: A basic problem for social psychology. In C. Nemeth (Ed.), *Social psychology: Classic and contemporary integrations* (pp. 1–51). Chigaco, IL: Rand McNally.

Levine, R.V., Martinez, T.S., Brase, G., & Sorenson, K. (1994). Helping in 36 US cities. *Journal of Personality and Social Psychology, 67*, 69–82.

Lewin, K. (1951). *Field theory in social science*. New York: Harper.

Lewis, H.B. (1971). *Shame and guilt in neurosis*. New York: International Universities Press.

Lickona, T. (1976). Research on Piaget's theory of moral development. In T. Lickona (Ed.), *Moral development and behavior* (pp. 219–240). New York: Holt.

Liebrand, W.B.G. (1984). The effect of social motives, communication and group size on behaviour in an N-person multi-stage mixed-motive game. *European Journal of Social Psychology, 14*, 239–264.

Lifton, R. (1968). *Death in life: Survivors of Hiroshima*. New York: Random House.

Lilli, W., & Luber, M. (2001). Solidarität aus sozialpsychologischer Sicht [Solidarity from a social-psychological point of view]. In H.W. Bierhoff & D. Fetchenhauer (Eds.), *Solidarität: Konflikt, Umwelt und Dritte Welt* [*Solidarity: Conflict, environment, and Third World*] (pp. 273–291). Opladen, Germany: Leske & Budrich.

Lott, A.J., Lott, B.E., & Walsh, M.L. (1970). Learning of paired associates relevant to differentially liked persons. *Journal of Personality and Social Psychology, 16*, 274–283.

Luks, A., & Payne, P. (1991). *The healing power of doing good: The health and spiritual benefits of helping others*. New York: Ballantine.

Lyman, S.M., & Scott, M.B. (1968). Coolness in everyday life. In S.M. Lyman & M.B. Scott (Eds.), *The sociology of the absurd* (pp. 145–157). Pacific Palisades, CA: Goodyear.

Lyubomirsky, S., & Nolen-Hoeksema, S. (1993). Self-perpetuating properties of dysphoric rumination. *Journal of Personality and Social Psychology, 63*, 339–349.

Macrae, C.N., & Bodenhausen, G.V. (2000). Social cognition: Thinking categorically about others. *Annual Review of Psychology, 51*, 93–120.

Macrae, C.N., & Johnston, L. (1998). Help, I need somebody: Automatic action and inaction. *Social Cognition, 16*, 400–417.

Maes, J. (1998). Immanent justice and ultimate justice. In L. Montada & M.J. Lerner (Eds.), *Responses to victimizations and belief in a just world* (pp. 9–40). New York: Plenum.

Magnusson, D., Bergman, L.R., Rudinger, G., & Törestad, B. (Eds.). (1994). *Problems and methods in longitudinal research: Stability and change*. Cambridge: Cambridge University Press.

McDougall, W. (1908). *An introduction to social psychology*. London: Methuen.

Mehrabian, A. (1970). The development and validation of measures of affiliative tendency and sensitivity to rejection. *Educational and Psychological Measurement, 30*, 417–428.

Mehrabian, A. (1977). Individual differences in stimulus screening and arousability. *Journal of Personality, 45*, 237–250.

Mehrabian, A., & Epstein, N. (1972). A measure of emotional empathy. *Journal of Personality, 40*, 525–543.

Mehrabian, A., & Russell, J.A. (1974). *An approach to environmental psychology*. Cambridge, MA: MIT Press.

Mehrabian, A., Young, A.L., & Sato, S.

(1988). Emotional empathy and associated individual differences. *Current Psychology: Research and Review*, 7, 221–240.

Messick, D.M., & Brewer, M.B. (1983). Solving social dilemmas: A review. In L. Wheeler & P. Shaver (Eds.), *Review of personality and social psychology* (Vol. 4, pp. 11–44). Beverly Hills, CA: Sage.

Meyer, W.U. (1982). Indirect communications about perceived ability estimates. *Journal of Educational Psychology*, 74, 888–897.

Midlarsky, E. (1971). Aiding under stress: The effects of competence, dependency, visibility, and fatalism. *Journal of Personality*, 39, 132–149.

Midlarsky, E. (1991). Helping as coping. In M.S. Clark (Ed.), *Prosocial behavior* (pp. 238–264). Newbury Park, CA: Sage.

Midlarsky, E., & Bryan, J.H. (1967). Training charity in children. *Journal of Personality and Social Psychology*, 5, 408–415.

Midlarsky, E., Bryan, J.H., & Brickman, P. (1973). Aversive approval: Interactive effects of modeling and reinforcement in altruistic behaviour. *Child Development*, 44, 321–328.

Midlarsky, E., Hannah, M.E., & Corley, R. (1995). Assessing adolescents' prosocial behavior: The family helping inventory. *Adolescence*, 30, 141–155.

Midlarsky, E., & Midlarsky, M. (1973). Some determinants of aiding under experimentally induced stress. *Journal of Personality*, 41, 305–327.

Midlarsky, M., & Midlarsky, E. (1976). Status inconsistency, aggressive attitude, and helping behavior. *Journal of Personality*, 44, 371–391.

Milgram, S. (1970). The experience of living in cities. *Science*, 167, 1461–1468.

Mill, J.S. (1985). *On liberty*. New York: Clarendon Press. (Original work published 1859.)

Miller, D.T. (1977). Altruism and threat to a belief in a just world. *Journal of Experimental Social Psychology*, 13, 113–124.

Miller, D.T., & McFarland, C. (1987). Pluralistic ignorance: When similarity is interpreted as dissimilarity. *Journal of Personality and Social Psychology*, 53, 298–305.

Miller, J.G. (1984). Culture and the development of everyday social explanation. *Journal of Personality and Social Psychology*, 46, 961–978.

Miller, J.G., Bersoff, D.M., & Harwood, R.L. (1990). Perceptions of social responsibility in India and in the United States: Moral imperatives or personal decisions? *Journal of Personality and Social Psychology*, 58, 33–47.

Miller, P.A., & Eisenberg, N. (1988). The relation of empathy to aggressive and externalizing/antisocial behavior. *Psychological Bulletin*, 103, 324–344.

Miller, R.L., Brickman, P., & Bolen, D. (1975). Attribution versus persuasion as a means for modifying behavior. *Journal of Personality and Social Psychology*, 31, 430–441.

Miller, R.L., Seligman, C., Clark, M.T., & Bush, M. (1976). Perceptual contrast versus reciprocal concession as mediators of induced compliance. *Canadian Journal of Behavioural Science*, 8, 401–409.

Mills, R.S.L., & Grusec, J.E. (1991). Cognitive, affective, and behavioral consequences of praising altruism. *Merrill-Palmer Quarterly*, 35, 299–326.

Mischel, W. (1973). Toward a cognitive social learning reconceptualization of personality. *Psychological Review*, 80, 252–283.

Misra, J., & Hicks, A. (1994). Catholicism and unionization in affluent postwar democracies. *American Sociological Review*, 59, 304–326.

Mitchell, D., Stotland, E., & Mathews, E. (1978). The role of instructions: Further validation of the fantasy-empathy scale. In E. Stotland, K.E. Mathews, S.E.

Sherman, R.O. Hansson, & B.Z. Richardson (Eds.), *Empathy, fantasy and helping* (pp. 45–50). Beverly Hills, CA: Sage.

Montada, L. (1998). Belief in a just world: A hybrid of justice motive and self-interest? In L. Montada & M.J. Lerner (Eds.), *Responses to victimization and belief in a just world* (pp. 217–246). New York: Plenum.

Montada, L. (2001a). Denial of responsibility. In A.E. Auhagen & H.W. Bierhoff (Eds.), *Responsibility—the many faces of a social phenomenon* (pp. 79–92). London: Routledge.

Montada, L. (2001b). Solidarität mit der Dritten Welt [Solidarity with the Third World]. In H.W. Bierhoff & D. Fetchenhauer (Eds.), *Solidarität: Konflikt, Umwelt und Dritte Welt* [*Solidarity: Conflict, environment, and Third World*] (pp. 65–92). Opladen, Germany: Leske & Budrich.

Montada, L., & Lerner, M.J. (Eds.). (1996). *Current societal concerns about justice.* New York: Plenum.

Montada, L., & Lerner, M.J. (Eds.). (1998). *Responses to victimizations and belief in a just world.* New York: Plenum.

Montada, L., Schmitt, M., & Dalbert, C. (1986). Thinking about justice and dealing with one's own privileges. In H.W. Bierhoff, R.L. Cohen, & J. Greenberg (Eds.), *Justice in social relations* (pp. 125–143). New York: Plenum.

Montada, L., Schmitt, M., & Dalbert, C. (1991). Prosocial commitments in the family: Situational, personality and systemic factors. In L. Montada & H.W. Bierhoff (Eds.), *Altruism in social systems* (pp. 177–203). Lewiston, NY: Hogrefe.

Montada, L., & Schneider, A. (1991). Justice and prosocial commitments. In L. Montada & H.W. Bierhoff (Eds.), *Altruism in social systems* (pp. 58–81). Lewiston, NY: Hogrefe.

Moore, B., & Underwood, B. (1981). The development of prosocial behavior. In S.S. Brehm, S.M. Kassin, & S.X. Gibbons (Eds.), *Developmental social psychology* (pp. 72–95) New York: Oxford University Press.

Morris, M.W., & Peng, K. (1994). Culture and cause: American and Chinese attributions for social and physical events. *Journal of Personality and Social Psychology, 67,* 949–971.

Moschner, B. (1998). Ehrenamtliches Engagement und soziale Verantwortung [Volunteerism and social responsibility]. In B. Reichle & M. Schmitt (Eds.), *Verantwortung, Gerechtigkeit und Moral* [*Responsibility, justice, and morality*]. Weinheim: Juventa.

Moss, M.K., & Page, R.A. (1972). Reinforcement and helping behavior. *Journal of Applied Social Psychology, 2,* 360–371.

Müller, G.F., & Bierhoff, H.W. (2001). Stimmungseinflüsse in Projektgruppen [Mood influences in project groups]. In R. Fisch & D. Beck (Eds.), *Projektgruppen in Organisationen* [*Project groups in organisations*]. Göttingen: Hogrefe.

Murray, H.A. (1962). *Explorations in personality.* New York: Science Editions.

Mussen, P., Harris, S., Rutherford, E., & Keasey, C.B. (1970). Honesty and altruism among preadolescents. *Developmental Psychology, 3,* 169–194.

Mussen, P.H., & Parker, A.L. (1965). Mother nurturance and girls' incidental imitative learning. *Journal of Personality and Social Psychology, 2,* 94–97.

Nadler, A. (1987). Determinants of help seeking behavior: The effects of helper's similarity, task centrality and recipient's self esteem. *European Journal of Social Psychology, 17,* 57–67.

Nadler, A. (1991). Help-seeking behavior: Psychological costs of instrumental benefits. In M.S. Clark (Ed.), *Prosocial behavior* (pp. 290–311). Newbury Park, CA: Sage.

Nadler, A., & Fisher, J.D. (1986). The role of threat to self-esteem and perceived control in recipient reaction to help: Theory development and empirical validation. In L. Berkowitz (Ed.), *Advances in experimental social psychology* (Vol. 19, pp. 81–122). Orlando, FL: Academic Press.

Nadler, A., Fisher, J.D., & Ben Itzhak, S. (1983). With a little help from my friends: Effect of single or multiple act aid as a function of donor and task characteristics. *Journal of Personality and Social Psychology, 44*, 310–321.

Nadler, A., Fisher, J.D., & Streufert, S. (1976). When helping hurts: Effects of donor–recipient similarity and recipient self-esteem on reactions to aid. *Journal of Personality, 44*, 392–409.

Nadler, A., Mayseless, O., Peri, N., & Chemerinski, A. (1985). Effects of opportunity to reciprocate and self-esteem on help-seeking behavior. *Journal of Personality, 53*, 23–35.

Neiderhiser, J.M., Reiss, D., & Hetherington, E.M. (1996). Genetically informative designs for distinguishing developmental pathways during adolescence: Responsible and antisocial behavior. *Development and Psychopathology, 8*, 779–791.

Nelson-LeGall, S., Gumerman, R.A., & Scott-Jones, D. (1983). Instrumental help-seeking and everyday problem-solving: A developmental perspective. In B.M. DePaulo, A. Nadler, & J.D. Fisher (Eds.), *New directions in helping* (Vol. 2, pp. 265–283). New York: Academic Press.

Neuberg, S.L., Cialdini, R.B., Brown, S.L., Luce, C., Sagarin, B.J., & Lewis, B.P. (1997). Does empathy lead to anything more than superficial helping? Comment on Batson et al. (1997). *Journal of Personality and Social Psychology, 73*, 510–516.

Neuf, H. (1997). *Determinanten des Eindenkens in andere Personen [Determinants of empathic cognitions]*. Münster: Waxmann.

Newman, R.S., & Goldin, L. (1990). Children's reluctance to seek help with schoolwork. *Journal of Educational Psychology, 82*, 92–100.

Oliner, S.P., & Oliner, P.M. (1988). *The altruistic personality: Rescuers of Jews in Nazi Europe*. New York: Free Press.

Olson, M. (1965). *The logic of collective action*. New Haven, CT: Yale University Press.

Omoto, A.M., & Snyder, M. (1995). Sustained helping without obligation: Motivation, longevity of service, and perceived attitude change among AIDS volunteers. *Journal of Personality and Social Psychology, 68*, 671–686.

Omoto, A.M., Snyder, M., & Martino, S.C. (2000). Volunteerism and the life course: Investigating age-related agendas for action. *Basic and Applied Social Psychology, 22*, 181–197.

Orbell, J.M., & Dawes, R.M. (1993). Social welfare, cooperators' advantage, and the option of not playing the game. *American Sociological Review, 58*, 787–800.

Organ, D.W. (1988). *Organizational citizenship behavior: The good soldier syndrome*. Lexington, MA: Lexington.

Organ, D.W., & Ryan, K. (1995). A meta-analytic review of attitudinal and dispositional predictors of organizational citizenship behaviour. *Personnel Psychology, 48*, 775–802.

Oskamp, S., Harrington, M.J., Edwards, T.C., Sherwood, D.L., Okuda, S.M., & Swanson, D.C. (1991). Factors influencing houshold recycling behavior. *Environment and Behavior, 23*, 494–519.

Oyserman, D., & Markus, H. (1990). Possible selves in balance: Implications for delinquency. *Journal of Social Issues, 46*(2), 141–157.

Parsons, T. (1964). *Social structure and personality*. New York: Free Press.

Penner, L.A., & Finkelstein, M.A. (1998). Dispositional and structural determinants of volunteerism. *Journal of Personality and Social Psychology, 74,* 525–537.

Penner, L.A., Midili, A.R., & Kegelmeyer, J. (1997). Beyond job attitudes: A personality and social psychology perspective on the causes of organizational citizenship behavior. *Human Performance, 10,* 111–131.

Perugini, M., & Gullucci, M. (in press). Individual differences and social norms: The distinction between reciprocators and prosocials. *European Journal of Personality, 15,* 519–535.

Peterson, T. (1993). The economics of organizations: The principle–agent relationship. *Acta Sociologica, 36,* 277–293.

Petty, R.E., & Wegener, D.T. (1999). The elaboration likelihood model: Current status and controversies. In S. Chaiken & Y. Trope (Eds.), *Dual-process theories in social psychology* (pp. 41–72). New York: Guilford.

Piaget, J. (1932). *The moral judgement of the child.* London: Routledge.

Piaget, J., & Inhelder, B. (1947). *La représentation de l'espace chez l'enfant* [*The child's conception of space*]. Paris: Presses Universitaires de France

Piliavin, I.M., Piliavin, J.A., & Rodin, J. (1975). Costs, diffusion, and the stigmatized victim. *Journal of Personality and Social Psychology, 32,* 429–438.

Piliavin, I.M., Rodin, J., & Piliavin, J.A. (1969). Good Samaritans: An underground phenomenon? *Journal of Personality and Social Psychology, 13,* 289–299.

Piliavin, J.A. (1989). The development of motives, self-identities, and values tied to blood donation: A Polish–American comparison study. In N. Eisenberg, J. Reykowski, & E. Staub (Eds.), *Social and moral values* (pp. 253–276). Hillsdale, NJ: Lawrence Erlbaum Associates Inc.

Piliavin, J.A., & Callero, P. (1991). *Giving blood: The development of an altruistic identity.* Baltimore, MD: Johns Hopkins University Press.

Piliavin, J.A., Dovidio, J.F., Gaertner, S.L., & Clark, R.D. (1981). *Emergency intervention.* New York: Academic Press.

Piliavin, J.A., & Piliavin, I.M. (1972). Effect of blood on reactions to a victim. *Journal of Personality and Social Psychology, 23,* 353–361.

Podsakoff, P.M., Ahearne, M., & MacKenzie, S.B. (1997). Organizational citizenship behavior and the quantity and quality of work group performance. *Journal of Applied Psychology, 82,* 262–270.

Podsakoff, P.M., MacKenzie, S.B., Paine, J.B., & Bachrach, D. (2000). Organizational citizenship behaviors: A critical review of the theoretical and empirical literature and suggestions for future research. *Journal of Management, 26,* 513–563.

Pomazal, R.J., & Jaccard, J.J. (1976). An informational approach to altruistic behavior. *Journal of Personality and Social Psychology, 33,* 317–326.

Prentice, D.A., & Miller, D.T. (1996). Pluralistic ignorance and the perpetuation of social norms by unwitting actors. In M.P. Zanna (Ed.), *Advances in experimental social psychology* (Vol. 28, pp. 161–209). San Diego, CA: Academic Press.

Pruitt, D.G. (1968). Reciprocity and credit building in a laboratory dyad. *Journal of Personality and Social Psychology, 8,* 143–147.

Pruitt, D.G., & Kimmel, M.J. (1977). Twenty years of experimental gaming: critique, synthesis, and suggestions for the future. *Annual Review of Psychology, 28,* 363–392.

Quiles, Z.N., & Bybee, J. (1997). Chronic and predispositional guilt: Relations to mental health, prosocial behavior, and

(1998). Representation of human rights across different national contexts: The role of democratic and non-democratic populations and governments. *European Journal of Social Psychology, 28,* 207–226.

Stapleton, R.E., Nacci, P., & Tedeschi, J.T. (1973). Interpersonal attraction and the reciprocation of benefits. *Journal of Personality and Social Psychology, 28,* 130–140.

Staub, E. (1970). A child in distress: The influence of age and number of witnesses on children's attempts to help. *Journal of Personality and Social Psychology, 28,* 199–205.

Staub, E. (1971). Helping a person in distress: The influence of implicit and explicit "rules" of conduct on children and adults. *Journal of Personality and Social Psychology, 17,* 137–144.

Staub, E. (1974). Helping a distressed person: Social, personality, and stimulus determinants. In L. Berkowitz (Ed.), *Advances in experimental social psychology* (Vol. 7, pp. 293–341). New York: Academic Press.

Staub, E. (1978). *Positive social behavior and morality* (Vol. 1). New York: Academic Press.

Steblay, N.M. (1987). Helping behavior in rural and urban environment: A meta-analysis. *Psychological Bulletin, 102,* 346–356.

Stegge, H., & Ferguson, T.J. (1990). *Child–Child Attribution and Reaction Survey (C-CARS)* [Unpublished instrument]. Utah State University.

Steins, G., & Wicklund, R.A. (1993). Zum Konzept der Perspektivenübernahme: Ein kritischer Überblick [On the concept of perspective taking: A critical overview]. *Psychologische Rundschau, 44,* 226–239.

Stepper, S., & Strack, F. (1993). Proprioceptive determinants of emotional and nonemotional feelings. *Journal of Personality and Social Psychology, 64,* 211–220.

Stevens, S.S. (1972). *Psychophysics and social scaling*. Morristown, NJ: General Learning Press.

Stinson, L., & Ickes, W. (1992). Empathic accuracy in the interactions of male friends versus male strangers. *Journal of Personality and Social Psychology, 62,* 787–797.

Stotland, E. (1969). Exploratory investigations of empathy. In L. Berkowitz (Ed.), *Advances in experimental social psychology* (Vol. 4, pp. 271–313). New York: Academic Press.

Strack, F., Stepper, L.L., & Martin, S. (1988). Inhibiting and facilitating conditions of the human smile: A non-obtrusive test of the facial-feedback hypothesis. *Journal of Personality and Social Psychology, 54,* 768–777.

Tajfel, H., & Turner, J. (1986). The social identity theory of intergroup behavior. In S. Worchel & W.G. Austin (Eds.), *Psychology of intergroup relations* (pp. 7–24). Chicago, IL: Nelson-Hall.

Tangney, J.P. (1991). Moral affect: The good, the bad, and the ugly. *Journal of Personality and Social Psychology, 61,* 598–607.

Tangney, J.P. (1998). How does guilt differ from shame? In J. Bybee (Ed.), *Guilt and children* (pp. 1–17). San Diego, CA: Academic Press.

Tangney, J.P., Niedenthal, P.M.. Covert, M.V., & Barlow, D.H. (1998). Are shame and guilt related to distinct self-discrepancies? A test of Higgins's (1987) hypotheses. *Journal of Personality and Social Psychology, 75,* 256–268.

Tangney, J.P., Wagner, P.E., Burggraf, S.A., Gramzow, R., & Fletcher, C. (1991). *Children's shame proneness, but not guilt proneness is related to emotional and behavioral maladjustment*. Poster presented at the meeting of the American Psychological Society, Washington, DC.

Tangney, J.P., Wagner, P., Fletcher, C., & Gramzow, R. (1992). Shamed into anger? The relation of shame and guilt to anger and self-reported aggression. *Journal of Personality and Social Psychology, 62*, 669–675.

Tangney, J.P., Wagner, P.E., & Gramzow, R. (1989). *The Test of Self-Conscious Affect*. Fairfax, VA: George Mason University.

Taylor, S., & Todd, P. (1995). An integrated model of waste management behavior: A test of household recycling and composting intentions. *Environment and Behavior, 27*, 603–630.

Taylor, S.E., & Brown, J. (1988). Illusion and well-being: A social psychological perspective on mental health. *Psychological Bulletin, 103*, 193–210.

Taylor, S.E., & Brown, J. (1994). Positive illusions and well-being revisited: Separating fact from fiction. *Psychological Bulletin, 116*, 21–27.

Taylor, S.E., & Dakof, G.A. (1987). Social support and the cancer patient. In S. Spacapan & S. Oskamp (Eds.), *The social psychology of health* (pp. 95–116). Newbury Park, CA: Sage.

Tesser, A. (1988). Toward a self-evaluation maintenance model of social behavior. In L. Berkowitz (Ed.), *Advances in experimental social psychology* (Vol. 21, pp. 181–227). San Diego, CA: Academic Press.

Tesser, A., & Smith, J. (1980). Some effects of friendship and task relevance on helping: You do not always help the one you like. *Journal of Experimental Social Psychology, 16*, 582–590.

Thome, H. (1999). Solidarity: Theoretical perspectives for empirical research. In K. Bayertz (Ed.), *Solidarity* (pp. 101–131). Dordrecht: Kluwer.

Thompson, R., & Hoffman, M.L. (1980). Empathy and the development of guilt in children. *Developmental Psychology, 16*, 155–156.

Tietz, W., & Bierhoff, H.W. (1996). Motive ehrenamtlicher Helfer: Wie entsteht soziales Engagement und wie wird es aufrechterhalten? [Motives of volunteers: How does social involvement develop and how is it maintained?] In H. Mandl (Ed.), *Bericht über den 40. Kongress der Deutschen Gesellschaft für Psychologie* [*Report of the 40th congress of the German Psychological Association*] (pp. 470–476). Göttingen: Hogrefe.

Toi, M., & Batson, C.D. (1982). More evidence that empathy is a source of altruistic motivation. *Journal of Personality and Social Psychology, 43*, 281–293.

Triandis, H.C. (1978). Some universals of social behavior. *Personality and Social Psychology Bulletin, 4*, 1–16.

Triandis, H.C. (1994). *Culture and social behavior*. New York: McGraw-Hill.

Triandis, H.C., Vassiliou, V., & Nassiakou, M. (1968). Three cross-cultural studies of subjective culture. *Journal of Personality and Social Psychology Monograph Supplement, 8(4/2)*, 1–42.

Triplett, N. (1897). The dynamogenic factors in pacemaking and competition. *American Journal of Psychology, 9*, 507–533.

Trivers, R.L. (1971). The evolution of reciprocal altruism. *Quarterly Review of Biology, 46*, 35–57.

Trommsdorff, G., Suzuki, T., & Sasaki, M. (1987). Soziale Ungleichheiten in Japan und der Bundesrepublik Deutschland [Social inequality in Japan and the Federal Republic of Germany]. *Kölner Zeitschrift für Soziologie und Sozialpsychologie, 39*, 496–515.

Twenge, J.M. (2000). The age of anxiety? Birth cohort change in anxiety and neuroticism, 1952–1993. *Journal of Personality and Social Psychology, 79*, 1007–1021.

Tyler, T.R. (1986). The psychology of leadership evaluation. In H.W. Bierhoff, R.L. Cohen, & J. Greenberg (Eds.), *Justice in social relations* (pp. 292–316). New York: Plenum.

Uleman, J.S. (1999). Spontaneous versus intentional inferences in impression formation. In S. Chaiken & Y. Trope (Eds.), *Dual-process theories in social psychology* (pp. 141–160). New York: Guilford Press.

Underwood, B., & Moore, B. (1982a). The generality of altruism in children. In N. Eisenberg (Ed.), *The development of prosocial behavior* (pp. 25–52). New York: Academic Press.

Underwood, B., & Moore, B. (1982b). Perspective-taking and altruism. *Psychological Bulletin, 91*, 143–173.

Van Lange, P.A.M. (1999). The pursuit of joint outcomes and equality in outcomes: An integrative model of social value orientation. *Journal of Personality and Social Psychology, 77*, 337–349.

Van Lange, P.A.M., & Kuhlman, D.M. (1994). Social value orientations and impressions of partner's honesty and intelligence: A test of the might versus morality effect. *Journal of Personality and Social Psychology, 67*, 126–141.

Vining, J., & Ebreo, A. (1992). Predicting recycling behavior from global and specific environmental attitudes and changes in recycling opportunities. *Journal of Applied Social Psychology, 22*, 1580–1607.

Voland, E. (1999). On the nature of solidarity. In K. Bayertz (Ed.), *Solidarity* (pp. 157–172). Dordrecht: Kluwer.

Wagner, C., & Wheeler, L. (1969). Model, need, and cost effects in helping behavior. *Journal of Personality and Social Psychology, 12*, 111–116.

Walster, E., Walster, G.W., & Berscheid, E. (1978). *Equity*. Boston: Allyn & Bacon.

Walters, R.H., Parke, R.D., & Cane, V.A. (1965). Timing of punishment and the observation of consequences to others as determinants of response inhibition. *Journal of Experimental Child Psychology, 2*, 10–30.

Watson, D., & Clark, L.A. (1992). Affects separable and inseparable: On the hierarchical arrangement of the negative affects. *Journal of Personality and Social Psychology, 62*, 489–505.

Watson, D., Clark, L.A., & Tellegen, A. (1988). Development and validation of brief measures of positive and negative affect: The PANAS scales. *Journal of Personality and Social Psychology, 54*, 1063–1070.

Weber, M. (1919/1989). *The profession of politics* [S. Draghici, Trans.]. Washington, DC: Plutarch Press.

Webster's New Encyclopedic Dictionary. (1993). New York: Black Dog & Leventhal.

Wegner, D.M., & Erber, R. (1993). Social foundations of mental control. In D.M. Wegner & J.W. Pennebaker (Eds.), *Handbook of mental control* (pp. 36–56). Englewood Cliffs, NJ: Prentice-Hall.

Weiner, B. (1980). A cognitive (attribution)–emotion–action model of motivated behavior: An analysis of judgments of help-giving. *Journal of Personality and Social Psychology, 39*, 186–200.

Weiner, B. (1995). *Judgments of responsibility: A foundation for a theory of social conduct*. New York: Guilford Press.

Weiner, B. (2001). An attributional approach to perceived responsibility for transgressions: Extensions to child abuse, punishment goals and political ideology. In A.E. Auhagen & H.W. Bierhoff (Eds.), *Responsibility—the many faces of a social phenomenon* (pp. 49–59). London: Routledge.

Weiss, R.F., Boyer, J.L., Lombardo, J.P., & Stich, M.H. (1973). Altruistic drive and altruistic reinforcement. *Journal of Personality and Social Psychology, 25*, 390–400.

Wentzel, K.R. (1993). Does being good make the grade? Social behavior and academic competence in middle school.

Journal of Educational Psychology, 85, 357–364.

Wentzel, K.R. (1994). Relations of social goal pursuit to social acceptance, classroom behavior, and perceived social support. *Journal of Educational Psychology, 86,* 173–182.

West, S.G., & Brown, T.J. (1975). Physical attractiveness, the severity of the emergency and helping: A field experiment and interpersonal simulation. *Journal of Experimental Social Psychology, 11,* 531–538.

Williams, C., & Bybee, J. (1994). What do children feel guilty about? Developmental and gender differences. *Developmental Psychology, 30,* 617–623.

Williams, K.B., & Williams, K.D. (1983a). Social inhibition and asking for help: The effects of number, strength, and immediacy of potential help givers. *Journal of Personality and Social Psychology, 44,* 67–77.

Williams, K.B., & Williams, K.D. (1983b). A social-impact perspective on the social inhibition of help-seeking. In B.M. DePaulo, A. Nadler, & J.D. Fisher (Eds.), *New directions in helping* (Vol. 2, pp. 187–204). New York: Academic Press.

Wills, T.A. (1991). Similarity and self-esteem in downward comparisons. In J. Suls & T.A. Wills (Eds.), *Social comparison* (pp. 51–78). Hillsdale, NJ: Lawrence Erlbaum Associates Inc.

Wispé, L. (1986). The distinction between sympathy and empathy: To call forth a concept, a word is needed. *Journal of Personality and Social Psychology, 50,* 314–321.

Witt, L.A., & Silver, N.C. (1994). The effects of social responsibility and satisfaction on extrarole behaviors. *Basic and Applied Social Psychology, 15,* 329–338.

Wortman, C.B., & Lehman, D.R. (1985). Reactions to victims of life crises: Support attempts that fail. In I.B. Sarason & B.R. Sarason (Eds.), *Social support: Theory, research and applications* (pp. 463–489). Dordrecht: Martinus Nijhoff.

Wrosch, C., & Heckhausen, J. (1999). Control processes before and after passing a developmental deadline: Activation and deactivation of intimate relationship goals. *Journal of Personality and Social Psychology, 77,* 415–427.

Yakimovich, D., & Saltz, E. (1971). Helping behavior: The cry for help. *Psychonomic Science, 23,* 427–428.

Yamagishi, T., & Sato, K. (1986). Motivational bases of the public goods problem. *Journal of Personality and Social Psychology, 50,* 67–73.

Yarrow, M.R., Scott, P.M., & Waxler, C.Z. (1973). Learning concern for others. *Developmental Psychology, 8,* 240–260.

Yarrow, M.R., & Waxler, C.Z. (1979). Observing interaction: A confrontation with methodology. In R.B. Cairns (Ed.), *The analysis of social interaction* (pp. 37–65). Hillsdale, NJ: Lawrence Erlbaum Associates Inc.

Young, S.K., Fox, N.A., & Zahn-Waxler, C. (1999). The relations between temperament and empathy in 2-year-olds. *Developmental Psychology, 35,* 1189–1197.

Zahn-Waxler, C., Kochanska, G., Krupnick, J., & McKnew, D. (1990). Patterns of guilt in children of depressed and well mothers. *Developmental Psychology, 26,* 51–59.

Zahn-Waxler, C., & Radke-Yarrow, M. (1982). The development of altruism: Alternative research strategies. In N. Eisenberg (Ed.), *The development of prosocial behavior* (pp. 109–137). New York: Academic Press.

Zahn-Waxler, C., Radke-Yarrow, M., Wagner, E., & Chapman, M. (1992a). Development of concern for others. *Developmental Psychology, 28,* 126–136.

Zahn-Waxler, C., & Robinson, J. (1995). Empathy and guilt: Early origins of feelings of responsibility. In J.P. Tangney & K.W. Fischer (Eds.), *Self-conscious emotions* (pp. 143–173). New York: Guilford Press.

Zahn-Waxler, C., Robinson, J.L., & Emde, R.N. (1992b). The development of empathy in twins. *Developmental Psychology, 28,* 1038–1047.

Zahn-Waxler, C., & Smith, D. (1992). The development of prosocial behavior. In V.B. VanHasselt & M. Hersen (Eds.), *Handbook of social development: A life-span perspective* (pp. 229–256). New York: Plenum.

Zajonc, R.B. (1965). Social facilitation. *Science, 149,* 269–274.

Zuckerman, M., Klorman, R., Larrance, D.T., & Spiegel, N.H. (1981). Facial, autonomic, and subjective components of emotion: The facial feedback hypothesis versus the externalizer–internalizer distinction. *Journal of Personality and Social Psychology, 41,* 929–944.

Author index

Abramson, L.Y., 137
Ackerman, P., 10
Ahearne, M., 304
Ahn, R., 133
Ainsworth, M.D.S., 137
Ajzen, I., 101, 165, 226,
229, 322
Albrecht, T.L., 10
Alexander, R.D., 144
Allen, H., 185
Allen, J.L., 201
Allen, N., 319, 321
Allen, N.J., 303
Alloy, L.B., 137
Allport, F.H., 234
Altmann, J., 48–49
Amato, P.R., 11, 14, 31–32,
34, 256
Anderson, N.R., 309
Archer, J., 63
Archer, R.L., 125,
203–204
Aron, A., 211
Aron, E.N., 211
Aronfreed, J., 115
Auhagen, A.E., 158,
161–162
Axelrod, L.J., 165
Axelrod, R., 291
Ayvalioglu, N., 32, 39

Bachrach, D., 301
Bae, H., 46
Bagozzi, R.P., 227

Bakan, D., 28
Bamberg, S., 166
Bandura, A., 73–78, 80–81,
235
Barlow, D.H., 145
Barnett, M.A., 124
Baron, R.A., 117, 239
Barrett, K.C., 143, 149
Batson, C.D., 10, 22, 41, 43,
97, 107, 110–111, 118,
130–133, 174, 189,
191–193, 196–197,
199–203, 205, 207–209,
211–212, 245, 287,
297–299, 319, 331–333
Baumann, D.J., 152, 191
Baumeister, R.F., 139–140,
143–144, 149, 329
Bayer, U., 332
Bayertz, K., 285–287
Bem, D., 99
Ben David, A., 150 174,
273
Ben-Itzhak, S., 261
Bennington, J., 158
Benson, S.M., 151, 169,
319
Bentler, P.M., 227
Bergman, L.R., 59
Bergson, H., 286
Berkowitz, L., 12, 15, 117,
130, 164, 168, 170,
246–247, 296, 301–302
Berliner, D., 149

Bernzweig, J., 70
Berscheid, E., 153
Bersoff, D.M., 159
Bettenhausen, K., 307
Bickman, L., 185
Bierhoff, H.W., 9, 18–19,
21, 28, 152, 154, 157, 161,
168, 170–172, 190, 247,
274, 279–280, 287,
296–297, 305, 308–310,
314, 316, 318–319,
321–322
Birch, K., 10
Bischof-Köhler, D., 121
Bissonnette, V., 135
Black, J.S., 165
Blake, R.R., 74,
Blehar, M.C., 137
Bless, E., 139, 150–151
Blöbaum, A., 165
Bodenhausen, G.V., 77
Boehnke, K., 44
Boggiano, A.K., 79
Bolen, D., 96
Bolen, M.H., 130
Borden, R., 232
Bornstein, R.F., 164, 302
Bowlby, J., 120, 144
Boyer, J.L., 88
Bradshaw, D., 144, 256
Brase, G., 13,
Braun, O., 2 55
Brehm, J.W. . 257, 267
Brehm, S.S., 257, 267

Williams, K.B., 256–257
Williams, K.D., 256–257, 284
Willits, J.E., 40
Wilson, M.S., 66
Wispé, L., 107, 126, 129
Witt, L.A., 169
Wolf, S., 31, 38
Word, L.E., 187, 236, 277–278
Wörsdörfer, C., 319

Wortman, C.B., 260
Wright, J.C., 81
Wrosch, C., 16

Xie, J.L., 45–46

Yakimovich, D., 236
Yamagishi, T., 289–290
Yarrow, M.R., 49–51, 80
Young, A.L., 123

Young, S.K., 64, 66,
Ypma, I., 32

Zahn-Waxler, C., 25, 51, 55, 59–66, 108, 112, 121, 140–143, 157, 159, 217, 276
Zajonc, R.B., 238
Zigler, E., 149
Zuckerman, M., 113

Subject index

Adherence to social rules 170–173, 296
Adult socialisation 72
Affective empathy 110
Age differences 59–72
Aggression 2, 4, 26–27, 47, 50, 74, 89, 141, 144–145, 161
Aggressive sanctioning 297
Affiliation 125
Affirmative action 297
AIDS 103, 294, 316–317, 320–321
Altruism 9–11, 27, 41–43, 54, 62, 64, 73, 82, 84–85, 90, 93–95, 97, 117, 131, 152, 177, 193, 196–205, 212, 264, 286–287, 293, 304–305, 308–310, 319, 325, 331–333 *see also* Helping behaviour; Altruistic behaviour; Values, altruistic
definition of 9–10
Altruistic motivation 39, 132, 192, 197, 212–213, 267, 297–298, 302, 316
Altruistic personality 3, 69, 177–178, 245–249, 320, 323, 330, 334
Ambiguity 187, 236

Anger 11–12, 14, 18, 28–29, 142, 145, 148–150, 160–161, 175, 252
Anonymity 204, 237, 289
Antisocial behaviour 2, 48, 51–53, 65, 149
Anxiety, 39, 130, 137, 143, 149, 169, 218, 227, 235
Approval 4, 15, 48, 67–68, 71, 77, 88–89, 96, 98, 102, 125, 152, 164, 181, 193, 207, 247
Approval orientation 67–68
Arousal *see also* Aversive arousal
empathic 112–119, 194–201
physiological 65, 179–184, 188–190, 204, 215–221, 238–239, 331
vicarious 107–112
Arousal: cost–reward model 177, 179–190, 334
Arousal scale of the semantic differential 125
Attachment 80, 120, 137, 144, 196, 209–210, 317–318, 321–322, 327
Attachment style 80, 137

Attention 18, 49–51, 76–77, 89–90, 92, 121, 188, 197, 213, 216–217, 219, 225, 228, 238–239, 290, 296, 335
Attitude 3, 15, 29, 77, 91, 94–95, 101, 166, 172, 226–227, 234, 258–260, 282, 296, 316, 319, 321–322 *see also* Attitude towards the act; Attitude–behaviour consistency; Attitude-behaviour model; Theory of planned behaviour; Theory of reasoned action; Ego-defensive function of attitude; Knowledge function of attitude; Social-adjustive function of attitude; Value-expressive function of attitude
Attitude towards the act 226
Attitude–behaviour consistency 77, 165
Attitude-behaviour model 166, 226–227
Attraction, interpersonal 198–199, 282, 322
Attraction–selection– attrition hypothesis 322

Attribution 27, 46, 67, 88, 96–99, 122, 159–160, 175, 189, 252–253, 267, 269, 293, 297 see also Attribution theory; Correspondence bias; Fundamental attribution error; Responsibility attribution; Strategic management of responsibility attributions

Attribution of responsibility see Responsibility attribution

Attribution theory 267

Audience inhibition 237–239

Autonomic Reactivity Scale 219

Autonomy 159, 164

Authoritarianism 15

Authority 164, 246, 285

Aversive arousal 182–184, 192, 197

Baby-cry helping task 217–218

Basic behaviour categories 48

Behavioural control 226

Betrayal 291

Biological factors 41–43, 46, 62, 286–287, 327–329

Blameworthiness 158, 163

Blaming the victim 109, 122, 150, 174

Blood donor 100–102

Boomerang effect 86, 91

Bystander effect 223–242

Bystander intervention 1, 29, 177, 179, 188, 190, 223, 257

California Psychological Inventory 123

Career advancement 317–318

Causality 162–163, 175

Child–Child Attribution and Reaction Survey 147, 149

Children, development of altruism in 59–72

Christian values 298

Civic virtue 304

Civil rights activist 87

Classical conditioning 88, 114–115, 119

Cognitive appraisal 227–228

Cohesiveness 282, 286

Collective identification 294

Collectivism 44, 294, 329

Common fate 190

Communication 10, 46, 81, 92, 96, 121, 231, 239, 241, 258, 290, 292, 305

Community concern 318

Compensation 119, 140, 144, 149–153

Compensation for stress at work 317–318

Competence 53, 66, 71, 76, 78, 102, 119, 130, 153, 190, 216, 220, 228, 246, 259, 268–269, 273–280, 321

Compliance 48, 50, 88, 92–93, 97, 99, 169, 215–216, 282, 284, 304–306, 334

Generalised 304–306, 310

Confession 141, 145, 147–149, 151, 169

Conformity 68, 77, 232

Consistency see Attitude–behaviour consistency

Contrast empathy 128

Controllability 157–158, 160–161

Coolness 235

Co-operation 43, 164, 184, 260, 263, 265–266, 284, 286–287–292, 295, 298, 301, 303, 322

Coping 76, 227–229

Correspondence bias 45–46

Cost–reward analyses 179–182, 202–203

Cross-cultural studies 328–329

Cry for help, 236–237

Cultural factors 25–40, 43–46, 235, 298–299, 326–329

Criminality 149

Decision-making models 223–229

Defence processes 225, 263, 268, 318

Definition of the situation 234–236

Delay of gratification 74

Demographic variables 16, 30–40, 55, 278, 326

Denial of discrimination 297

Denial of responsibility 151, 173–175

Dependency 2, 12, 50, 71, 127, 164, 253–254, 260, 266, 283–284, 301–302

cause of 160–161

–responsibility hypothesis 267, 301–302

Depression 149, 154, 307

Devaluation 109, 252, 262

of donors 257–266

of victims 109

Developmental task 16

Diffusion of responsibility 22, 32, 38, 174, 188, 224–225, 228, 230, 232–233, 239–242, 329

Reciprocity 43, 46, 62, 68, 253, 255, 262–267, 287, 291–293 *see also* Generalised Reciprocity; Reciprocal altruism; Reciprocity ideology; Symbolic reciprocity

Reciprocity ideology 266, 327

Reinforcement 3, 68, 73–74, 77, 80, 87–90, 92, 98, 117, 159, 182–184, 191, 193, 207 *see also* Positive Reinforcement

Relative deprivation 293–294, 334

Religion 46, 298–299, 321, 323

Reproductive success 42, 329

Resistance to temptation 169

Responsibility 4, 6, 12, 18, 26, 38–40, 46, 58, 68, 90–91, 104, 109, 115, 124, 132–133, 135, 138–157, 169, 197–204, 218–219, 235, 239, 241–244, 248, 252, 262–263, 270, 275, 288–289, 294 *see also* Dependency–responsibility hypothesis; Denial of responsibility; Personal responsibility; Political responsibility; Responsibility attribution; Social Responsibility Scale environmental 165–167 social 12, 40, 46, 109, 115, 140–142, 145–158, 218–221, 252, 261–263, 266, 279–280, 283–284, 288–289

Responsibility attribution 160–164, 166–167, 173–174

Responsibility denial *see* Denial of responsibility

Retaliation 160–161, 291

Rewards 77, 80–81, 90–91, 116, 152, 156, 191, 193, 202–203, 205, 266, 268, 287, 307

Role identity 101–103, 305, 319–320, 323

Rural–urban differences 30–38

Sadness 60, 113–114, 148, 152, 207–211, 218

Sanction 284, 291, 297

School 45, 51–53, 259, 329

Shame 140, 142, 145–148

Secondary appraisal 227

Self-concept 96, 149, 248, 259

Self-consequences 268

Self-control 28, 73, 81–82, 158–159, 169, 173, 219, 235, 289

Self-controlled learning 254

Self-efficacy 75–76

Self enhancement

Self-esteem 144, 179, 247, 252, 255, 258–264, 268–269, 317–318, 321

Self experience 317

Self-focus 77–78

Self-help groups 287, 314

Self-interest 164, 178–180, 289–291

Self–other differentiation 119–122

Self-perception 99, 294, 319

Self-presentation 235, 251

Self-recognition 121

Self-reinforcement *see* Reinforcement

Self-reward 152, 192,

Self-serving bias 46

Self transcendence 299

Semantic differential 125

Shyness 65, 130

Similarity 4, 11–12, 14, 40, 64, 128, 136, 158, 172, 182, 190, 199, 209–210, 235, 245, 255, 258–260, 263, 268, 286

Skin conductance 216

Social-adjustive function of attitude 316

Social attachment 317–318, 321

Social comparison 75, 78, 114, 235–236, 258–259

Social cues 235, 237

Social desirability 147, 181, 218, 319

Social dilemma 288–292, 334

Social discrimination *see* Discrimination, social

Social exchange *see* Exchange, social

Social facilitation 237–239, 242

Social identity 293–294

Social impact theory 232–233, 256–257

Social inhibition 2, 22, 65, 75, 177, 188, 223, 229–230, 236–237, 239–241

Social intelligence 291

Socialisation 25–30, 43–46, 62, 64, 72–103, 134, 142–143, 152, 159, 191, 207, 279, 286–287, 295, 307–308, 319, 327–329

Social learning 3, 134 acquisition of new behaviour patterns 73–74 facilitation of performance 74 inhibition of performance 73–75 symbolic representation 75

Social loafing 284